ARCANA VII

ARCANA VII
MUSICIANS ON MUSIC

EDITED BY
JOHN ZORN

HIPS ROAD 2014

Book design by Heung-Heung Chin.

First published in 2014
ISBN 978-0-9788337-4-9
ISBN 0-9788337-4-0
Printed on acid-free paper
Printed and bound in the United States of America

Hips Road
200 East 10th Street #126
New York, NY 10003
http://www.tzadik.com

Distributed to the trade by D.A.P. / Distributed Art Publishers
155 Avenue of the Americas, Second Floor
New York, NY 10013

Orders: (800) 338-2665 Tel: (212) 627-1999
Fax: (212) 627-9484

CONTENTS

PREFACE

The Lyre of Orpheus

JOHN ZORN

"Resist much. Obey Little."
—Walt Whitman

May your vision be always clear, honest and imaginative; your work well crafted and cathartic. May you ever take the dangerous path, the one that is difficult, winding, perilous; leading to unknown valleys, dark forests, bottomless caverns; to secret temples, impassible mountains and inaccessible peaks breaking through the clouds. May they bring you to a transcendental world filled with truth, beauty and goodness. May your melodies soar to the heavens, your rhythms flow without pause, your harmonies resound with the healing power of love—frighteningly real and visceral.

Let moonlight fill your hand, the sun fill your heart such that no fear might stray you from your path, nor prevent you from advancing. Let no doubt divert you from the zone of creative light, from the flow, from being in the very center of life's eternal energy—the energy of imagination, mystery and beauty. Let your work encompass all things and flash like lightening with the white hot magic of the strange and the beautiful. Let no one and nothing get in your way. Let no part of the illusory world of falseness, greed and fashion distract you from your struggle, which is the invention/discovery/creation of that perfect vision of creative light. Let your deepest dreams and wildest fantasies lead you toward the fulfillment of the purest creative acts. Let your connection to the immutable aeons light the way. Take the hard road and never despair. Revel in the struggle and never give up. Never stop for a moment's rest.

—John Zorn, *NYC 2014*

ARCANA VII

CHAPTER 1

THE BABY'S FLYING CIRCUS

IRVINE ARDITTI

Once upon a time, there was a baby who some say had a bad knock on the head. Other less kind folks say that his mother, who loved him dearly, once dropped him on his head because she could not stand the noise he was creating. Standing on tiptoes, he used to play with a wireless, (a radio, for today's folk), and was especially interested in the short wave band. With the volume turned up full, this wireless emitted burbles and gargles of extraordinary quality and some say that there were many performances of short wave pieces in East London in the '50s long before Stockhausen even thought of writing them. We mention this giant of new music as not so many years later, the baby, now turned youth became enamored with this composer's music. In fact his first trip outside the UK was to Germany to hear the Giant's music.

Some years later, when the youth had formed a chamber music ensemble called a string quartet, he asked the Giant if he would write a work for this ensemble. "Ensembles like that I don't write for," said the Giant. "I only write for much weirder combinations of instruments." "Oh" said the youth, immediately thinking of stopping his violin studies and learning the flugelhorn or bass flute. But then he thought of the implications of carrying around such a whopper...

The youth would manage to attain the support of other such musicians and festival directors to advance on the Giant at odd moments, like the end of concerts, where he might be a little more susceptive to his request to write a string quartet. Many years passed and there was no positive or forward motion with this idea.

And Then...

The Giant had this dream about 4 helicopters, each carrying one string quartet member around in the air, each learning how to count in foreign languages and playing their boring regular instruments.

And Then the Giant Became Inspired...

He told the first distinguished quartet member that the piece might present a challenge for the promoter, but that if it was a festival with a good team, they would be able to solve all the requirements of the score.

Over the next year he scored the piece for the now, ~~4 babies, 4 helicopters~~, ooopps sorry, I mean he scored the piece for 4 helicopters, 4 television channels, 4 technicians and 4 distinguished quartet members, concert hall with 4 television monitors to show live on stage what the distinguished ***maestri*** would be getting up to in the air. When the work was finished he sent the score to the leader of the quartet, who was in charge of such things. When the leader read the instructions in the score, he collapsed on the floor with amazement. You may not think this is unusual for someone who remembers so well being a baby, but I think he got a bang on the head rather similar to the one he may or may or not have had, when he was a real baby...

After that he rose to the challenge by persuading the directors of the famous Austrian festival in Salzburg that this was not such a crazy idea at all, and maybe this was the direction string quartets were going to go in, in the future. Alas, green parties, health food, vitamin pills and all that crap, got in the way and this famous festival decided that it did not want nasty green army helicopters flying around the city depositing fumes and making horrid drone noises and not the nice chuggy-chuggy sounds that the Giant had scored the piece for.

Holland: to the Rescue...

The famous Holland festival in Amsterdam decided it could cope with Giants, ex-Babies and all else that might pollute its wonderful city.

Surely this was the most logical place for the premiere of such a piece. With so many pot-heads about, no one would be able to tell that it was a normal boring string quartet being drowned-out by 4 wonderful grass-hoping helicopters.

The now famous, soon to become infamous string quartet worked intensively with the Giant, without the intrusion of helicopters, in order to be able to master the intricacies of this wonderful score and perform this delicate piece of chamber music. Without being able to hear their colleagues, they found a way to solve the problems of rhythm, playing together and not playing together, with a "click" track, provided by one of the Giants own babies. The problems of tuning were left to the imagination of the musicians and a final "La" on the tarmac.

Finally the helicopter rehearsal day arrived and the quartet were required to employ all their expert abilities to cope with the tilting experience, stomachs left on the ground feeling and all the wonderful things that you cannot experience in the concert hall. (Unless you are of nervous disposition, take beta-blockers, and basically should not be playing your instrument in public.) Of course being babies at heart, they loved all of this and at one point, one of them forgot to play the piece and started improvising, giving himself a chance to see the wonderful view of the cafés below. The Giant was not impressed with this and cast a long glare that was felt from within the helicopter. All the musicians rallied together and gave more than 100% concentration for the three performances that took place within one day. After the first performance, the Giant ushered them into the concert hall and asked the leader how the experience had been for him, playing in a helicopter. The leader was so ecstatic that he could not contain himself and said, that he thought that all quartet literature should be played from helicopters in the future!

At the end of the day, the esteemed *maestri* and the composer were exhausted but elevated by this incredible experience. The Giant had found a way to write a string quartet, which he obviously was not originally comfortable with. He had added a truly original composition to the rich repertoire of quartet music. The first maestro had had a lifelong dream come true.

CHAPTER 2

HARDCORE ELECTRONICS

The Music is People!

CHUCK BETTIS

The year was 1989. I was 13 years old and had just started to attend D.C. hardcore shows. The community embraced and nurtured young misfits like me, breaking down barriers with direct communication. Shows were affordable ($5) and were ALWAYS all ages. The idea was that no one should be excluded because of their age or financial situation. These shows opened up a world to many young people who were inspired by the intense performances and thereby motivated to start their own bands. Such was the case for me: I started playing guitar when I was 14. By age 16 I was asked to play bass in my first real band, called Smooch. We got our first gig from Bikini Kill, an extremely confrontational punk band and one of the pioneers of the radical feminist Riot-Grrrl movement. I sent Kathleen Hanna (Bikini Kill's singer) a fan letter along with a demo tape of Smooch without the intention of soliciting a gig. I honestly only wanted her insight into my music. To my surprise, she called me up and asked us to play our first show, kickstarting my musical career. That is when the backbone of the hardcore community really solidified for me.

This immediacy of hardcore punk affected me at a root level. One night after a show, while conversing with the singer/guitar player of a band I just saw that night, I mentioned how I needed a new living situation. Within a week, I was moved into a group house known as The Embassy (all the D.C. group houses had names) that also housed various members of bands I was regularly checking out at the time. I was 18, living in this punk house, and singing in an oddball hardcore band called The Meta-matics. My lyrical content was a verbal left-leaning newspaper of the atrocities happening in the world, which was a typical characteristic of hardcore songs those days. We were a band that incorporated various musical ideas not typically attributed to hardcore music and joyously experimented with different approaches strictly for the love of sound. Despite this quirky aspect, the community was still there to nurture one of their own, even if it was for a group out of step with their musical paradigm. On one of our typical days after practice, a friend asked if he could hear the recording of the Meta-matics rehearsal. Upon giving him our latest recordings, we were offered to tour with his band. This led to a number of tours with other bands that would give us a much wider exposure. At the same time, in retrospect, misfits like Meta-matics might have opened the door to other uncategorizable musicians to jump in and create music within the D.C. scene. The mutual support of each others' musical pursuits was essential for growth in D.C.

Perhaps ironically, bands in D.C. normally had short life spans. The Meta-matics dissolved within a year and half. Shortly after this, I was offered to join a band called All Scars and began singing and playing trumpet with them. The band itself started off as a revolving cast of veterans of D.C. hardcore's past, sometimes with members from Fugazi, Beefeater, and Nation of Ulysses joining on an impromptu-basis. This band fully embraced improvisation as we attempted to distance ourselves from the confines of hardcore music while working within its established instrumentation framework. This particular band situation allowed me to have room to further explore different elements of the trumpet as well as the use of my voice as textural instruments, both of which I had not been able to experiment with in my previous bands. This group embraced the joy of free improvisation, allowing each musician to explore his own pursuits, akin to the element of mutual aid cultivated in the D.C. hardcore punk scene. Once again, the community supported us by taking us on tour, putting out our records, and attending our shows.

I then took the do-it-yourself ethos from the hardcore community and utilized it to curate a music series to support the burgeoning experimental music scene in Washington, D.C. This bi-monthly series received plenty of the support from the community from the beginning; punks came to check out their bandmates and other familiar faces creating experimental sounds, breathing fresh air into the scene.

These years were a time of deep "crate digging"—we were fiendishly searching for new sounds to inspire our musical creations. Mile high stacks of mix-tapes were traded back and forth between friends for years prior to this. We were always trying to surprise each other with new and exciting music. 1996 seemed to be a year no different than any other. Yet, one fateful day, while trying to fill the last small blank space at the end of a tape, I made my first attempt at making electronic music. I went into my shared rehearsal space, plugged in all of the guitar pedals I could find and had them feedback into each other. This was before any of us had even heard any abstract electronic music; the thrill and excitement from hearing the rich and alien textures emerging in conjunction with the spontaneity involved in the construction of these sounds sparked a love that is still with me to this day.

This coincidental discovery of electronic music was a total liberation from what I felt was the sonic strangle-hold that traditional rock instruments embodied. For a long time prior, I was unable shake the rich history attached to the guitar, bass, and trumpet, instruments I had been playing up to this point. However, my interest began leaning more and more towards a fully electronic music. For several years the musical output of All Scars paralleled my solo electronics (under guise of Trance And The Arcade) without much crossover. Therefore, I abandoned the guitar and bass altogether, eventually leaving my trumpet as well. I began to focus strictly on electronic instruments which seemed to have endless sonic capabilities.

Originally I was recording live (aka no overdubs) using the built-in condenser mic on one of those very cheap Realistic QTR-72 cassette tape recorders. It captured the sound of the room as well as the newly discovered guitar pedal instrument (which was simply one flanger, one delay, and one distortion pedal hooked up to each other) through amps. The audio quality was poor, and I aimed for better fidelity as well as a wider sonic palette. Eventually I started using the studio as an instrument by incorporating overdubbing and multitracking with the assistance of a Tascam 4-track tape recorder. I finally felt as if the sonic possibilities were endless, though there was a catch: there were limitations with the equipment I had in terms of implementing my 4-track compositions live. That created a dilemma. My intention had always been to present my music in a live context, so over the next few months I amassed a very personalized arsenal of noisemakers: a suitcase filled to the brim with various guitar pedals, a Roland SH-101 synthesizer with a handmade wooden case that was heavier than the synth itself, and a backpack filled with all kinds of bizarre electronics (the Simmons "clap trap," a device that only created hand clapping sounds, broken delay pedals that didn't delay the signal properly, a sampler filled with sounds sourced from my kitchen appliances, a Roland CompuRhythm 68 drum machine for some low end pulses, as well as three Boss Dr. Pad drum pads that I would play by punching them.) After years of touring up and down the East coast of the United States, during which I was constantly tearing up my shoulder muscles, this setup became physically detrimental to my health. I yearned for a lighter and more portable set-up. Around this time, I experienced Ikue Mori, Peter Rehberg, and Marcus Schmickler on separate occasions performing mind-altering live music on a laptop computer, and my days of lugging around heavy hardware were over.

Here I was with my first laptop computer, feeling more free and refreshed than ever. However, the first issue I encountered with this new instrument was my lack of experience with computers, except for checking my email. I didn't know where to start or what programs to use to create the sounds in my head. There was not a community of musicians in my area who were going in the direction I wanted to go with the computer, that is to turn it into a real time instrument I could improvise on. At some point I came across a bunch of software, but they were all poorly designed, sounded like shit and could not perform in real time. For quite some time before I knew what I was doing on my computer, a typical gig night would involve multiple programs running simultaneously that would often crash my computer. Those programs were soft synths, samplers, and drum machines; most of them cease to exist for good reason and their names are irrelevant here.

Frustrations built up, and gradually my technical needs solidified: creating my own synthesizers, samplers, and effects that are controlled by my voice and external midi hardware. Eventually, I became aware of Max/Msp (or as it is presently known simply as Max), a software and visual object-based musical language program where one can design his own instrument from scratch. When I first acquired this software, I was naively under the impression it would come as a readymade instrument. To my surprise, the software only came with a blank canvas called a "patch," along with a few sample patches. To give you an idea of Max terminology; a patch can contain several "objects" (visual boxes that contain tiny code to do something specific such as create sounds, visuals, connect midi controllers, control lights and/or other hardware, etc.), which you can connect to other objects via virtual patchords to do something specific. The system is very much like a modular synthesizer. However, my initial encounter with Max obviously did not come with any of the above description. Sitting in front of the computer, literally staring at this language which I couldn't even comprehend, I wondered to myself, "What the fuck is this?" However, despite my initial doubt about continuing to use the program as a musical tool, there was a solid ground of support from other Max enthusiasts. The online forum for Max users was instrumental to my technical development, and I could also participate in supporting others with their problem solving. Again, much like the mutual-aid in the D.C. music milieu, a solid community support was present with this software, which continues to satisfy my needs and defy my expectations. Max has become the single instrument that I have stuck with for the past 15 years.

In my youth I was greatly influenced by the Washington, D.C. hardcore community which set a moral compass that eventually led me to where I am today. The music was as serious as your life; it was faster and louder than most music of the time, and was filled with a passion and intensity that conveyed its message, which was politically heavy. People gave their all to the music and lived the life they sang about. We lived in group houses, went to protests together, took each other on tour, attended each other's shows and never took any shit. Yes, this kind of community is hard to maintain—everybody needs to make a living, and some struggle more than others. This is not news in New York City, where I am living today. Throughout the years my instrumentation has changed, and the meaning of terms like community/punk/D.C. might have changed also—but the do-it-yourself attitude has remained the most crucial theme in my music—thanks to continuous support from like-minded people in the community (whether the word community stands ideologically, geologically or musically.) Collaboration is a constant—vital and necessary, whether in the realm of digital circuitry or of analog flesh. But collaboration also means taking care of each other.

CHAPTER
3

ABRAXAS TOUR 2014

Realities of a European Tour

SHANIR EZRA BLUMENKRANZ

February 5, 2014—Travel Day

Leave home in NYC 1:15PM ~ Car will not start until 1:45PM ~ Pickup band 2PM ~ Drive to parking lot in Irvington, NJ ~ Take shuttle to Newark Airport ~ Check in for flight 3:30PM ~ Flight scheduled to leave 5:35PM to Dusseldorf with one stop in Geneva ~ Board airplane 4:50PM ~ Flight crew arrives 1 hour late ~ Pilots arrive 2 hours late ~ Pilots find a problem with the airplane ~ Flight cancelled ~ Flight rebooked for 9PM ~ Actual departure 10PM

February 6, 2014—Koln, Germany

Land in Geneva ~ Miss connection to Dusseldorf ~ Flight rebooked to Dusseldorf with stop in Munich ~ Land in Dusseldorf 4:15PM ~ 1 hour drive directly to venue in Koln ~ Soundcheck 5:45PM–7PM ~ Dinner 7:15PM–8:15PM ~ Concert starts 8:45PM ~ Band plays 2 sets ~ Hotel check-in 12AM

February 7, 2014—Innsbruck, Austria

Hotel breakfast 6:30AM ~ Lobby Call 7AM ~ Train departs from Koln 7:55AM to Innsbruck with stop in Munich ~ Arrive Innsbruck 3:30PM ~ Hotel check-in 4PM~ Lobby call 5:30PM ~ Soundcheck 6PM–7:30PM ~ Dinner with booking agents 7:30PM–8:30PM ~ Concert starts 9:15PM ~ Band plays 2 sets ~ Back to hotel 12:30AM

February 8, 2014—Maribor, Slovenia

Hotel breakfast 7AM ~ Lobby call 7:40AM ~ Train departs from Innsbruck 8:24AM ~ Arrive Graz 2:14PM ~ 1 hour drive to Maribor ~ Hotel check-in

3:30PM ~ Lunch with promoter 4PM–5:15PM ~ Back to hotel 5:30PM ~ Lobby call 6:30PM ~ Interview 6:45PM–7:15PM ~ Soundcheck 7PM–8PM ~ Concert starts 8:45PM ~ Band plays 2 sets ~ Late dinner with promoter 12AM ~ Back to hotel 1:30AM

February 9, 2014—Bern, Switzerland

Hotel breakfast 9:30AM ~ Lobby call 11:30AM ~ 1.5 hour drive from Maribor to Ljubljana Airport ~ Flight departs 2:20PM ~ Arrive Zurich 3:35PM ~ 1.5 hour drive directly to the venue in Bern ~ Soundcheck 5:15PM–6:45PM ~ Dinner 7PM–8:15PM ~ Concert starts 8:45PM ~ Band plays 2 sets ~ Hotel check-in 1AM

February 10, 2014—Bolzano, Italy

Hotel breakfast 6:30AM ~ Lobby call 6:45AM ~ Train departs from Bern 7:34AM with stops in Milan and Verona ~ Arrive in Bolzano 2:48PM ~ Hotel check-in 3:15PM ~ Soundcheck 6PM–7PM ~ Dinner with promoter 7:15PM–8:30PM ~ Concert starts 9:15PM ~ Band plays 2 sets ~ Late dinner 12AM ~ Back to hotel 1AM

February 11, 2014—Travel Day

Hotel breakfast 9:30AM ~ Lobby call 11:35AM ~ Train departs from Bolzano 12:34AM with a stop in Innsbruck ~ Arrive in Zurich 7:20PM ~ Hotel check-in 7:45PM ~ Dinner 10PM ~ Back to hotel 11:30PM

February 12, 2014—Zurich, Switzerland

Hotel breakfast 9:30AM ~ Lobby call 4:30PM ~ Soundcheck 5PM–6:45PM ~ Dinner 7PM–8PM ~ Concert starts 8:45PM ~ Band plays 2 sets ~ Back to hotel 1:15AM

February 13, 2014—Vienna, Austria

Lobby call 5:50AM ~ Train departs from Zurich 6:40AM ~ Arrive in Vienna 2:30PM ~ Hotel check-in 3PM ~ Lobby call 5:30PM ~ Soundcheck 6PM–7:15PM ~ Dinner 7:30PM–8:15PM ~ Concert starts 8:45PM ~ Band plays 2 sets ~ Back to hotel 12:30AM ~ Late dinner 1AM–2:15AM ~ Back to hotel 2:30AM

February 14, 2014—Saalfelden, Austria

Hotel breakfast 9AM ~ Lobby call 9:45AM ~ Train departs from Vienna 10:30AM with a stop in Salzburg ~ Arrive in Saalfelden 2:54PM ~ Hotel check-in 3:30PM ~ Lobby call 4:30PM ~ Soundcheck 5PM–6:30PM ~ Dinner 6:45PM–8PM ~ Concert starts 8:15PM ~ Band plays 2 sets ~ Back to hotel 12AM

February 15, 2014—Travel Day

Hotel breakfast 7AM ~ Lobby call 7:55AM ~ Train departs Saalfelden 8:50AM with stops in Worgl, Innsbruck and Verona ~ Arrive in Milan 4:55PM ~ Hotel check-in 5:30PM ~ Interview 6:30PM ~ Lobby call 8:30PM ~ Dinner 9PM ~ Back to hotel 11:45PM

February 16, 2014—Milan, Italy

Hotel Breakfast 7:45AM ~ Lobby call 8:30AM ~ Soundcheck 9PM–10:30PM ~ Concert starts 11AM ~ Band plays one set (90 mins) ~ Lunch with promoter 2PM ~ Back to hotel 5PM ~ Dinner 8:30PM ~ Back to hotel 12AM ~ Band meeting 12:30AM

February 17, 2014—Travel Day

Lobby call 6:30AM ~ Flight departs from Milan Airport 9:10AM with a stop in Dusseldorf ~ Arrive to Newark Airport 3:05PM ~ Take shuttle to parking lot in Irvington, NJ ~ Arrive home in NYC 5:30PM

CHAPTER 4

THE OVERDUB

Showing Up for the Recording Session and Delivering the Magic Take

ROB BURGER

Being on a session—contributing to someone else's recording project—requires a very different approach than when composing and orchestrating my own music and/or leading my own ensembles. Often I find myself in a situation where I'm in the studio and interacting creatively with singers, other musicians, or producers whom I don't know very well and I'm called upon to make great music happen in a short amount of time. It's a common occurrence that I have never heard this music before and I don't have time to wait for musical ideas to come to me. I need to generate them quickly and apply them accordingly. It's been said numerous times before that "music is a language of its own" and nowhere is that more true than in the recording studio. The music so often speaks for itself—at various stages of the recording process—in terms of what it needs more of, less of, what needs to be cut, changed, embellished, rearranged, or left alone. The music "speaks" that, in *musical* ways, but we artists speak the language of pedestrians too (albeit not always very well). We attempt to communicate our musical ideas in another language—in most cases where I'm involved, the English language. This is where the recording process gets tricky.

If an artist has a specific idea, somehow that idea needs to be first communicated, and then interpreted. There is much subjectivity in this process, and also an enormous need for trust. The best kinds of recording sessions to me are the ones where two components are in balance:

> 1. The artist has a clear vision of both generally what they want their end product to sound like, and specifically what they would like me to perform; and
>
> 2. That artist is equally as open to having me apply my own vision to their music. Clear vision and openness—the magic duo. I've always been drawn to projects that allow a musician to blur this

line. When these two components are in balance, I have the experience of contributing to a piece of music by doing precisely what's called for stylistically, and tastefully filling a void, while also maintaining a strong sense of individuality. This is always what I strive for when I walk into the studio.

Often an artist (or director) doesn't know exactly how to articulate what they want to hear and therefore I'm called to bring something unique or perhaps specific to the table without much communication. Magic needs to happen right away; there is no time to waste. Before a session, I make certain the appropriate tools and proper equipment will be made available to me at the studio or I bring along some of my personal instrument collection. Having a variety of unusual instruments set up, tuned, and ready to play can lead to an unconventional or naive approach to the music, therefore sparking inspiration. When I arrive at an overdubbing session, I generally ask to first have a cursory listen to the piece of music we are working on and I then take notes. If there is written sheet music, I read the chart and look and listen for holes, or opportunities. Sometimes holes must remain holes and other times they are begging for something. If the artist doesn't write music, I'm happy to create my own road map. Doing this preliminary work is important as it saves precious studio time and also immerses me in playing the music and achieving a take. As an improvisor and eclectic listener, I find I am able to tune into my "inner radio," referencing or pulling from a multitude of styles, and then channeling them through my instrument. I've always been a proponent of going back in time, that is, back to the source from where the music I'm listening to is derived. Bringing my sense of musical history to the process helps me allocate strong new ideas that I must bring to the table to ally with the other musicians and to elevate the music.

Over the years, I've become adept at entering the studio environment confidently, gaining trust from the artist to improvise and/or orchestrate my own parts, while allotting the time to take creative chances. I've learned to take direction, add what's missing, and do all I can to inspire the artist or composer. I tend to think like an orchestrator as I improvise, reacting melodically but also exercising restraint and patience, playing when necessary, but choosing notes assertively. The most important things I've learned in my experiences in the studio are to put my full self into it, but also to remain somewhat detached from my own parts; to know collaboration at its deepest, most musical level, and also to know it's not "my" gig. I enter with an enthusiastic and focused attitude about each project and I do my absolute best, reminding myself that each take exists only for that moment in time and in that sense, each take is "the one" whether or not it's the chosen one in the end. But I also listen for when it's time to let go of what I'm working on, move ahead, get paid, and go home.

CHAPTER
5

BASIC ORGANIZATION OF PITCH AND TIME IN PIERRE BOULEZ'S "MESSAGESQUISSE"

JAY CAMPBELL

I first met Pierre Boulez when I was 19, playing for a lecture-performance led by Boulez on his 1976 work *Messagesquisse.* His candid unveiling of certain compositional underpinnings, as well as unexpected homages, were luckily recorded and I feel that it would be worthwhile to finally document some of them.

I have always been surprised by the lack of attention given to *Messagesquisse*. It is an unusual piece for Boulez, who, in other works, generally masks compositional scaffolding itself quite well. But *Messagesquisse* puts its inner machinery on clear display[1] and, for that reason, serves as ideal territory for exploring both the precision and freedom of Boulez's writing. Despite its small size, typically clocking in at around 8 minutes, there is a striking richness of material that Boulez further explores even after the last double bar, later recycling elements of *Messagesquisse* in major pieces like *Repons, Derive 1, Incises,* and *sur Incises.*

That said, going through the entire piece measure-by-measure, mindlessly ferreting out each permutation, would be tedious and would demonstrate little. Rather, the goal at hand will be to broadly explore how Boulez generates a wealth of material from limited pitch resources, and their relationship to the expansion/contraction of temporal space throughout the four sections of *Messagesquisse*. Hopefully, this primer will provide a glimpse into both its internal logic and Boulez's generative procedures beyond just the examples given, and perhaps be helpful for anybody who might want to study it further.

For anyone who may be new to the idea of rotation, it is simply starting on a pitch of any given set that is not the first one: S-A-C-H-E-R, A-C-H-E-R-S, C-H-E-R-S-A, and so on.

1. "...it's really not a complicated piece. I prefer it that way if the writer has a kind of secret or mystery, but here there is no secret. It was written for a festive occasion, and that's why I wanted to bring out the text and make it simply virtuosic. And it was conceived for Rostropovich, the great cello virtuoso. I wanted to really display this virtuosity. And a kind of virtuosity that is not full of anxiety, but rather quite the opposite: it is a virtuosity that is quite at peace with itself...simple."

* * *

The row starting on S would be considered rotational level zero, A would be level 1, and so on. Additionally, the 6 x 6 x 6 cube, shown below, will be used sometimes to navigate the different rotational areas in a more visually intuitive way:

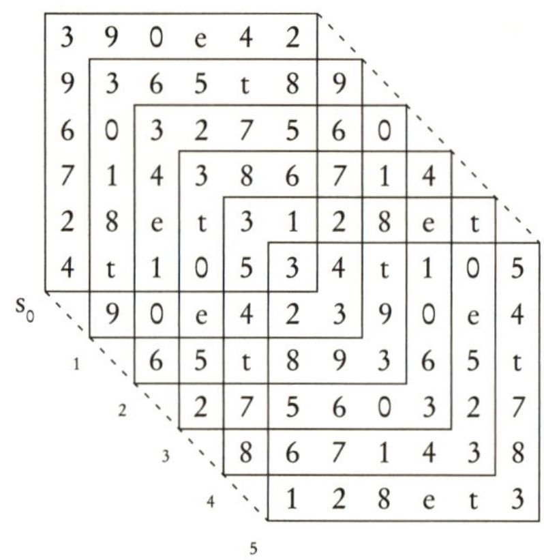

To find S_4R_3, for example, one would find the fifth rotational level (note: the first, original level is labeled as S_0) and then find the retrograde ending on pc 3: in this case, the very top-most row. Additionally, pc 11 and 10 are represented by "e" and "t", respectively.

A very brief context of the work: on the occasion of Paul Sacher's 70th birthday, Pierre Boulez and eleven other composers—Luciano Berio, Witold Lutoslawski, Henri Dutilleux, and Benjamin Britten, to name a few—were asked to write solo cello pieces for Rostropovich, built around a hexachord derived from the letters of Sacher's last name:

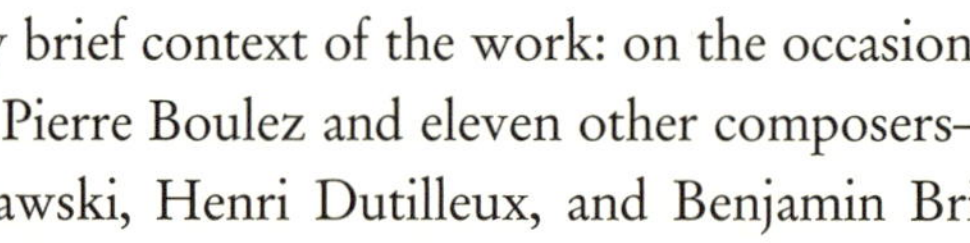

It is already at this early stage that Boulez departs from the crowd. Not only did Boulez submit the score past the deadline, but also broke the rules of the commission by expanding from solo cello to six-cello ensemble plus soloist.[2] While Boulez gave a sympathetic but frank

2. "...that is 70 years; with the 7th cellist being the most important along with 6 others each symbolic of a decade."

recollection[3] of the first time he heard Rostropovich play the solo part, the premiere was ultimately cancelled and the first performance of *Messagesquisse* was given the following year by cellists from Ensemble Intercontemporain and two European orchestras.

3. "You see, it was written for Rostropovich, and Rostropovich was not the slowest person in the world. And when he wanted to work, he did as much as he wanted to. [...] We met in London once where he was supposed to play the piece, but I heard a lot of open strings and not exactly every note I wrote. [...] It's not really a piece one can improvise."

I

A few pervasive elements throughout *Messagesquisse* are established immediately at the opening: most obviously, its harmonic nucleus; secondly, the function of the ensemble, in relation to the solo line, as merely an extension or shadow; and thirdly, the layering effect of stacking each cellist, in succession, at each pitch of the hexachord.

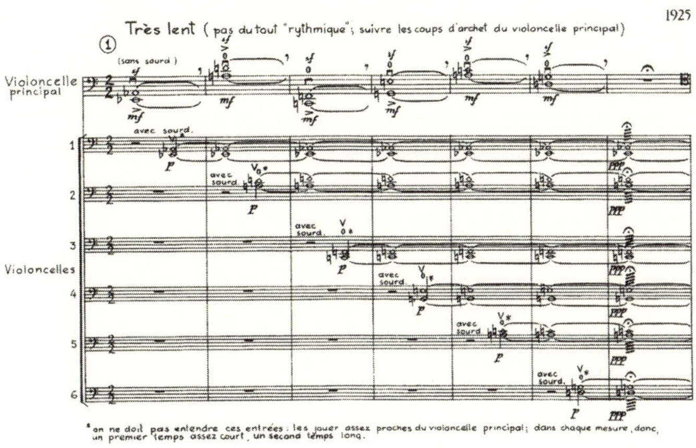

Example 1: the opening six measures of *Messagesquisse*, stacking S-A-C-H-E-R.
Pierre Boulez *Messagesquisse* | *für Violoncello solo und 6 Violoncelli*

With these features defined, the first of many permutational games begins, cycling through S_0P3 through S_5P3, exhausting all rotational levels. At each succession of rotational level, the pitches from the *previous* level are woven, additively, as grace notes, onto the corresponding pitches of the *new* level until, by the last phrase, every rotation except the original row form, S_0, is presented, horizontally, in the solo line (Example 2.)

The second layer of this game is the rhythmic representation of the letters SACHER in Morse alphabet, tapped out *col legno*, by the ensemble (shown in the right-most side of Example 2.) When the solo line starts each new permutation, another letter in Morse alphabet is added, stacking on top of each other in an aleatoric loop; thus, by the sixth phrase, all rotational levels of P3 are exhausted while the Morse rhythm corresponding to each letter is played freely, creating an intricate web of material, all derived from SACHER. The timbral complexity of this texture is further augmented by indicating for each ensemble member to move the *col legno* contact-point, resulting in a quasi-electronic sounding, indeterminate slew of overtones.[4]

4. "Do you know what that is? Morse alphabet. That is S, A, C, H, E, and, R. These multiply and are played not only as col legno, but as different positions of col legno. [...] You can hear all the different high overtones. You can hear all six letters struck, one above the other. [...] That is the message."

tempo (8ths)	S 3	A 9	C 0	H e	E 4	R 2						dynamics	morse
36–40		3	6	5	t	8	9					p	
46–48			3	$^{6}2$	$^{5}7$	$^{t}5$	$^{8}6$	$^{9}0$				mp	. . .
56–58				3	$^{62}8$	$^{57}6$	$^{t5}7$	$^{86}1$	$^{90}4$			mf	- . - .
72–76					3	$^{628}1$	$^{576}2$	$^{5t7}8$	^{816}e	^{904}t		f	. . . .
92–96						3	$^{6812}4$	^{2576}t	$^{5t78}1$	$^{e168}0$	$^{90t4}5$	ff	-
116						. . .			(S)			fff	(repeated)
111						. -			(A)			f	
108						- . - .			(C)			mf	
104						. . . .			(H)			mp	
99						-			(E)			p	
96						. - .			(R)			pp	

Example 2: Graph of the opening and first cadenza.

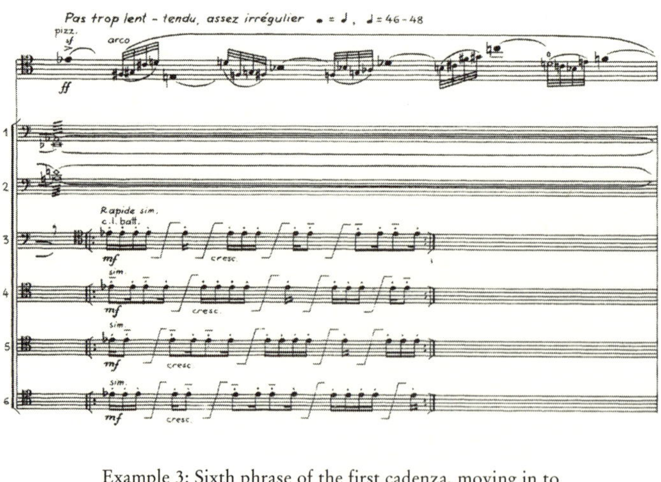

Example 3: Sixth phrase of the first cadenza, moving in to the last pizzicato/Morse iterationof SACHER in the solo line.

As one can see in Example 2, integrated pitch and contour patterns are established that will continue to appear throughout the score, with a particular gravitation to pc 3 as an axial pitch. Throughout the piece, this centricity will be a frequent presence, with pc 3 as a point of arrival and departure between rotational levels.

II

While all the musical material so far has been, as one would expect, referential to Paul Sacher, it is worth mentioning now that there are two somewhat quirky structural homages in this score. In the following section, marked *très rapide*, the simultaneous rhythmic expansion/contraction on the most local, note-to-note level against the gradual expansion/contraction of a deeper level is—as related by Boulez—a small nod to the *Allegro misterioso* movement of Alban Berg's *Lyrische Suite.*[5] As we will see in a moment, the large form of this section is, essentially, a passacaglia that expands and contracts at different structural levels.

The most immediately perceptible feature of the musical surface is, despite perpetual 16th notes, the sensation of acceleration and deceleration. This mobility is achieved by a rhythmic scheme of lengthening or shortening the distance between each accent: the aforementioned *local* expansion/contraction. That is, the first accent begins a unit of six, the second accent begins a unit of five, then four and so on, at which point the pattern either reverses or the pitch-center of the phrase is forcefully moved by a tutti outburst from the ensemble.

These local rhythmic fluctuations lay nested within a gradual dilation and constriction of phrase lengths, punctuated by shifts of pitch-center. Whenever the axial pitch changes, that particular phrase lasts slightly longer or shorter than the previous one.

5. "[...] It is a passacaglia on the name 'Sacher.' And at the same time, it is an homage to Alban Berg's Allegro misterioso, because the Allegro misterioso is built the exact same way: on rows which consist of 12 tones, each becoming shorter and shorter, while growing larger. This material morphs itself but you hear the same tones in their respective category."

pitch center	length bars)	distance between accents (16ths)
9	2	6
0	4	6
e	4	6
4	6	9
2	14	9, 11
9	6	11
0	20	13
e		13
4	16	13
2	8	13
90e42 (coda)		

Example 4: Reduction of the second section's temporal scheme.
Bar lengths grow or shorten with each pitch-succession of the long-range passacaglia.

The micro/macro dichotomy is applied to the domain of pitch as well: as noted before, the shifts of pitch-center over the course of this 91-measure section create a hierarchy of row-forms. While at the local level, rows are completed every measure, the long-range motion of pitch-centers functions as a passacaglia, slowly cycling twice through a partial collection, [9, 0, e, 4, 2]. The omission of pc 3 here also raises the implication of a larger harmonic framework, where the gravity towards pc 3 in the first section would serve as the first pillar of an even deeper background organization.

The local pitch material is extrapolated from these pitch-centers by, again, various rotations. Pitches are generated by straight-forward matrix organization, with each square transposed to the pitch-center of each phrase and arranged according to order patterns. An example of this process can be demonstrated from matrices of the first four measures:

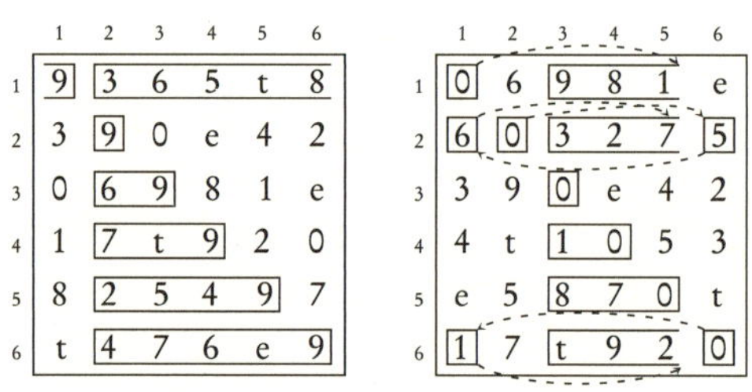

1 6 5 4 3 2	=	9 8 t 5 6 3	2 6 1 5 4 3	=	0 5 6 7 2 3
6 5 4 3 2	=	9 e 6 7 4	6 1 5 4 3	=	0 1 2 9 t
5 4 3 2	=	9 4 5 2	1 5 4 3	=	0 1 8 9
4 3 2	=	9 t 7	5 4 3	=	0 7 8
3 2	=	9 6	5 3	=	0 1
2	=	9	3	=	0

Example 5: The ordering scheme for the first two measures of the second section.

Corresponding to the left matrix of Example 5:

Corresponding to the right matrix:

As one can see, pitches here can be determined by a patterning of order-positions, corresponding both vertically and horizontally: that is, the ordering of row *positions* on a transposed matrix reflects the correct pitch-class *succession* on the musical surface, as well as the correct sequence of row-forms themselves. While this could also be done on the 6 x 6 x 6 cube, each rotational level is additionally transposed around the central pitch of each phrase, which would be not only tedious to graphically represent but ultimately useless, as it would be too visually disorienting to serve any illuminative purpose.

III

The multiple SACHER references have, so far, only been articulated separately, and until the third section—a second cadenza—a fully comprehensive integration of these facets has yet to be presented. This single, tightly integrated musical line is the first real display of compositional virtuosity; a game on SACHER around the rotational cube that weaves together previous compositional ideas, each evolving in multiple directions.

The six phrases of the cadenza are each divided into two parts: five unmetered pitches, and then the sixth as a refrain. The long-range rhythmic scheme resembles a gradual balancing between two opposite trajectories: the refrain gaining notes while losing tempo, versus the first half of the phrase, losing notes while gaining tempo. Similarly, while the main pitches of each phrase completes one retrograde row form, moving up one rotational area per phrase, the grace-notes attached to each pitch are derived from diagonals across rotational levels, as shown in Example 6. These two permutations are assigned timbral profiles: the diagonals of the first phrase are marked *pizzicato, ordinario*, while the refrain—punctuating, in order, each Morse letter of

SACHER—and its associated grace-note diagonal are indicated by *arco, sul tasto.*

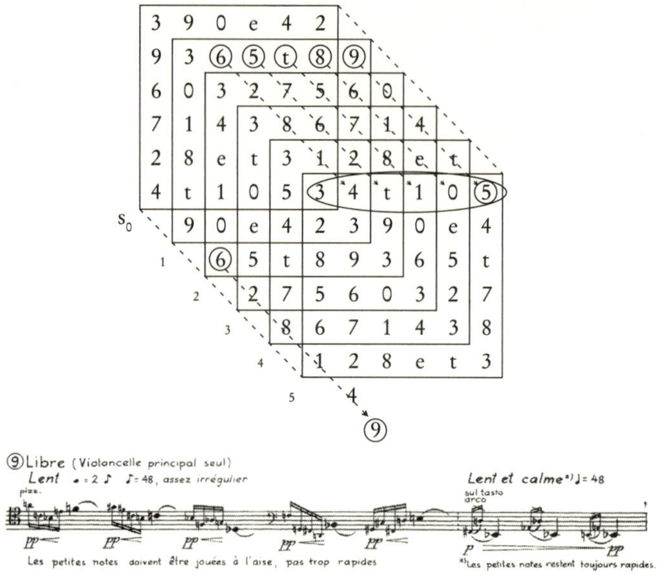

Example 6: First bar of the cadenza.
Grace-notes correspond to diagonals along the matrix, while main pitches are a horizontal completion of S_5R3.

With each successive phrase, diagonal movement is increasingly disrupted by *ponticello* horizontal statements of P3 in different rotational levels, always eliding with the terminal pitch of the preceding diagonal. As the amount of grace-notes shorten by one note per phrase—four in the first phrase, three in the second, and so on—each horizontal row form is on a higher rotational level than the previous one: from S_4R3 (shown below in Example 7) until S_0R3.

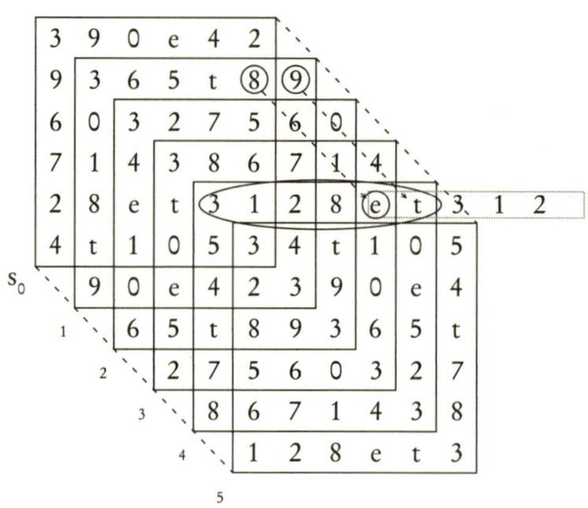

Example 7: The first horizontal disruption, assigned *arco sul ponticello* across S_4P3.

IV

The pitches of the concluding coda—surprisingly, a loose homage to the finale of Chopin's *op. 58* by rhythmic profile—are formed, like the first section, around the pc 3 diagonal. Similar to the long-range movement of pitch-center in second section, each downbeat constitutes an expanding vertical pitch-class succession, indicated by square vertical boxes in Example 8, while the pitches *within* each measure cycle, horizontally, through one rotational level per each measure. By beginning each phrase on pc 3 and adding only what is directly above pc 3 on the matrix, phrase lengths naturally expand in direct proportion to the size of the pitch collection. Boulez directly reflects this in the orchestration: as the pitch material becomes denser, so does the orchestration. By adding one player at the final pitch-class of each vertical succession, the entire ensemble is eventually playing through the entirety of the farthest rotational level simultaneously.

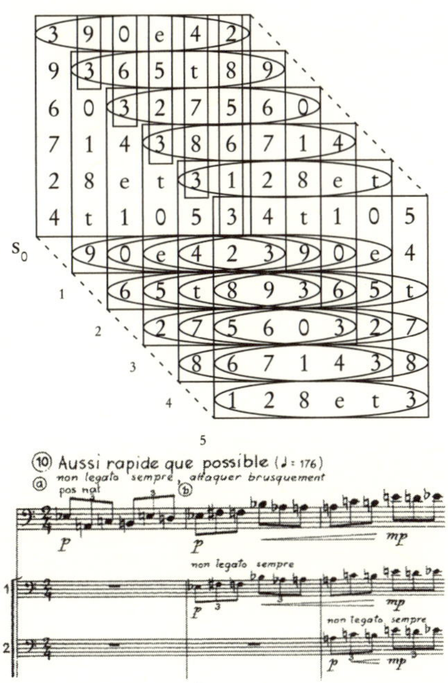

Example 8: First diagonal across pc 3, generating the pitches of the final section.
The first three measures are shown, corresponding to S_0P3 and S_1P3 of the rotational cube.

While the diagonal and vertical elements are clear in Example 8, it is easier to see the additive pattern through each rotational layer if the matrix is pulled apart into discrete squares:

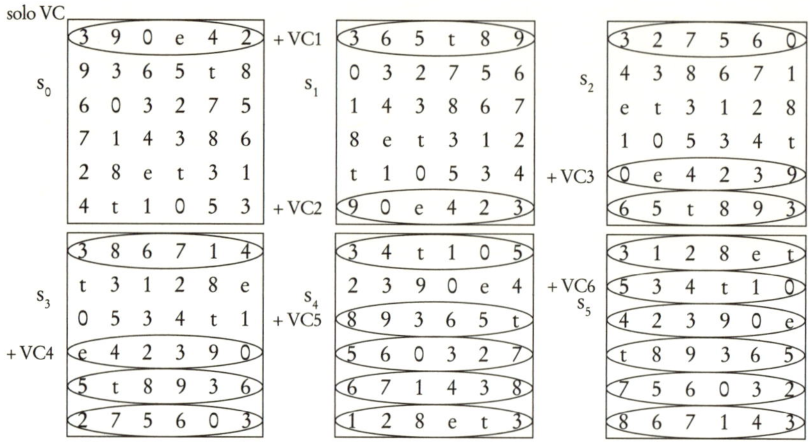

Example 9: The rotational cube, untangled, from Example 8.

Upon completing the sixth rotational level, the remainder of matrix is then introduced (Example 10), presenting all row-forms not used in Examples 8/9, getting shorter by one row until the entire rotational cube has been completed. However, unlike the beginning of this section—adding a new player for each rotational area—the density of orchestration here does not change. Each permutation is *not* punctuated, given the sense of a much longer phrase. Despite each rotational area shortening, the musical surface gives the impression of expansion.

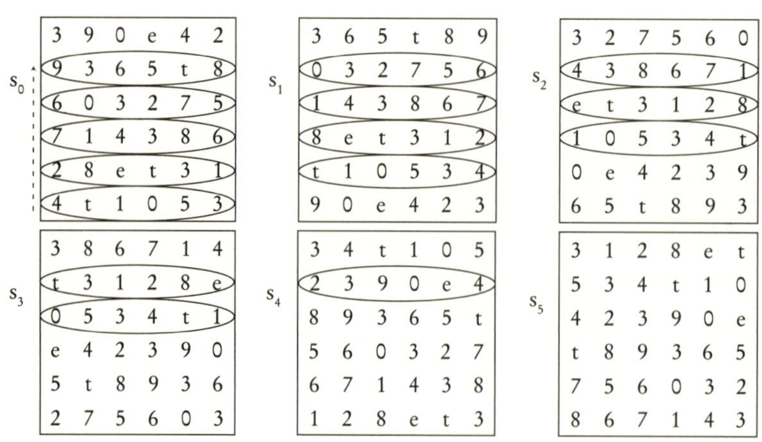

Example 10: The first five bars from the remainder of the rotational matrix, after Examples 8 and 9.

The return to the original row form is delayed and the opposite diagonal (from the upper-right corner of the matrix) is then completed, shown in Example 11. The chief difference here is that the ensemble does not follow the soloist into the next row form; rather, each ensemble member stays on the respective row at which they entered, cycling through as many permutations as possible. Thus by the time the soloist reaches the end of the diagonal, every possible rotational level of every row form of S_0 will be playing simultaneously, both horizontally and vertically.

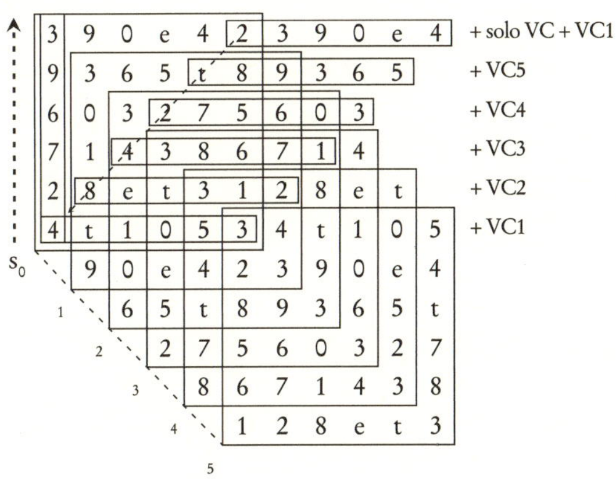

Example 11: Final diagonal with each cellist staying within, and rotating through, their own row form until the entirety of S_0 is articulated simultaneously.

The ensemble continues to cycle through their respective row forms for the last four measures, exhausting the entirety of S_0 with every measure, while the solo line reinforces this centricity, ascending from P4 to P3.

As with any good composition, a multitude of features omitted here could be repeatedly examined and reexamined. Similarly, there is an abundance of different ways to understand what *was* mentioned. However, by examining even a small selection of compositional procedures, one thing becomes overwhelmingly evident: for Boulez, form does not inherently supercede content. Deviations from established patterns are frequent; while they always fall within the general parameters of the operations used, sometimes there is no simple explanation for certain compositional choices at the point-to-point level.[6] Much of *Messagesquisse* defies the application of any comprehensive "equation" and often, the local connections are composed intuitively, in service to the musical surface rather than the compositional system.

6. For example, the pitch ordering of grace-notes in the second cadenza. While the notes are certainly to be found on the grid, there is no discernable ordering pattern.

CHAPTER
6

THE WALKS AND THE TAPES

EUGENE CHADBOURNE

Details of the roundtrip walks I took daily in the '70s from uptown to downtown Manhattan came back to me in the Fall of 2013 while playing a week long residency at The Stone. Memories of producing material on cassette had also been churned up recently by a loyal mail order customer's suggestions regarding CD versions of these works; some needed a better digital mastering and some had never had one at all.

My walks had inspired musical theorizing based around the choices I would make on a route from northwest to southeast, basically a grid with set characteristics as well as a few major variations. I would be starting and returning to the apartment I shared with my oldest brother on the corner of 72nd and Central Park West. The downtown destinations were usually rehearsals, movies or gigs.

On these walks I considered taking notes keeping track of my routes and eventually tried recording details about how long I would walk in a straight line in any one direction and when I would make a turn and in what direction.

In Manhattan all kinds of people walk for all kinds of reasons but for one and all the decision whether to turn or not is most likely governed by the crossing light—the idea is to keep moving.

Momentum and the perception thereof is a popular motivator with improvising but what I was thinking about on the walks was using spontaneous decisions about my route as factors in a composition. An all-encompassing body of notation could be created, similar to the Manhattan grid. The exact details of the walk could govern what parts of the notation are played in a given performance.

This notation was subsequently created and provided some interesting moments in practice sessions. Yet the manipulation by literally pedestrian design of notated music was clearly not where the excitement was in my solo music at the time, nor did I seek out the company of eager sight readers for an ensemble interpretation—despite the legitimacy that would have given my experiment, the equivalent of getting a group of people to take the exact walk I did at the exact time, turning my private experience into a public parade or march.

Examining a list of nearly 100 titles created as cassettes, I tend to pick out and hope I can find masters for productions that represent the total opposite of public performance or social participation in the creation of music. I recalled *Fake Fight* as involving hundreds of hours of delicious isolation, ear lobes deep in experimental mayhem, following no rules and with no one breathing over my shoulder. I was happy to find the cassette master and looked forward to listening to it while remastering.

Fake Fight had originated as a score that nobody could make much sense out of, with notated material originating in the master grid for the proposed musical interpretation of my walks, lifted whole cloth and dropped in a different setting where its meaning could change. "Fake fight" was the name of a grade school game, you have a pretend fight not only to imitate on screen action but to attract and mess with the attention of disciplinarians who might come a running, eager to break up a fight and ignorant of the fake fight concept.

Notions of low key civil disobedience and its relationship with improvisation took over the analysis of my walks, a development that came back to me as I relived much of the same route decades later with all of the same factors at play in both life and music. It isn't just the crossing signal i.e. rules of right and wrong governing decisions whether to turn or go straight. This is Manhattan after all and jay-walking will occur not only at the intersection but at any point on the block when a break occurs in the traffic.

Sometimes it is indiscretions with drivers that create such moments of freedom for a pedestrian, the way a fumble by one member of a band is an opportunity for another and then the whole thing seems great and well-planned in retrospect.

The study of such traffic patterns is instructive for anyone planning to spend time in improvising ensembles. It is easy to see, for example, how freedom of movement can be wonderfully desirable on an individual level but can result in varying degrees of discomfort if there are too many people doing what they want at once.

Having one of my 2013 walks take place on the day of the New

York Marathon seems initially to be a total fuck up, as well as ironic in that I had spent time studying computer-created routes from uptown to downtown, assuming a grandiose lesson or at least humorous comparison could be made between downloaded music and downloaded routes.

The complexity of following paths through Central Park—twisting and turning to economize on distance without losing sense of direction—could well be simplified by digital directions but the theory was not put to the test that day because all routes east through the mighty park were blocked.

Freedom of movement was a theme of *Fake Fight* and not just because basic material had been lifted from my walking notes notation. The score was offered to the Rova Saxophone Quartet of San Francisco who had just pulled off a tour of the Soviet Union at the height of the Reagan era.

Homeland Security presence, post 9-11 multiplied by the Boston Marathon bombing, meant my status as an individual was suspended for several miles, I was part of a thousand orchestras being herded toward the loud and noisy Times Square, where overlapping restaurant soundtracks and street noise put me into a mind-set developed on walks in the city of Amsterdam.

I concentrate on the sounds around me and see how long I can listen as if to a piece of music, how long it will seem to be an interesting piece of music and at what point is it so totally boring that it impossible to even consider it a piece of music any longer.

When Rova told me they couldn't figure out how to make music from my score, I volunteered to take recordings of theirs from the Russian tour and manipulate them on my own in my home studio.

The material arrived and I used speed to seed and spawn new growth, blossoms and fruit, the juice of which took on aspects of a plumbing leak. I had turntables with four possible speeds, so could take the LPs and either slow them down or speed them up. I developed automatic ways of making the LPs skip and recorded these, sometimes several skipping LPs at once, at various speeds. I used tape to further stretch or compact the speed. I made tape recordings of the LPs moving at highest speed, the tape running at slowest speed. Then I could play that tape at high speed. I developed ways of playing an entire side of an album in a matter of seconds. Then I would take these blips and slow them down again.

It wasn't long before the LPs were so mutilated from my experimentation that they weren't much use but nonetheless I had at least 16 hours of material on ¼ inch reel to reel tape; a labyrinth but not without an exit. Armed with a razor blade I would slash down to between 75 and 90 minutes, starting somewhere and when I got lost I would backtrack to a point of comfort, begin anew and concentrate on where the point is where there needs to be another edit to keep things interesting.

Getting lost is the difference between the Amsterdam walks and the Manhattan walks. In the latter case I rarely get lost unless I come off a subway and forget my sense of direction. Amsterdam is all about getting lost, even when and especially when running errands. Even before one has a chance to possibly get lost, across the avenue from the Central Station, there is the possibility to stand in front of the hotel where a famous jazzman met his end, the one and only Chet Baker whose biographical film portrait is entitled *Let's Get Lost.*

My Amsterdam routes, better described as "how I get lost", have some detail similar to Manhattan. I might turn right or left or stay straight based on a traffic signal, the presence of a nice walking bridge or an impassable canal.

Progress also comes to a halt following the general rule known as "enforced canal sit"—if there is an open bench by a canal and the weather is nice, I stop and sit for a spell. The process can also include redirecting myself toward certain neighborhoods where I can dependably find something good to listen to—pile ups of music, noisy wildlife, flamboyant chatter in overlapping languages.

I create my own fade outs, fade ins and mixes by walking towards or away from factors. I do repeats by backtracking, intentionally or otherwise. In many Dutch and Belgian towns it is possible to walk in grand circles without having any idea what is happening, hours of effort are expended and I am back where I started out—a happy conclusion or not what I wanted at all.

Despite the hours of Rovadaptations I also utilized soundtrack material pilfered from sources I decided to make note of while listening to *Fake Fight* during the digital remastering process.

John Wayne's opus *The Green Berets* was the source of several quotes including a Vietnam fact unfortunate for many but fortunately not me: "Out here, due process is a bullet."

At the end of the first cassette side, Ronald Reagan is heard repeating the phrase "America is great because America is good." The number of repetitions depended on the quality of cassette used for the dub. Name brand entities such as Sony provided up to 92 minutes on a C-90 so Reagan would go on and on, allowing time to mull over the Great Communicator's words. As a music critic, I knew "great" was better than "good." One had to be first good but it was a big step earning the great part, it didn't work automatically as Reagan was suggesting.

The cheapest tape stock on earth came from McCrory's dime-store store chain including Rose's, an actual 90 minutes was a rarity with these jokers, the norm was 88 and if the dub wasn't started at the very earliest possible second a listener could wind up not hearing Reagan's comment at all. Conservatives can balance this disappointment with the knowledge that profits from these discount shops fund all manner of right-wing mischief.

Even withstanding the 92-minute version of the Reagan quote, the largest amount of material came from one of Eddie Romero's *Blood Island* films that I had discovered and enjoyed in Calgary doing what John Wayne didn't want me to do, dodge the draft. Furthermore I had seen them in the glory days of that city's notorious grindhouse, The Tivoli Cinema.

The soundtrack music had a particular identity impossible to shake despite speeding up and processing through various masking filters. It could never be made to sound like anything the Rova group had played and retained its melodic nature no matter what I did to it. I speculated whether the film could be interpreted to have anything seriously to do with the Cold War or the USSR or Ronald Reagan. It was about an isolated dictator and weird scientific experiments and was filmed under the nose of Reagan's buddy President Marcos so maybe it did.

Mainly I theorized the process of composing and recording would be all the more enjoyable if I really loved the material I worked with, love being defined as anything I like as much or more than an Eddie Romero film.

To express this love and because I had no better idea, I had *Fake Fight* end the same way the Romero film did, with the Mad Doctor's voice narrating over the majestic end theme: "Cowardly...sniveling fools...I accept forgiveness of no one. I alone am answerable for what I am. I will not serve but I also am...and will not be... overcome."

This side ended somewhere close to the 40-minute mark so even the cheap tapes would have the full ending. Switching to Fortress Audio, a North Carolina supplier that created cassettes to perfect custom lengths, standardized the entire catalog so now every customer hears a piece that ends the same way.

My walks end at destinations or when I absolutely run out of steam, sometimes this happens concurrently or it can be like a decision made composing or improvising. If I am in the listening mode, the switch to a moving vehicle results in different sorts of stimulus. Manhattan cab drivers ask as a matter of routine what route I prefer but despite my hours of research into the topic, I still prefer to tell them I am no expert, same as when musicians ask "How will we know when it's the end?"

—Greensboro, North Carolina December 13, 2013

CHAPTER
7

SYNCHONICITIES

Intuitive, Metaphysical and Historical Influences in Three Compositions

GLORIA COATES

My Musical Landscape

Beyond the spheres that
Orbit our sun
Across the stars
Through black holes that
Lace the inner realm,
Shapes like dippers, kites and
Strings of pearls—
Sounds that echo—
Crusts of dried
Orbs
Whizzing, whirling, twirling,
Crashing,
Swirling through
Timeless space in
Circles round, oblong, and
Elliptical—

Through the
Vortex of my singing soul
Transformed from
Sounds and
Shapes of
Shadows
Shimmering
Into my
Now-a-nights
Day—

Nowadays
Transformed to
Musical
Calligraphy.

—Gloria Coates, *March 2002*

The relationship between creativity and metaphysical events has convinced me that some Higher Power is at work in music. Of course, there are many types of music such as improvisation or writing for films or dance that demand different approaches from mine, and I am not sure to what extent, if at all, those mysterious events occur to them. Each composer and musician has his own experience, so I will only write about my own approach to composing and some of the metaphysical happenings around and during the act of creation in three of my works.

For those young composers seeking detailed technical advice about my technique, this article might be a disappointment, for there is no single way that I compose. Each work has its own destiny propelled by an inner demand from the music itself as it is being formed. Even the notation I developed often changes with each work, which usually is derived from an incipient method of notation I had used in a previous work.

I believe that a young composer should know historically and technically what has been written before, not only so that he can use previous principles of form and structure if he wishes in his own works, but also, so that he does not repeat the past.

My favorite composers who have influenced me are J.S. Bach and Orlande de Lassus. I also am indebted to Beethoven for his tight forms that are remarkable in content, especially in his piano sonatas.

Being from Wisconsin, I was exposed to Freethinkers, a movement in Germany of liberal intellectuals, many of whom emigrated to the United States between 1850 and 1885, primarily to Wisconsin; this included families of both Otto Luening's and my own. There is still an enclave of Freethinkers in Sauk County, Wisconsin. Many ideals of the Freethinkers influenced the Progressive Party, primarily those of social reforms. (They themselves had difficulty agreeing on their own policies.) My father was one of the founders of the Progressive Party with the La Follettes, State Senator Roland Kannenberg, an innovator of social reforms. Many of his ideas and manner of thinking influenced me to search for truth instead of accepting dogma. Among the Freethinkers' beliefs are compassion for needless suffering, social progress, humanitarian values such as those found in art, music, literature, and the advancement of knowledge. (During his campaign, Abraham Lincoln went to Wisconsin to talk to and win the support of the Freethinkers who joined the Union army, many of whom died in battle.)

Music making in early America was always somewhat free in that one was forced to create his own rules, often because of lack of instruments but also the scarcity of instruction and implementation of musical rules.

Perhaps the most important composer was a poor tanner named William Billings (1746–1800) who wrote that in composing music "Nature is the best dictator." (I have used Quotations from William Billings' *Jargon* and Supply Belcher (1750–1836) in my *Symphony No. 14*).

My own method of composing shifts somewhat with each work.

Depending on what I want to say in a piece, there will be pre-compositional research. When this is finished, the major task is to clear my mind of all problems and ideas that might be bothering me. This might take days or weeks or even months. It is not the same as transcendental meditation. (I had spent six weeks at the Mt. Tremper Zen Monastery in Upstate New York meditating, but this was not exactly the type of concentration I needed to compose, for my clear mind must extend over long periods of time, and after the Zen meditation it did not.) After this has been resolved, and I am free, I can work, but only if the spirit descends. In this concentration there are emotional, technical, and spiritual forces that become integrated or appear to occur in and out during the process. Sometimes there is a "flow" as if the music is rapidly coming through me. Other times there is a struggle. Sometimes I will put away an unsuccessful attempt and later, often overnight, the musical idea will be there, sometimes in a different form from the original.

Every piece I write usually begins with the uncertainty as to whether or not it will come into being. The fact that Haydn always prayed before composing, and his fears being similar to mine, gives me consolation and allows me to continue composing.

During and around many of my compositions, there are metaphysical events that have occurred. I will discuss three of the various compositions that have been haunted with mystical events:

Symphony No. 1 (Music on Open Strings), *Symphony No. 4*

(Chiaroscuro) and the chamber opera, *Stolen Identity.*

Symphony No. 1 (Music on Open Strings) by Gloria Coates

A commission for a work for string orchestra from the Rhineland Chamber Orchestra in 1973 following a concert with the first five of my *Emily Dickinson Songs* was somewhat unsettling for me, as I was new in Germany and had never written for string orchestra. Not knowing where to begin, I remembered Alexander Tcherepnin writing down a series of Chinese pentatonic scales for me in 1962 at the Mozarteum in Salzburg, and telling me that I might be interested in using one of them some day. Looking through them, I selected one that had the tones C, D♭, F, G♭, and B♭. Working diligently for over a week, (but not at a deep level,) I produced a work for string orchestra. (There were no computers then, nor copy machines, nor cell phones, so whatever I did compose took considerable time and effort.)

Alas, when playing through my new piece on the piano, I discovered it sounded somewhat pseudo-Chinese and had more than an element of artificiality. What a waste of time and effort! I tore it up and immediately threw it in the wastebasket. I began wondering if I could ever write the piece in time, as the deadline was approaching in 2 months. I felt frustrated with myself and began to doubt if I could ever compose again. I went to bed disappointed with an aching "feeling in my bones."

Upon waking the next morning, I suddenly seemed to know what might solve the problem for the use of that pentatonic scale. Perhaps I could tune the strings of the different instruments to that Chinese scale. After calculating and comparing the notes to the strings and intervals needed, I saw that this was possible. Ideas began to spin through my mind...colors, intervals, patterns, new instrumental sounds and forms.

Bringing out my manuscript paper and pen, I wrote out the retuning of the various strings to the pentatonic scale, and created a little melody played, by necessity, in a mosaic pattern among the instruments. "The colors of the instruments on the open strings should be rough sounding," I thought, "which would go with the primitive melody." Then I had the various tuned instruments drop out of the melodic line as each set played a new color element and rhythm. Each time the melody repeated, two more groups would transform themselves until all the instruments were in a whirl of sound colors and rhythms. In the next movement I used the instrumental patterns derived from the first movement in a scherzo form with glissandi going in upward directions in pitch, often pizzicati, and I used percussive instrumental sounds made by tapping on the instruments in various ways.

I felt a need to return to normal tuning at the end of this piece, so I took our minor scale and turned it on its side in a vertical position which was formed, in truth, by the open strings of all the instruments in their normal tuning. The tones from these open strings I used as a starting point for glissandi, which in various divisions and rhythms, developed microtonally in a more or less refracted mirror canon ascending in quarter tones and returning in whole and half steps to its original position. This movement ended solidly in a long crescendo on open strings in all the instruments. In the original version, I had decided to have the players tune their instruments in a loosely timed movement between the second and final movements. This is the version I brought to the Rhineland Chamber Orchestra rehearsal in 1973.

There were two rehearsals. At the first rehearsal, various members of the orchestra vehemently protested. One woman shouted that there was no melody in the piece and that it could not be considered music. I pointed out the Chinese melody in the first movement. A passer by came into the rehearsal hall and was very excited about the work, having heard it from the street as she walked past and wanted to know who wrote it and when it would be performed. This was my only consolation.

Although the young Alicja Mounk was willing to conduct the piece, it was eventually decided to be performed without a conductor. This did not really work with the rhythmic patterns; the last movement sounded like an old fashioned washing machine because of the accents created for keeping in time! The head of new music from the WDR had decided to attend the premier, but for fear of an almost certain bad performance, I decided to take the piece off the concert. They substituted mine with a piece by Bacewiecz, a Polish woman composer. I learned later that there was a plan by a conservative composer to attack my work in a lecture on their series the following day entitled *Pollution in the New Music....*

I tried twice to interest someone in the score. Once was for Munich's Musica Viva under Wolfgang Fortner. He did not even look at the score, but sent it back untouched.

Another was Richard Kapp, a truly wonderful conductor living in New York who wanted to premier it with the New York Virtuosi. Eventually I learned that the copiest I had hired in London was late with the copying, and I had to have him send it on to Kapp without my seeing it. It turned out that the score and parts had so many mistakes that it was impossible to play the piece. Another failed attempt.

About that time, around 1973, I had a meeting with Stuart Pope at Boosey and Hawkes who was interested in using it in the educational department. I did not think it should be in that department, so I did not accept the offer to publish it there. However, he did suggest that the retuning movement might be better if written out. This was an excellent suggestion, for it gave me courage to do something I had thought would be too difficult. As it happened, I hit a "flow" and sitting in a library, I wrote the movement in a half hour. The retuning of the original scordatura to the normal tuning of the instruments creates glissandi which cascade in polyphonic phrases while the players are playing their instruments. I now think it is perhaps the most interesting part of the entire work. Nevertheless, the manuscript stayed in a drawer for a few more years waiting for its premiere.

Then a new music troop, a bag-piping ensemble from Warsaw had a concert in Munich. I attended, and was invited to go out with them afterwards. I mentioned my piece to the leader of the group, Zygmunt Krause. He gave me the address of Warsaw Autumn Festival, and told me to send the score to the committee. The piece was accepted by the committee and was to be performed by the Polish Chamber Orchestra under Jerzy Maksymiuk at the next Warsaw Autumn Festival in 1978.

Even in Poland at the new music festival there was opposition to the work from the musicians in the orchestra during the first rehearsal. They did not want to play on open strings and did not like the raw sound. They also insisted that it would be impossible to create the pianissimo at the beginning of the first movement and then crescendo on the open strings. They demonstrated this impossibility to me, and then played the piece with normal tuning, stopping the strings for the pitches. As much as they liked the sound, it was too refined a sound for what I wanted. I told them I would try to find a solution. I left perplexed and somewhat upset, not being sure what to do. Should I insist on the open strings without a crescendo and have a weak beginning? This was a possibility. There was one more rehearsal the next day.

I was housed by the festival committee in the famous old Bristol Hotel formerly owned by the Polish political leader and pianist Pederewski, and now in 1978, in need of repair, a sort of glimmering decadence. My room was on the fourth floor overlooking a plaza.

That night my sleep was restless, and around 4AM I began trying to solve the problem of the crescendo in the first movement without which would change all the colors as well as the meaning of the composition, for it would not be played on the open strings. As I pondered this situation, it occurred to me to use the bow instead of the strings for the crescendo. If the hairs on the bow were to be very loose and hanging, one could play across the strings very softly. There were rests built into the piece in the mosaic pattern, so the players could tighten their bow hairs during the rests. As the bow hairs would become tighter, a crescendo might be possible so that towards the end of the mosaic section, one could reach the highest dynamic level creating a great crescendo. I also thought the piece might work better with microphones on or near the instruments for it was to be performed in the enormous philharmonic hall. I would have to check on that possibility. The problem was that the only rehearsal was in a few hours, and I had to know if this would work before suggesting it at the rehearsal. There would be no time to experiment.

Dawn was breaking, and it was around 5AM. I was pacing the room wondering how I could manage to find a stringed instrument, when I looked down from the little balcony of my room and saw a lone figure walking across the plaza. He was carrying a case. "Could it be a physician on a night emergency call," I wondered, "or could it be a case with a stringed instrument inside?" I threw on my coat, found the elevator still out of service for the night, so I ran down the four flights of the spiral staircase and out the door facing the plaza to see if he were still there. There was no one. Suddenly behind a column pasted with festival posters I saw him anxiously looking at his watch.

I hurried up to him and discovered he could not understand me as he spoke no English, German or French. I made motions as if playing a violin and he pointed to his watch and then to a poster on the column announcing a concert from Krakow that had finished performing that night. I then pointed to my name on the same poster, and the concert that was in one day. He then became interested in helping me.

We went inside the hotel and woke the sleeping night watchman who spoke German. He was able to translate my requests about the bow hairs. The violinist from Krakow began playing with the loose hairs and gradually tightening the bow as he played various tones. It worked. There was a crescendo!

At the rehearsal I explained the process to the musicians and concertmaster. They all seemed delighted with the new technique...sometimes playfully looping the bow hairs around their instruments. Afterwards I was able to contact Josef Patkowski, director of the electronic studio. He graciously supplied microphones for the performance.

The piece finally had its premiere on September 20, 1978 in the Philharmonic of Warsaw by the Polish Chamber Orchestra under Jerzy Maksymiuk. I was exhausted from all the stress leading up to that performance, but was relieved it was well received. Shaken, I only wanted to return to my room afterwards and recover. This was too bad as one of my favorite composers, Arvo Paert, congratulated me enthusiastically and asked me to join him and his wife. I could only drag myself back to the hotel. Throughout the press, *Music on Open Strings* was selected as one of the high points of the festival. In *Melos Neue Zeitschrift fuer Musik* Detlef Gojowy wrote, "It was hailed by the public as the cutting edge of experimental music. It is the beginning of the very origin of the elementary musical material."

The Bavarian Radio's new music department ordered the tape of this performance from Polish Radio which was later broadcast. Without my knowledge, it was programmed for a concert on Musica Viva by Juergen Meyer Josten who succeeded Wolfgang Fortner as artistic director. This was the first time in the 35-year history of Musica Viva that an orchestral work by a woman composer was performed on this festival initiated by Karl Amadeus Hartmann after World War II. It was a success, but more important, a breakthrough for the many women composers that followed through the years. This performance was produced on an LP recording by Sonoton and was one of the nineteen finalists for the 1986 Koussevitzsky International Record Award that honors a living composer for an important work. I dedicated this work to the memory of Alexander Tcherepnin.

The metaphysical happening of seeing a man with a case in the early morning hours at a time that I needed an instrument so desperately, and finding his case to contain a violin was, for me, a miracle.

Symphony No. 4 (Chiaroscuro) by Gloria Coates

In October of 1983 the Kronos Quartet had recorded three of my string quartets for the South German Radio in Stuttgart, the BBC had recorded

Music On Open Strings with the London Sinfonia under Richard Pitman, and I left London for northern Wisconsin to see my sick father and to help drive him to the hospital in Madison.

He went through various tests, and the doctors did not know how much time he had. After two weeks, I had to return to Munich, so I said good bye to him, and felt as if it were the last time. In Munich I telephoned him daily. Usually there was someone with him for the night.

About two weeks after I returned, I telephoned to my sister-in-law and was told he was doing well. She told me that nobody was with him that night. This upset me, but I was too far away to do anything from Munich.

I went to bed. About five in the morning, I awoke with an extremely empty and sad feeling, as if I were parting again from my father. I put the radio on and began to walk about the room. The feeling got worse suddenly, and I fell on the bed sobbing. I felt as if something, almost like a long breath, were leaving me from the top of my head...and I remember whispering and repeating the words, "Don't leave me," Through my tears I could hear music from the radio. It was playing Purcell's aria from *Dido and Aeneas* "*When I Am Laid in Earth*," an aria I had sung many times and knew well. The text is "When I am laid in earth, may my wrongs create no trouble in thy breast. Remember me, but forget my fate." (This is a passacaglia in form with a choral-like theme under the melody.) I became more aware of reality and stopped crying.

The room seemed to be flooded with light, an unnatural light that illuminated even the objects around me, giving them a warm glow. I fell asleep with a feeling of being comforted. Later, around noon, the telephone rang. It was my mother who was crying. In tears, she told me that my father had died. It was the same time as my own feeling of grief in the early morning hours.

In the months that followed, I went through the process of mourning, but always wondered about this metaphysical happening. Because of my grief, it was not until a year had passed before I decided to translate this experience into music. A commission from Klaus Hashagen of Ars Nova Ensemble Nuremberg was pending, and I turned to this for my vehicle of expression. It takes the form of three parts; the first is that of my metaphysical experience with my father's death. The second represents the conflicts in the family following his death. The third movement is derived from a dream I had almost a year later that resolves problems he had in his life and my relationship to them. It was the acceptance of his life's message and death. I also painted a painting about the third movement and put some of the music notes from the manuscript in the painting. This chamber music version titled *Transitions* was first performed at a Musica Viva Concert in Munich by the Ars Nova Ensemble under the baton of Werner Heider on June 23, 1985.

Illumination is the first movement which is in the form of a passacaglia. It uses the passacaglia theme from the Purcell work layered under and around the music. Circling this theme are forms representing the events of that morning in a collage of canonic materials. It culminates with the Purcell melody played by flutes in a polyphonic texture, leading to a final climax.

The second movement, *Mystical Plosives*, is a percussive and more aggressive expression representing the feelings and conflicts within the family surrounding my father's life and death.

The third movement titled *Dream Sequence*, is based on a dream I had a year after my father's death. I was traveling in a rectangular black car on a wide highway with many lanes leading upward to my childhood home. My mother, sister and brother are with me. En route, we stop at a wayside to rest. Other cars move past. Suddenly a woman composer appears, and she is taken into the car with my family, and I am left outside alone. While waiting, I see a car with the deceased former partner of my father. I hail her car, and we proceed to my house where she drops me off. My brother runs towards me crying and motioning that I go inside and that my father is on the phone and wants to talk to me. As I enter I see my sister and mother sitting side by side crying on a bench. I go to the telephone and hear his voice asking me to come to visit him. He will pick me up at a particular place half way between. I am hesitant and full of anxiety as I do not know how to get there, and my car has already departed.

Suddenly I see my father in an office dressed in a grey pin striped suit lying across his desk. His partner enters, takes his pulse and raises his hand. She exclaims vehemently and repeatedly that he is dead. This ends the dream.

After several years, in 1990, I had the opportunity to orchestrate this work, and it was premiered in Stuttgart as *Chiaroscuro* (*Symphony No. 4*) by the Stuttgart Philharmonic under Wolf-Dieter Hauschild at an exhibition of paintings by the Thiele-Zoll artist pair and recorded by a coproduction of the West German Radio Cologne (WDR) and the Bavarian Radio Munich (BR).

The orchestral version was premiered on June 22, 1990. It is dedicated to the memory of my father. I consider it to be my best work.

Stolen Identity, a chamber opera in one act by Gloria Coates

The research on this chamber opera began around 1994 when I became personally interested in the problem concerning musical copyright. This was near the beginning of the age of the internet as well as technical advances in the reproduction of music, books, and other materials. Even an identity could be stolen!

Already around 1992, composer Morton Gould, who was then President of ASCAP, offered me a position checking music for plagiarism. I was unable to accept, but know he was aware then of the increasing threats to individual artistic works. In 1994 in a discussion with Libby van Cleve, now the new director of Oral History of American Music at Yale University and a talented oboist, expressed her concern that the internet might undermine all copyrights because of the immense spectrum of reproduction possibilities.

Soon after, I happened to meet with a very important US copyright attorney active in the arts. We discussed plagiarism in music, and he seemed to think that it was a compliment to the composer for his/her music to be copied, and that the originator could best fight back by promoting his own music so that it would be known beyond that of the plagiarist. Somehow, this seemed to be the best solution, for if a composer has a new idea and much of his music featuring it is stolen, and if the original composer tries to stop the music from spreading by suing the plagiarist, then he is likewise, to some degree, putting a halt to his own ideas. It seems counter-productive, in any case. Of course, giving credit to the originator by the copiest is always desired, but this does not usually happen without a nudge. One must believe that history will eventually prove the truth, albeit often after the death of the composer.

In the year 2010 I went to bed one night thinking about various of my musical works that had been copied and sometimes even published, and wondered about it until I fell asleep. In the morning, I awoke with a strong urge to write down the details of a dream I had that night:

A young girl is standing in a large nest bordered with sticks made from criss-crossed bows of stringed instruments. She is looking for her bird who has not returned to the nest. Upon his return, he is injured. She must leave him to search for healing herbs. While she is away, a wandering thief spies the bird and realizes it is the magic musical bird he has been seeking all his life. He is able to overpower the weak bird, stabbing him with the bows from the side of the nest. He has a bag and as the bows pierce the bird's sides, instead of blood, music flows out. The thief catches the music in his bag.

Finally there are six wounds. The bird collapses. At this moment, a loud clap of thunder sounds as the girl returns with the healing herbs in the form of a wreath. The thief is frightened and drops his bag of music as he flees the scene. Seeing her bird wounded or dead from the stick wounds, the girl bends over him and places the wreath of healing herbs on his head. She sees it is too late. She then decides to pull out the bows from his sides.

As she pulls out the sticks from the bird's sides, the music returns into the bird. He begins to expand and seems to become stronger.

The last of the six bows is removed and the bird can stand again. They rejoice. The bird tells her about the thief and what happened to him. He sees the bag on the bottom of the nest. They laugh as a quote by Abraham Lincoln seems to disperse the gloom, "You can fool some of the people some of the time, but not all of the people all of the time."

This story seemed ideal for an opera. I then filled in some details and titled it *Stolen Identity.*

The orchestra is composed of a string quartet, percussion and piano. I wrote the spoken text myself which carries the action of the play. The arias use poems by Emily Dickinson, Paul Celan, and Alexandra Coates. There is a second version with a spoken text by Edgar Allen Poe as well. Thus, it is a Singspiel related to the early Miracle Plays from the Middle Ages. It also has a similar content.

The Carl Orff Institute in Munich had wanted a concert of my music for 2012, and I suggested the opera. The idea was enthusiastically received by the director Thomas Roesch. Because of financial problems, the opera was performed in concert version only on April 26, 2012, in the Carl Orff Institute in Munich, Germany.

The Performers were: April Fredrick, soprano, Nicholas Clapton, counter-tenor, Gary Martin, bass baritone, with instrumentalists: Peter Sheppard-Skaerved and Mihailo Trandafilovski, violins, Morgan Goff, viola, Neil Heyde, cello, Stephan Blum, percussion, and Eva Schieferstein, piano.

As I was finishing writing the orchestration for the opera, I decided to go downtown to find bird whistles to use as a musical element in the nest scenes. I happened to try a shop which had various hardware and other items. I could not find a bird whistle that suited me, but I happened to see a shelf of masks and noticed a paper-mâché mask which seemed perfect for the thief, so bought it. I asked about the origin of the mask, and the clerk said the design was originally from Venice. They produced a short description about it. It was a copy of a Renaissance mask used also by the protagonist in the Commedia dell'Arte named Zanni, a clever and humorously sly joker or thief. Zanni represented the simple, common people of the day.

Returning home, I went to the computer to do more research on the mask. As I began, the doorbell rang. It was the postman with a small package. Opening it, I saw there were three CDs that were sent to me from the Tcherepnin Society in New York. I did not expect them. I looked at them. One was from a program at Carnegie Hall with works by Tcherepnin's students including one of mine entitled *Tones in Overtones*. Performed by Stephen Gosling, pianist, it was entitled *Alexander Tcherepnin and his Students.*

The second was the complete piano concertos of Alexander Tcherepnin.

The third was piano music by Alexander Tcherepnin's father Nikolai Tcherepnin. There in Nikolai Tcherepnin's CD was his music for the *14 Sketches on Pictures from the Russian Alphabet, Opus 38.* The sketches are based on a children's book with the paintings by Alexander Benois, great uncle of Alexander Tcherepnin. The paintings for the book by Alexander Benois appear in the booklet of the CD. I looked up Benois in the computer, and on the same page was a painting with the Harlequin (Zanni) character holding a mask similar to the one I had just bought. A small bag hung at his side. The scene was that of the Commedia dell'Arte.

On the other side of the page was a portrait of Benois painted by Leon Bakst, who with Benois and Diagilev started the important Symbolist *World of Art* magazine (1898–1904) which was the leading propagation of the communication of modern ideas on art as a form of mystical experience. Nikolai Tcherepnin composed and conducted for the Ballet Russe at that time and was a part of the group of innovators.

Alexander Tcherepnin knew and saw the beginning of my first opera based on Poe's *Fall of the House of Usher* in 1962 at the Mozarteum while working with him. Tcherepnin encouraged me to finish it as no one had written this opera then, and Debussy's was unfinished. However, I never felt the need after that summer, and composing chamber music and orchestral music led me in another direction. Almost every time Tcherepnin saw me he would remind me to finish the opera before someone else wrote it. As history has proved, it finally was too late for me, as many versions appeared on the market including that of Debussy's which had been finished. There was no need for mine.

However, with a different chamber opera, and the echos of Tcherepnin via the mask, the knock on the door with the CDs, and Benois's paintings of the Commedia dell'Arte with the very mask appearing on the internet ....altogether seemed to say something to me. Perhaps it was mystically a happy nod from Tcherepnin acknowledging that I had finally finished an opera.

Beyond the spheres that
Orbit our sun
Across the stars
Through black holes that
Lace the inner realm,
Shapes like dippers, kites and
Strings of pearls—
Sounds that echo—
Crusts of dried
Orbs
Whizzing, whirling, twirling,
Crashing,
Swirling through
Timeless space in
Circles round, oblong, and
Elliptical.
Through the
Vortex of my singing soul
Transformed...

January 2014

CHAPTER 8

JACQUES DEMIERRE IN CONVERSATION WITH GUILLAUME BELHOMME

JACQUES DEMIERRE

There are different ways of breaking stones—as the poet Charles Péguy once showed—whether we pave pathways or build cathedrals. With *Breaking Stone* (Tzadik 9001), Jacques Demierre has shown it again recently. From inside his piano, here he is, running through the layers of a musical art "in balance" with his own existence, in order to bring to surface stones of memory and fragments of forgetfulness that he shapes freely with the hammers. In conversation, the sparks of the pianist are as generous—and itinerant—as he is: the latest one reaching all the way to Tuscany.

Jacques: In the '80s, I had met Luciano Berio on the occasion of an interview for the first issue of the magazine *Contrechamps* devoted to him. Berio received us in Radicondoli, not far from Siena, around a pasta meal he had prepared himself. The house was magnificent, on top of a hill surrounded by vineyards. To the question whether the peaceful and harmonious atmosphere of the place inspired him in his work, he replied that almost all of his music had been written in hotel rooms. Today I understand better why the music and the thought of Luciano Berio have been so important to me. I could see entwined in the work of this composer a great deal of my own concerns at that time—concerns that have not left me and resonate to this day under different forms in my music. Besides the question of improvisation and musical forms related to jazz and the practice of experimentation, I find in it a lot of founding elements of my work: the interest in voice, the relation between language and music, the link with experiments in linguistics, in particular with the research of Ferdinand de Saussure. But above all, there is the relation to sound, which underlies the universality of the experience of language and opens a field of possibilities where making sense, giving form, composing with materials belonging to different worlds would become a significant part of my life as a musician.

Guillaume: Your interest in speech and language, you once told me, has brought you to think of voice as a "material" somewhat apart, because capable of sound as much as of sense. Berio used to say that language was "*the house of life* (...) and a wonderful machine which incessantly makes sense," adding that "music is another machine that amplifies and transcribes sense on another level of intelligence and perception."[1]

Was your relation to the piano, your first instrument, modified by your interest in linguistics and the work of Saussure in particular? Did you feel the need to approach it in another way so that it could "speak" in its turn—even "sing the words," to quote Berio speaking of the effect the instruments in Debussy had on him?

1. Berio, Luciano, *Entretiens avec Rossana Dalmonte*, translated into French by Martin Kaltnenecker, JC Lattès, Paris, 1983.

Jacques: The piano was already there, in progress, influenced by the blues, rock, jazz and contemporary music, at the time when I discovered linguistics. It was like a revelation, I was discovering a domain where sense and sound worked in a space of complementarity. It was a real shock because, immersed in musicology on one hand, while playing jazz and contemporary music on the other, I saw an ideal place where both theoretical thought and the practice of sound could coexist. The reality was of course more complex than that, but the encounter was radically decisive. In fact, it was mostly the encounter with Luis Prieto, the Argentinean linguist and semiologist whose classes I was following at the University of Geneva, that was decisive. Paradoxically, through a love for Argentinean tango, which we both shared, he opened my mind to this discipline through his very rigorous thought, while at the same time he managed to make me give up, in favor of music and piano, the path of linguistics which I had provisionally intended to pursue. A pianist infatuated by tango—he had hesitated for a long time between piano and linguistics in his youth—he used to repeat at each of our meetings how much better it would be for me to continue with music, where undoubtedly I would find a more enriching and essential interior space. Unconsciously, I followed his advice. I continued playing tangos too, while keeping speech and language at the core of my piano and music. But it took time for the piano to "speak in its turn," as in *Breaking Stone* for instance. It was first by the intercession of pure listening that I could approach the piano differently. I would hear the voice and the piano of bluesmen pianists/singers such as Champion Jack Dupree or Memphis Slim as a single unique sound. I wouldn't hear a vocal melody and accompanying piano. I could see the projection of the words through the body, the musician's mouth, with all the linguistic accidents that speech entails, as well as the action of bodily movement liberating through the fingers the sounds of the piano. Their pianos were speaking in me, their words were playing the blues. I remember how as a teenager, alone at the harmonica I would play the songs of Sonny Terry and Brownie McGhee, where the sound of my single instrument, through my breath only, was at once the expression of the voice and that of the instruments. My piano would also speak when, playing a jazz standard—something that after all happened only very rarely on stage—I could not imagine the improvisation without taking into account the original words of the standard in question: I could hear in each pitch of the initial melody its vocalic and consonantic origin. I wanted not only to play an extension of the sense of each word, but also to trace a prolongation of the purely acoustic aspect of the text of the song. I was trying to spell out, by means of the twelve half tones I was using then, the undetermined noised reality of the intermingled consonants and vowels. Later, there were productions such as *Fabrik-Songs,* a project for solo piano based on the songs of Kurt Weill and Hanns Eisler. Songs whose texts, without exception, were all written by Bertolt Brecht. It was a music without words, where the piano, literally, made off with the words. But it took them to better render them after, once it had passed them through its pianistic acoustic and gestural filter. Later still, the project *Avec* for prepared piano on the poems of the French poet Guillevic again charged the piano alone with the mission of uttering the poetic word. This time what was at stake was the tension between each poem spread spatially over the score and the blank space of this same page dictated by the typographic layout. Tracing diagonals of sense between imaginary buccal points of articulation, locating the poems over the space of the page and handing out to the public, while still playing, the already interpreted scores.

Guillaume: I'm delighted to hear of your affinity for tango (which was first instrumental, then sung, like your music in a way…). The writer Ramón Gómez de la Serna has written that tango comes "at once from dance, from song, and from a certain funeral music (played discretely beside the coffin holding the departed's corpse)."[2] This might strike you as strange, but I

2. Gomez de la Serna, Ramón, *Interprétation du tango*, translated into French by Danièle Robert, André Dimanche, Marseille, 1993.

recognize these three things in your music.

Jacques: Not strange, on the contrary. I see in this comparison a continuity between several elements that have always been very important to my work. In large part, I see the body's movement as the basis of my instrumental sound, in that both are rooted in a relation to time, duration. Singing, especially in tango, is never far from speech, even in counter-relief. And it's a small step from this black piece of furniture to a coffin. The body of the sound lies in the vibration of this fragile sheet of spruce, the soundboard. For a long time I used to begin my day as a pianist by playing tangos, without realizing that in doing so I was, as always, at the heart of this acoustic-linguistic dynamic between sound and meaning. I remember a concert Roberto Goyeneche gave in Buenos Aires; he was already very old, sick, gaunt but elegant, and his voice, backed by a bandoneon, a guitar and a double bass, was nothing but a trace of itself, but more than ever it told of this strength of speech. There was no longer a melody on one side and an uttered text on the other, even masterfully united. I was like all those young children who, until a certain age, can't yet distinguish the text from its melodic movement when they hear a song. They can't say the text without the melody, no more than they could sing the melody without the text. Goyeneche's porteño speech had that effect on me, it was an astounding balance of sound and sense within the space of performed poetic speech. Of course, alongside my wonder at this unheard-of balance, I felt tempted towards the utopia of a "music of meaning" as Roland Barthes writes, of a language "enlarged, (...) even denatured, until it formed an immense fabric of sound in which the semantic apparatus would find itself deactivated: the phonic, metric, vocal signifier would unfurl in all its sumptuousness, without ever letting a sign arise from it (...)" But I also think, like Barthes, that "there always remains too much meaning for language to fulfill a *jouissance* appropriate to its material."[3] If one wants to tackle such material as speech and language, then to work on acoustic writing and to improvise on qualities of relation between sound and sense seems of greater interest to me than their absolute independence in regard to each other, or even than to work on quantities.

3. Barthes, Roland, *Œuvres Complètes, IV. Livres, textes, entretiens: 1972–1976*, Le Seuil, Paris 2002.

Guillaume: We could crudely paraphrase that last quotation of Barthes:

language, "in all its senses," can never be too "sensual." In spite of everything, you keep looking after this, working on the "nature of the relations between sound and meaning" as you say, and in my opinion—if you'll forgive the risky undertaking—you do it "by the coffin which holds the body of the departed." Is it not through your mourning of this "music of meaning" that you are able to compose with an ear both for the music of sense and the sense of the music? In fact, couldn't your experiments in this domain be compared to building a new language?

Jacques: At a certain moment there was a—slightly naïve—temptation to think that music could be seen as a language. Under the influence of advances in linguistics at the time, research in musical semiology laid some tracks in that direction. To me, ethnolinguistics and ethnomusicology seemed interesting paths because they were faced with unknown linguistic or musical systems and had to propose descriptions that, to my ear, often sounded like compositional structures. But pretty quickly that began to seem a dead end. Instead, listening to John Cage's music and reading his texts led me to accept the autonomy of the elements at play: where listening allows a work of balance and complementarity in a space of continuous transformations. Instead of leading me off towards the utopia of a new language, my consideration of both the music of sense and the sense of music spurred me still more to work towards an equilibrium of opposed elements. I don't seek to marshal these elements to build a new acoustic reality, rather I try to refine their positioning and interactions within a whole of complementary objects in movement. This idea of complementary movement and equilibrium gradually took hold in my work. And it's still happening. Some improbable encounters have also influenced me in this direction: while I was working on a musical project in Bolivia, I met an old man sitting on a bench in a park in Sucre. We struck up a conversation and I told him about my work in sound. He listened, replied nothing for a moment, then began to speak with a voice that seemed to come from very far away. He was a philosopher, a retired military man, a shaman—with as skillful a handle on philosophical reflection combining European thought with the mythologies of the Andean high plateaus, as on the narration of several pirogue expeditions up Amazon rivers, punctuated by piranha attacks and the revelation of old Nazis hidden in inaccessible prairies. He started telling me how the "law of equilibrium" had imposed itself upon him little by little, and how much his own life, as well as that of the world today, owed to this fundamental law. Amidst a silence, he stood up, took three steps and turned back to me saying "*no te olvides: la ley del equilibrio....*" I haven't forgotten.

Guillaume: You conceded a few moments ago that in *Breaking Stone* the piano in fact "speaks." Is this piece, in your opinion, a "tell-tale" example of the search for equilibrium? Do you distinguish it from those "songs without words," if you will, that you composed when you adapted Weill and Eisler in *Fabrik-Songs*, or when you transformed Guillevic texts into musical scores in *Avec* or, again, evoked the Alps of your childhood in *Sumpatheia*?

Jacques: In *Breaking Stone*, the setting is a search for equilibrium between the body, the spoken text and the piano. It isn't a matter of a completely "equal" equilibrium, in which the overall tension would be equally and constantly distributed over these three entities. A homogenous system which doesn't transform over time doesn't seem particularly convincing to me. For me there is a high-wire zone, in which precisely I do my work of equilibrium. A zone which runs from absolute equilibrium, never attained, to avowed disequilibrium, which I try to avoid, and inside this zone the body, the text and the piano constantly reevaluate their mutual interactions. These interactions are multiple: the sound of the voice, amplified, is projected against the instrument's soundboard, casting it into resonance and allowing me to play with the voice by the technical means of the piano; I play the voice and the piano becomes a mouth in turn, the spectrum of the voice shading my piano colorations. This is not spectacle, but rather something intimately organic. The spoken text and the piano find themselves united by the intermediary of the body. The voice articulates the text, the body, finding its places of articulation in the piano's space, articulates the voice. *Breaking Stone* takes the measure of these three territories. These "songs without words" for solo piano that you spoke of as well, *Fabrik-Songs* and *Avec*, are distinct from *Breaking Stone* in that the accent is placed on the text as the generator of music and sounds. The relation of equilibrium is more at the level of the construction. In *Fabrik-Songs*, I play and improvise music—*Songs*—that Weill and Eisler wrote to texts by Bertolt Brecht. The idea was to extend the poetic range of the texts through improvisation, based on the notion of the rhythmic predetermination of music in relation to text, which Kurt Weill evokes when he writes of the gestural nature of music. ("Music can notate the accents of a language, the distribution of long and short syllables, and especially the pauses [...] Moreover, it is possible to interpret a phrase in all sorts of ways. [...] However, this rhythmic setting that one gets from a text affords only the rudiments of a gestural music. The specific work of the musician begins only once he finds the contact between the word and what he wants to convey by music's other means of expression."[4]) Thus the oral, performative dimension, which in this project is buried in the piano's melodic-rhythmic structures, leaves its mark on the songs in counter-relief. In *Avec*, Guillevic's poems find themselves arranged as a graphic score, in which the space on the page and the poetic meaning become musical text. First, the poems are simultaneously read and interpreted on the piano, then, as the piece progresses, the pages of the score are gradually distributed to the audience and silently read by each spectator. Gradually, the auditory space fills with silent poetry readings and wordless piano sounds. In homage to the poet Guillevic, the inscribed text remains on the score-sheet and never gains full oral expression, instead leaving the stage to the duo of body and piano. In this sense, *Breaking Stone* is the first live meeting of three territories: word, body and piano. The performance aspect is crucial—that's where the piece's real poetic and musical text is played, not in the words on the page or the indications on the score. The poetic-musical text exists and bodies forth only in this meeting, at the very moment of the performance, between speech, body and piano. This is writing as such, inscribed in the instant across these three territories.

4. Weill, Kurt, *«A propos du caractère gestuel de la musique»*, in Contrechamps *#4*, L'Age d'Homme, Lausanne, 1985.

Guillaume: In what way does the "written word" influence your work as a composer generally—regardless whether it loses all established meaning, or even disappears, as if dissolved in music? Could one say that your readings depend on the memories that suffuse many of your compositions?

Jacques: The relation between the "written word" and my work as a composer initially consisted in setting things to music. This is a rather traditional approach, but it did take into account the achievements of contemporary experimentation and of concrete and electro-acoustic music in their use of the speaking and singing voice (here pieces such as *Thema* (*Omaggio a*

Joyce) for instance were decisive). The writing of certain poets—e.e. cummings, James Joyce—also marked me a lot, opening textual spaces of otherness. Alongside this compositional work of setting texts to music, a sort of displacement of the text happened inside of me. There were revelations, like the German poet Gerhard Rühm, performing his texts or playing them on the piano in a purely acoustic translation. Or else my telephone encounter with the poet Ghérasim Luca whose writing I greatly admired. I didn't know him personally, so I called him to ask his permission to set to music one of his poems. Of course he refused, but above all he took the time to explain his answer. We spoke a very long time about this issue of sound and text. He explained to me his intention in detail—how much care he took to introduce an explicitly acoustic dimension in his poetic material, which thus finally should not need to be set to music: if a sound dimension is already present, the acoustic form will fully reveal itself at the moment of the spoken performance. Thus in my work as a composer, in my "musical settings," the text gradually found another place: from the page and the score it moved to the mouth. But I needed to put this text into my own body, I had to put it in my mouth, make it sound out, manage to listen to its unfurling on the inside. Only progressively did sound poetry furrow its space in me, settled in my body, in my buccal territory, soon spreading itself to the entire breathing apparatus. This movement accelerated significantly in the duo collaboration with Vincent Barras—performer, poet and historian of medicine. We have worked and are still working on the materiality of language and speech in a four-hand process of writing/composition. After having written *anatomic* poems, we followed up on this over several years with a project on Ferdinand de Saussure, the founder of contemporary linguistics. The text of *Breaking Stone* in fact has its origin in *Voicing through Saussure*, where the fragments of languages analyzed by the Genevan linguist are reworked and recomposed, and then performed in their concrete and embodied reality in a speech liberating a linguistic flood of small particles of verbal matter. In *Breaking Stone* this flood is in a way processed, as when one speaks of signal processing in real time, by the piano play and the movements necessary to it. Our next project as a duo continues this long-term work of sound poetry on the origin of Indo-European languages. The point is to start out from these moments of conversation that contain, alongside the apparent discourse conveying the "content" or the meaning, all that mass of "parasitic" sound events—accents, stammers, sighs, hesitations, gaps, noises ... This piece, based on conversation as a genre and as a material, will narrate the duo's poetics. The work on sound poetry with Vincent Barras plays the role of a mirror, which is essential to my musical work with piano and voice. Thanks to this proximity, to this poetic and acoustic genealogy I can envisage with more clarity and distance the eminently musical aspect of *Breaking Stone*. The breaths, for instance, are on one hand part of the system of organization and construction of *Breaking Stone*, while on the other hand they organize the poetic system of the duo Vincent Barras & Jacques Demierre. The same physical act belongs in each case to radically separate systems of composition.

Guillaume: Your regard for these "parasitic sound events" might find an echo in the concerns of several contemporary composers (Cage or Globokar, to mention just two), and we see it in yet another of your fields of action—improvisation. Saussure, who inspired your work as a composer, was also the father of modern semiotics. Did you take an interest in this field of knowledge as an improviser? And, while you are improvising, how do you manage this complex relation between what is heard and what makes meaning?

Jacques: I believe that my work of sound poetry on speech—that is, according to the Saussurean distinction, on the private, personal, non-codified, unpolished surface of linguistic expression that stands in contrast with language or the social, collective, polished and codified side of this same expression—has had a strong influence on the way I envision musical improvisation. Performed poetic speech allows one to embrace "democratically" all the events in the production of sound, not just those that work directly towards meaning and language, but also all those that make it possible to hear the fundamentally concrete and material dimension of speech -sound residues, lisps, breaths, noises accompanying a discourse, "in other words, according to the felicitous phrase by Michel de Certeau, 'the grass between the paving stones' that punctuates ordinary language and conversation."[5] In my improvisation work, I have gradually appropriated the "grass between the paving stones" of my piano playing. This shift didn't happen in a day, because in order for these "absurd" noises to start making sense, I had to make them mine at

5. Barras, Vincent, "Parole performée", *Communications*, No. 92, 2013, quoting Certeau(de), Michel, «Utopies vocales: glossolalies», *Traverses*, No. 20, 1980.

each concert, during each performance. I couldn't work on them off stage—wanting to find pertinence to their accidental dimension was impossible at another time, their sense escaped me, it was only through contact with the live performance that I opened to the inscription of their sense in me. Nonetheless, the linguistic pair language/speech is not fully operational in music, it cannot be transposed as it is. If poetic work on speech allows one to add everything that makes noise to that which refers to language, improvisation work in general, and especially for me on the piano, does not refer to any codified or socially shared musical "language." Here the boundaries between what makes sense and what smacks of absurdity are less stable. The action of identifying purely acoustic pertinence is based on another type of relation between semantic organization and sound matter. And as semiotics had convinced me, sometimes *a contrario*, that music was not a language, the comparison stopped there, somewhat brusquely. How are we then to understand the gesture of improvisation and its attempt to signify a world of sound in constant change? I wrote in a previous article that "sound improvisation is the result of an encounter: that between a body and a sound. The two of them share the same space."[6]

This statement is really about the idea of movement, a movement that we perceive through hearing: first the movement of sound, which spreads incessantly, but also, and through it, the movement of life itself, which is in perpetual transformation. It is thanks to hearing that we enter in contact with the continuous vital movement that surrounds us incessantly. One cannot escape this primordial movement, nor escape hearing it. Short of piercing your eardrums, which is a sort of acoustic suicide, you cannot not listen. Listening transmits this propensity for movement that life manifests to the improvising body, and it is this improvising body that resonates directly with the vital flux. Improvisation, at each concert, puts into play the primary relation with the movement of life. The body reenacts each time its presence to the world by integrating this essential activity into its own motor activity. The improvising body re-elaborates this initial rhythmic gesture—which precedes any concept—and its infinite transformations. The improviser is a body in movement run through by thrusts, jolts, quivers, sudden energy releases, he is a place of transmutation in the alchemic sense of the word. But no loneliness in this seismic surge. Vibration, the wave phenomenon inherent to listening, links the improvising body with

6. Demierre, Jacques, «Cause et effet, sur l'improvisation sonore», in *Corps, son et geste*, Mômeludies, Lyon, 2012.

the other bodies that share the same field of sound disturbance. We are all subject to the movement of vital energy and to that of spreading sound: the sound body of the improviser sets off a vibration gesture in the acoustic space surrounding him and the eardrums of the listener share the sound fluctuations that affect at the same moment the eardrums of the improvising musician. This is almost a mimetic process—not just the bodies, but also the objects—loudspeaker membranes, mics, materials of the constructed environment—they all partake of that global movement constantly fed and transformed through the particularities of each body, animated or not. What is heard and what makes sense at the moment of sound improvisation is essentially constructed and thought through the listening body in movement. The musical meaning emerges from practice, and is expressed in all these occurrences through what is at once a fiercely individual and a profoundly collective experience.

Guillaume: Berio used to say that improvisation "poses problems, above all because there isn't a real unanimity of discourse among the participants, but only, at times, a unanimity of behavior."[7] How does this apply to your improvisations with other musicians? For example let's take your (remarkable, I must say) collaboration with Urs Leimgruber and Barre Phillips: do the three of you try to "figure as one," as the single body that meets the sound, in your earlier definition? Do you all conceive of this experiment in the same way beforehand, and do you all hope for the same outcome?

7. Berio, Luciano, *op. cit.*

Jacques: For the musicians of the LDP trio, it's not at all a matter of "figuring as one body"—but rather, on the contrary, of opening their playing to the experience of a "sound body" which results from the improvised situation itself, and whose parts together characterize the improvised instant in terms of an instrumental, architectural, and aural space. This might finally be no different from what we call the trio's sound, or that of any band which has developed its own. Once the concert begins, each musical gesture enacts a corresponding change in the relation between the instruments' particular conditions of production, the transmission of sound in the acoustic space, and the reception of the acoustic signal played by the musicians. As soon as there is improvisation, everything is heard, everything is tested, everything is listened to, not only the circumstances of what each musician plays instrumentally, but the architectural or natural characteristics of the physical environment, as well as each individuals' personal acoustic fabrication, both subjective and objective, in simultaneously perceiving this music and these sounds. At the crucial moment of playing, all of the elements of sound production, of acoustic propagation and reception, which compose the continuous state of improvised flux and are simultaneously caught in its flow—all of these elements are intimately and organically conditioned by each other, without however being completely dependent on each other. One could even speak of a "conditioned co-production of phenomena" to borrow from Buddhist terminology, in the sense that no acoustic phenomenon exists without being compounded of multiple conditions and itself becoming the condition of a new phenomenon. Improvisation is a state of constant flux, a succession of acts of knowledge which never cease to replace and mutually condition each other. It's the same for the musicians in this trio navigating at the heart of this conjunction of transitory and acoustic circumstances. Each musician is conditioned by the other two, without however being dependent upon them. The trio with Barre and Urs was—and still is—an incredible space of trust and experimentation. A trust which has helped me to accept a certain state of mental confusion and emptiness at the moment of improvising, in order to move towards a greater receptivity to what is happening. And an experimentation which, since the beginning, has emphasized the idea of responsibility rather than freedom. No improviser is entirely free in his improvisation. He can, on the other hand, be entirely responsible in the way he takes charge of the continual acoustic effects which influence the "acoustic body" that issues from the united presence of these musicians, from their playing and place. Improvisation—or on-the-spot composition, if you prefer, for actions also write—swings from dependence to independence, cause and effect. An improvised instant is the result of past improvised instants and conspires to create future ones. Playing with the trio has also made me feel a sort of perceptive intelligence that is at work in improvisation, that incites us to shun appropriation and so helps us to let go of thought and be more present to experience. As for listening, that's absolutely central to the playing between Barre, Urs and me. It's a listening which allows us to appropriate the present, a listening which constructs, which shapes the acoustic real and gives a being to the acoustic temporal flux. For music is above all duration, and improvisation is extent and alteration. The trio works a great deal with accident, with fortuitous and unforeseen occurrence. The unexpected tells of passing time and acts as a tool for generating and transforming the never-silent flux of our acoustic world. Every musician tracks down the unexpected, but without looking for it. Each remains open to his own surprise. Nonetheless, this availability to what happens at the moment of playing still doesn't mean that the musicians "figure as one body." No one is master of the others' activities, and these other two acoustic sources will redound upon his own activity, upon his own acoustic source. Each musician's sound is reflected, in every sense of the word, in the activities of the others. It's an approach to music and improvisation that supposes a particular relation to our individual faculties, not only to our consciousness, but also to all the resources of our bodies. Within these collective acoustic reflections, the musician's attitude might recall the writings of Chuang Tzu, tutelary figure of Taoist thought, translated and annotated by the Sinologue Jean-François Billetter: "The perfect man uses his mind as a mirror—accompanying nothing that leaves, nor running to meet what comes, welcoming everything but keeping nothing, and thus embracing beings without ever coming to harm."[8] The musician improviser plays this mirror, receives what offers itself to him without in doing so losing contact with his most spontaneous and most complete faculties. As he keeps nothing, he "reacts in a new way each time." Mastery of an instrument and of improvisation causes a kind of forgetting, a return to confusion and void. The improviser has to trust his body, his consciousness has to trust his body, for him to be able to "integrate the forces of nature acting within him." The improviser's consciousness is like a surprised witness, rejoicing in what's taking place. What Billeter—in glossing the thought of Chuang Tzu—calls the different regimes of activity profoundly resonates in my work as an improviser and composer, for he proposes a conception of the body "as the whole of our faculties, of our resources, of our strengths, known and unknown to us, therefore as a world without discernible limits where consciousness now disappears, now detaches itself to varying degrees according to the regimes of our activity."

8. Billeter, Jean-François, *Leçons sur Tchouang-Tseu*, Allia, Paris, 2002.

Guillaume: In an interview for *le son du grisli*, still on the subject of LDP, you once said that you play "also with memory, because paradoxically, without memory there is no improvisation. Each new concert is thus constructed from the memory of the last concert played. And I like the idea that this trio is a real band, with the sound of a band, and that between tours the music of the band continues (...)"[9] If you and I both agree on the influence of a past music on the music that is being made, we get back to the notion of memory ... Since your first steps with the instrument your piano seems filled with it—from compositions feeding on memories to improvisations creating new ones. What does the piano retain of you, that you are aware of?

9. Le son du grisli, *Interview de Jacques Demierre*, Octobre 2011, available on http://grisli.canalblog.com/tag/Jacques%20Demierre

Jacques: It is not so much the concrete memory that interests me as the mechanism of memory itself. Working with a memory holds nothing nostalgic for me, on the contrary, it has to do with the present moment: it is exactly here that the articulation of my present by the mechanism of memory becomes visible. Whether with the trio Leimgruber-Demierre-Phillips, or solo or simply in my everyday life, the identity of what I produce acoustically comes as much from what I remember as from what I have forgotten. It is the mechanism of memory that allows me to say that the trio LDP has been playing a single concert lasting already almost 15 years. The silence between each performance is simply a little bit longer than the silences performed on stage. Our listening to the trio does not stop with the end of the concert, it extends, creates incessantly a dynamic link with memory until the next live meeting of the three musicians. On one hand, listening renews itself continuously and slides a window always open on the present, instant after instant. On the other hand, memory agglutinates the fragments of this irreversible itinerary, continuing the work of integration already started by the listening, which modifies the temporal reality of each acoustic instant. The practice of listening is fundamentally integrative. It stretches the present moment, letting resonate within itself what has happened in the previous moment and revealing already what the coming instant will hold. It produces a material of the perceived instant fit to be memorized. For instance when I was making the project *Fabrik-Songs* I had decided to let memory play with the initial material—that is the *Songs* of Weill and Eisler. One concert after another, my memory worked as a filter, as a plug-in processing in real time the original music. I would play with what came to memory at the moment of the concert, and thus also implicitly with what the mechanism of memory had decided not to keep. All that was audible was marked at once by the trace of memory and by that of forgetting. But the memory-object or the forgetfulness-object as such is much less fascinating than the way of remembering it or that of forgetting it. If I think of the piano today, of the piano instrument, I do not see it as a place of memory, or as a place of forgetfulness, but as an empty place, an emptiness liable to receive anything. In the beginning the piano used to be a sort of interface between my interior world and the outside world; it played sometimes the role of a decompression chamber between the two. For a long time the piano sound carried a strong emotional charge—it was hard for me to let my working sounds be heard, they were too intimate, too open, too risky. But paradoxically, despite this relation of intimacy, I've always loved playing solo. In spite of the extreme exposure that the fact of being alone on stage entails, I also knew that I was in an almost sacred space that no one was going to profane. The piano solo thus became a space of great tranquility, of elected loneliness and exchange with the public. A link of presence to presence emerged gradually before the physical relation with the instrument could fully reveal itself as material for play. Writing and performing pieces of "musical theater" probably accelerated this movement by putting the accent on the extension of the acoustic territory of the piano and the pianist. The widening of the playing field went together with a repositioning in regard to the instrument: I was no longer playing the piano; I was playing *with* the piano. Now that the instrument was in a way put at a distance I could observe it, see it in its totality, not just envisage it through its keyboard but consider it as a field of possibilities, where two bodies—that of the instrument and that of the player—reunite and face off. This body-to-body confrontation had the positive consequence of making me love all the pianos that I would be brought to encounter. Each piano is unique—there are no good or bad pianos. It's a question of listening point since it is always possible to strike up an acoustic and musical relation with any instrument. Besides, each piano carries in it all the music, all the sounds already played in the history of piano. By playing a C in a certain way I glide along the traces of all the C's played by all the pianos that ever existed. To play the piano is also to play with these multiple strata of meaning, arranged in profound and superficial layers that constitute the starting material for a work in sound. The geological metaphor is extended today in a project in progress entitled *The Well-Measured Piano* where the music produced results from a work of measurement—that of the instrument's geometry on the basis of which the pianist constructs his discourse. Lines, surfaces, volumes—everything allows itself to be heard progressively in an acoustic and architectural body-to-body encounter, where the pianist topographer extracts the rhythms, the matter and the musical forms of the territory which is the piano.

Guillaume: Certain people have made a specialty out of playing "ruined" pianos. Could this practice interest you? In the end, without a piano, would you still be making music as a pianist?

Jacques: I don't particularly have a fetish either for wrecked pianos or brand-spanking-new ones. Anything can be an object of worship, but I'd rather concentrate on what I'm doing and not on what kind of piano I'm using. Certain pre-conceived ideas, like preferring a piano just out of the factory to one in ruins, or the opposite, could interfere negatively with my activity as a pianist. I'd have the impression, in categorizing things in this way, of being limited by my own restrictions, of reducing the possibilities offered by a playing activity that rests on an empty space, open to everything. There's the desire to understand the piano experience as direct experience, desire to enter directly into the phenomenon. When I play *with* a piano, I observe it and I force myself to abandon all preconceived ideas. I try simply to listen, to observe its manner of being. It's an attitude, in fact, that one can take in any situation, with or without a piano...

Translation: Petya Ivanova and Peter Behrman de Sinéty

CHAPTER
9

A WHOLE LOT OF SORROW

BRYCE DESSNER

Having spent most of my life making music with my twin brother, Aaron, I often think I was born to collaborate. Aaron and I have spent the better part of our adult lives collaborating on writing songs for our rock band The National. We work very closely together and have such an intimate knowledge of each other's musical minds, that we often easily finish the others thoughts and songs. The band itself is a collaborative project that involves another set of brothers, Scott and Bryan Devendorf (bass and drums), and our singer Matt Berninger. Playing in a collaborative rock band can be equally exhilarating and maddening, we are five opinionated minds often with conflicting ideas about creative direction, but the ultimate result I think is far superior to what any of us would do alone.

My musical and collaborative life also extends beyond the band and I have created several large collaborative performances with other composers and visual artists in recent years including *The Long Count* (2009), a 70-minute song cycle written for the BAM Next Wave Festival with my brother Aaron and visual artist Matthew Ritchie, as well as *Planetarium* (2011) a 60-minute work written with my friends Nico Muhly and Sufjan Stevens for the Sydney Opera House, Muziekgebouw Eindhoven and the Barbican. In 2015 we will celebrate the 10th anniversary of the *Music Now Festival* in Cincinnati, Ohio, which I founded in 2006 as a yearly collaborative new works festival. I'm drawn to these projects because it is always a tremendous learning experience to inhabit someone else's creative space for a time, to learn how another songwriter or composer works, or to get inside the ideas of a visual artist.

In November of 2011 we received an interesting proposal for a collaboration from Icelandic visual/performance artist Ragnar Kartjanson, in which he suggested doing a daylong performance of a song by The National, called *Sorrow*. Ragnar's plan was to set the band up at PS 1

MoMA in New York and have us perform the song, which is just 3½ minutes long, on loop from sunrise to sunset. In his letter Ragnar wrote about the mantra-like character of the song and his interest in making the music "sculptural." He was fascinated by the way bands will play the same song every night while touring, and how fans will often listen to that same song "over and over in their everyday lives." As our tours have gotten bigger over the years, moving into larger venues and longer set-lengths, we have grown accustomed to playing two and a half hour shows for thousands of people. The idea of playing the same song for hours in a museum, however, was something unimaginable.

Sorrow is a song from our fifth record, *High Violet* (2010). Although it is not one of the "hits," it's a dark and subtle song that people love and the lyrics are even bleaker than our characteristically melancholy fare:

Sorrow found me when I was young
Sorrow waited, sorrow won
Sorrow they put me on the pill
It's in my honey, it's in my milk

Don't leave my hyper-heart alone on the water
Cover me in rag and bone, sympathy
'cos I don't want to get over you

Sorrow's my body on the waves
Sorrow's the girl inside my cake
I live in a city that sorrow built
It's in my honey, it's in my milk

Don't leave my hyper-heart alone on the water
Cover me in rag and bone, sympathy
'cos I don't want to get over you

I have heard from Scandinavians before that *Sorrow* strikes a particular chord for them. A Finnish violinist friend of mine, Pekka Kuusisto, once accosted me backstage after a National show in Helsinki and said, "Bryce, do you know that *Sorrrrrrrow* (the Finns, like the Icelanders, roll their R's quite beautifully) could be our National Anthem." There is something cathartic in exploring the darker corners of human emotions through music, especially at a rock show where it becomes a communal event shared by so many people. Usually we put *Sorrow* in the set between more up-beat songs, and it works well in that way. To play *Sorrow* on its own for several hours would be something else entirely, a journey into total darkness.

Ragnar's idea was for the band to set up on a stage exactly as we would to play a normal show. He planned to light the whole affair like a rock show with "smoke and white spotlights." The crew would build a sound stage in the Buckminster Fuller designed geodesic dome at PS 1. The band would enter at noon and proceed to play the song on loop for 6 hours straight until the museum closed. After several conversations we had settled on 6 hours, as opposed to sunrise to sunset, which would be roughly 120 versions of the song. The dome could hold 500 people and the museum planned to let in up to 5,000 in the surrounding courtyards, with people rotating in and out to catch part of the performance. In discussing this with Ragnar and the band we decided that we would not deviate from the actual form of the song, meaning we would not "jam" during the performance.

There are several things about *Sorrow* that posed serious issues for an epic version like this. Probably the most difficult of these is the 16th note hi-hat pattern, which our drummer Bryan Devendorf plays throughout the song. We decided that Bryan would take breaks as needed from playing the constant hi-hat but that the rest of us would play the song as we always do, and just repeat back to the beginning at the end of the form.

Sorrow is based on a four-note descending bass line A-G♯-F♯-E, which repeats endlessly throughout the song. Ragnar imagined that something which already repeats itself for 4 minutes straight might be able to go on much longer. When asked about our music a few years ago by the *New York Times Magazine*, composer Steve Reich also singled out *Sorrow*. Reich said of *Sorrow*, "A-major is their gold key. The melody note will be repeated but the bass and harmony will change. You'll find it all over my music, a lot in the *Mother Goose* of Ravel, and as far back as Bach. It works very well." I think Steve also heard the cyclical pattern in the song and it appealed to him. Ragnar intuitively knew that something which functions in this way could take on a timeless open form, like an Indian raga.

We are by no means unique in writing about sorrow in our songs. As a classical guitar student in the '90s at Yale some of my favorite repertoire were the lute songs by Elizabethan composer/lutenist John Dowland

(1563–1626). One of those songs, *Flow my Tears*, was one that Dowland himself made multiple versions of, including his well-known *Lachrimae*. Dowland (and *Lachrimae* in particular) is often cited as an early example of when melancholy became its own subject for a piece of music, as composers began to allow non-sacred ideas and emotions to be the primary purpose of a musical composition around the end of the 16th century. Unrelated to our collaboration with Ragnar, I recently composed my own *Lachrimae* for string orchestra (for the Amsterdam Sinfonietta), which uses a few quotes from Dowland's string consort version of the piece as a inspiration for my own music.

The music critic Alex Ross writes in *Listen to This*, a collection of his articles on music for the New Yorker, that, "If the chaconne is a mercurial thing, radically changing its meaning as it moves through space and time, these motifs of weeping and longing bring out profound continuities in musical history. They almost seem to possess intrinsic significance, as if they were fragments of a strand of music DNA." Ross points out an interesting thread in musical history of the falling four-note bass line to represent sorrow. (We did not know this when we wrote our song.) To illustrate this common trope of a descending bass line Ross cites the Dowland, flamenco music, and Bob Dylan to name but a few. According to Ross, Stravinsky once said, "I consider music by its very nature powerless to *express* anything." And yet Ross notes that despite his words, when Stravinsky composed the opening lament of his ballet *Orpheus*, he used the same four-note descending figure that has represented sorrow for at least a thousand years.

Often when working with visual artist or dancers, the music is at the service of some larger aesthetic agenda or narrative. An ambitious visual artist can sometimes dominate a collaboration in a way where the music feels almost like underscoring or illustrative. In Ragnar's case he is actually making the music the piece, they are one and the same. In his proposal to PS 1 he wrote, "I am obsessed by the song *Sorrow* by the National and want to create a piece that serves the song." The idea of creating a work of art that "serves" the song was part of what was unique about Ragnar's thinking. Usually a song would be in service of an installation, or a particular scene in a movie for instance. But Ragnar prefers to set in motion a certain idea or framework, and then allow the players to be the subject themselves and to self-realize the work, all within the paradigm he has set up. The music somehow stands on its own more powerfully because it is not taking its cues from the visual framing.

The project with Ragnar got me thinking a lot about form and length in music. Ragnar has done quite a few projects using prolonged musical performance in his installations. A few years ago for Performa in New York he staged a 12-hour version of the final aria from Mozart's *Marriage to Figaro* with full costuming and accompaniment. The composer Caroline Shaw, who played violin in Ragnar's *Figaro* as part of the ensemble ACME, recently told me that the 12-hour Mozart was one of her greatest experiences. One can see how Ragnar's work owes some debt to Marina Abramovic's performance art. Her recent retrospective at MoMA featured many of her endurance performance pieces as well as a new work *The artist is present*, (also the title of the exhibition) in which she sat facing individual visitors to the exhibition for the entire time the museum was open each day. She appeared in the piece everyday of the month-long show.

I also recently saw the re-staging of Philip Glass' 1976 5-hour plus masterpiece, *Einstein on the Beach* at the Brooklyn Academy of Music. The piece itself unfolds at a glacial pace, and while the music doesn't repeat exactly in the way we would do in *A Whole of Sorrow*, there is an overwhelming sense of re-visiting the same themes and phrases over and over again. In their original statement about the piece, Philip Glass and director Robert Wilson suggested that the audience should feel that they could come and go from the performance. During the performance of Einstein I never once felt like leaving, every moment felt riveting and vivid. Glass recently told me that his own sense of proportion and form in music grew out of his experience of learning Indian music and collaborating with Ravi Shankar.

In suggesting that we play the same song for 6 hours, Ragnar was referencing these epic works of Abramovic and Glass, but also hinting at something more subversive. *Sorrow* is a pop song that states most of what it has to say in the first 30 seconds, while works like Glass' *Einstein* are fundamentally defined by their long and slow unfolding form. Our *Sorrow* relates far more to 4 minutes pop songs than say these epic contemporary works by Glass and Abramovic. By framing *Sorrow* in this way Ragnar is firmly basing his work in popular culture and but also challenging the way we listen to music.

Before our performance of *A Whole Lot of Sorrow* at PS 1, we agreed that Ragnar would bring us a tray of food (oddly, crab sandwiches, and later chocolate) and water every hour. As previously mentioned, we agreed not to alter the form of the song. We would play it the same length each time. We were surprised that the room was full and more like a rock club than we had expected, the white ceiling of the dome and white draping around the stage (not to mention the dry ice Ragnar had brought in) made everything seem like an odd stylized movie set. The first version of the song was our closest to the record, we each played as we would in a normal concert.

The way things developed throughout the afternoon, Matt never changed anything about his vocal line, repeating verbatim the melody and words each time almost like a kirtan singer. But I think the rest of us never played it the same way twice. Within a few versions I was taking the song pretty far off course from my normal live parts, eventually re-harmonizing it and making every version a new challenge to find different colors on the guitar and ideas for the song. In one particularly insane version a few hours in, I did a feedback guitar solo with my head up against the amp. (by that time Matt was in such a state of trance I don't think he noticed) By the end of the 6 hours it had gone through some pretty wild permutations, but we never altered the actual form of the song. The only person who didn't play full tilt the whole 6 hours was our drummer who would take a song-length break every hour or so.

Within 20 minutes some kind of fatigue set in, and by an hour a kind of hallucinatory feeling, your hands even start to numb a little. And then all of the sudden you lose complete sense of time. I think somewhere around the 3-hour mark or so I started to float in a meditative state, allowing myself to fully inhabit the music. And beyond I felt a kind of freedom with the instrument, as if the song would play itself and I could do something else entirely with the music, while still playing it. The musicians became so free in repeating the song, that eventually we could all inhabit separate spheres, and still arrive at the same end point. I think there were moments where the music congealed incredibly tightly, the rhythms in the drums and bass perfectly aligned, and then other versions where we were on totally different planets.

By the end of the 6 hours we had performed *Sorrow* 128 times. In the weeks after the performance fan community boards held discussions about which version of *Sorrow* they preferred (some shaky YouTube footage had been recorded of the first couple hours. Ragnar did a six-camera shoot of the performance, which will be edited and released in the future). It was pretty amusing to see how people would say, "I prefer *Sorrow no. 27.*"

The most surprising thing about the experience was definitely the fact that the most of audience stayed put for the whole show. We expected to be in a museum gallery with people wandering in and out of the installation. My experience of most art events or openings is most people don't listen, or even really look at the art all that much. Or like Glass' *Einstein*, I imagined people would feel free to wander in and out of the dome. But in this case there were at least 200–300 people who were there for most of the 6 hours, often singing every word. It felt very much like a punk rock show from the early days of the band in a sweaty basement club. By the end Matt had lost his voice and fumbled a verse and the audience felt it and rose up around him, singing the whole song really loud. After 15 years of touring that was definitely one of the most amazing experiences we have had as a band.

Ragnar's *A Whole lot of Sorrow* wasn't about us as individuals, but about the band itself. It brought us together, closer in a way than anything has in years. We are band that doesn't communicate so much about these things, but in this case the experience was so ecstatic that we all agreed something special had taken place.

But I think more than that maybe we found some new magic or mystery in our music. That in those four chords and that simple melody and lyrics there is some power. I think Ragnar took a sliver of a pop song and turned it into an epic art experience. And he did it with a playful energy and a joy about the process that we all found infectious. He set up a game for us to play and then he set us free.

CHAPTER
10

WHAT DO I MEAN WHEN I TELL YOU A STORY

DU YUN

Day 1

A **cow walks** past a crane; a horse is amused.
I'm wondering what to write today.

/// The radio is on. iTunes is playing some audio files.
Cue the Spotify list. Make a queue on Grooveshark.
Audit them all together. Cross-fade in my own head. ///

Determining what to write seems to be the most formidable. When compelled by a certain idea (*catching the fish* David Lynch would say), I become obsessed with a voodoo of notion. Until the piece stops, months, if not years, have passed. Yet the universe has continued to move on, and the notion of the piece morphs too.

/// Silence. ///

And yet I have to write. The necessity feels rooted in some fatal mortality. Still, I feel like maybe I should instead make the conscious choice to write. Like maybe I should stop and whether this is something I choose to write, something that could exist longer than my imminent decaying body... (?)

An open secret is that many composers are revisionists to some degree: Stravinsky is quite mischievous, and Elliot Carter plays a game or two based on his systematic charts: Change the tempo, change the pitches... *Oh, it just sounds lovely*, they tell you later.

Day 2

I just finished my new opera, *Angel's Bone*. In the piece, many musical elements surfaced: Russian Orthodox tradition, English Renaissance, Webern modernism, a punk sensibility or two... Wait. To be honest, I don't really know the definitions of those terms. They're a bunch of words really. Styles are elusive. Some writers report that certain artists use a flux of styles in an organic way. The truth has nothing to do with being, or not being organic. Rather, sounding "organic" requires a meticulous process of auditing over and over, rinse and repeat, and over some more. At the beginning of every new workday, and sometimes during working pauses, I listen to my ideas and meditate on my intentions all over again. I follow my gut, ponder the same questions until I pin down every detail. My intuitions need to be examined. Not unlike a sculptor we composers first see a shape and later on we carve the miniature details to serve the larger form.

Styles are not meant to be confining, but rather to allow space for anticipation and reinterpretation. It is often the missed detail that can launch or renew a tired or trained relationship, whether between the objectified and the creator or amongst the works themselves.

Simply mixing and matching is a univocal approach. Styles can be similar. It's as though the more places one travels, the more one finds the similarities between the diverse cultures. Locate the similarities, celebrate the differences, and exacerbate their respective inherent dramas.

/// Day 1 again. ///

Today I went to a concert branded as Eastern Music.

"Stop playing the pentatonic scales as Chinese music!" My thoughts went on:

"Focus instead on pitches outside of the scales. I'm not even talking about microtones. Any scale is a starting point."

To be a good cook, one must know about every flavor, and concentrate on the nuances in-between; the physicality of how to tell a story is essential. Stop writing a synopsis as replacement for your fiction. Boney skeletons.

Day 5

I tell people I do not live in Brooklyn. The urgency of artists grouping together makes me quite nauseous. My home is my own battleground. I haven't been out for a few days in a row. Brooklyn artists? Music brewed in Brooklyn?? I hear my brain slow-cooking a gradual and massive implosion. Every time we mention a Brooklyn artist, a Buddha is laughing somewhere.

Why would I leave my homeland just to steep myself in a borough of music? Do not expect to know who I am and have been just because of how my music sounds or how I dress. Do not form a new type of racism.

Localism should indeed be celebrated. But when implant-ism becomes so shallow, and confined to one very small geographic region it becomes puritanical to the world.

Rebellion.

Let's talk about rebellion then. What does it mean? What are we rebelling against? The rules? The system? What is a system? Nothing works if there is no system or organism. We could pretend that many laws and matters work within chaos. But chaos is also a type of an organism such that one can also start to perceive patterns in it, and notice that it has its own breathing mechanism.

Enough about being a rebel. Rebellion is extreme adolescence. Youth is a bygone drug. So is the glorification of being old. It is the ever-present wonderment that we hold onto to understand ourselves, and each other, that will eventually emancipate us.

The rules themselves can be beautiful in an original and pure form, connected to the core principles they were initially created to protect. And yet strangely, those same rules inevitably become distilled, then diluted, revised, and distant from that core. From that process, conformity ensues.

The most powerful and effect-lasting rebellions and revolutions start from within.

But without a consciousness of criticism, we are a bunch of drunken juveniles just liming about.

Forget some systems too.

When we are all living on a planet that functions subject to the laws of physics, do not pretend we function without gravity. Respect. Expand. Protect. Expand more.

Have a compassionate ear, and fight like water. Killing me softly.

Have wonderment, regardless of age and whichever culture and society you live within.

The instant affect comes from the *rebel*; the long-lasting effect is born out of an evolution.

Day 6

Here are the statistics of the gender ratio of composition students in every conservatory of music in China: 1:10. The one represents a male composer.

This is contrary to what's happening in the U.S. One might think this ratio is promising for women artists there; however, it actually results in attitudes that reveal an entrenched systemic misogyny: When female students were rare they were cast aside as inferior and curious anomalies, but now when male students are rare, they are treated as a special species needing to be protected. Once again, women are treated as inferior. Even beyond this, and other clear-cut instances of misogyny, it seems the system of cultivating well-rounded composers works against women. Most notably, there are no allowances for women who are mothers or wish to become mothers, with no concept of a "maternity leave" for women artists. As a result, if women do choose to become a mother, they risk losing long-term opportunities, and being seen as dropping from a world that demands a constant production of new work.

But here, in the U.S. and Europe, and in many other countries we woman composers still have the liberty to choose to exist in a fabricated reality that our works are celebrated solely because of our merit. Not a single female composer wants to be considered based on gender, but simply as a composer. To be able to do this, in fact, is tremendous gender freedom at practice.

And let's be honest, all this is not as immediately urgent as a life at stake. In many other societies, the crisis that affects women remains profound, and deeply rooted. There, women face danger for simply expressing their own thoughts and opinions. But that shouldn't lessen the importance of the continuing feminist fight here, both for our society and importantly, to continually fuel the fires for the feminist fight throughout the world. The hope is that the rest of the world could eventually evolve, with each society expressing different shapes, forms and narratives.

Still, no outsider can go directly into a society to "save" that society. No one wants to be pitifully rescued. We should support each other, but give each other enough room to allow each other to form individual ideas; we should not judge with our own prejudice.

As the "system," we should cultivate an environment in which judgment would cultivate a well-rounded artist, with less bias, less labels.

To women artists everywhere: do not be defeated even before we can possibly stand up. Being human is the hardest.

Simple. Sisterhood. Brotherhood. *Humanhood.*

Day 7

Let's think about music again, and its social pertinence.

It's important for art to reflect society as it is, and not what pretends to be.

I worked with amateur poets, like those who write out of a poetry house in Sharjah, United Arab Emirates, and those who perform in courtyard spaces and poetry clubs—I saw and heard people whose subject speaks directly and honestly about the hidden aspects of society and a heritage that people tend to ignore. By calling attention to these aspects of society, these poets advocate for change.

The acknowledgement of multiplicity and contingency of contexts in which to place oneself also implies a sense of movement and change.

Day 8

In interviews, given my cultural background, reporters gravitate to ask me issues about politics. But these are hard to answer. In some countries, the political regimes and their corresponding ideologies change so rapidly that people don't have a chance to keep track of the changes. However, I might know some people living within the system.

Artists have the responsibility to make their works reflect the societies in which they live. While mass-market artists often inject social awareness into their work, why do the artists who work in "serious art" lag behind?

/// Resilience. ///

Day 14

When A Tiger Meets Everything.

Giving a title to a work is at once arbitrary and fatal. It is like christening a baby with a bestowed good wish. Many reasons go into the naming—Fortune, Luck, Kismet, Numeric fortuity. It seems like a willpower synchronicity.

Some people hear my violin and piano piece, *When a tiger meets a Rosa Rugosa*, and say "here is the section of the tiger, ahh, there comes another section of rosa rugosa, here they meet and now they fight, now they reconcile..." But, as a matter of fact, the title is from a Chinese translation of a poem by the English poet Siegfried Sasson: *In me, past, present, future meet... In me the tiger sniffs the rose.* In the Chinese rendering, it has become: *embodying a tiger, smell the rose slowly*, followed by two phrases added by an unknown: *Tearing up, after the banquet.* Together, these four translation phrases have become a Zen vernacular.

I do not mind people's (mis)interpretations. The content of a piece could also be just in transit, scripted in translations. What is the original? When does the translation become more vernacular than the original? I think in the end, if the work evokes a profound intangible, we will reach to the same location of the other side of this river of Lethe.

Every time I write a piece, I fall in love a little. This act of falling in and out of the most intuitive sense is gripping. Some say it's a calling, I named it *falling in love constantly*.

Secular and sacred.

The abyss of a breath. Of how people tell a story shapes how we are able to behold our breath. The sound I make is a catalyst of a synthesis of what I'm trying to tell you.

Day 19

/// Creating a piece is to fall in love. ///

Falling in love fast while having the idea first is infatuation. Skill and patience ensue to make the narrative work.

A crane flies by.

Today and yesterday, I was asked again if I write my music to reflect current events.

I answered. I hesitated. I answered more. I thought hard. To me, current events are not an immediate mirror. I think there are things I shouldn't choose to say. But when I look at contemporary women and men, how can I not reflect our personal and universal stories in my work?

I believe that one of the artists' roles is to create greater diversity and provide a platform in which our society can take a break and listen and look inward, to breathe and think, to ponder and live again. A non-profit product can be meaningless, and a deeply commercialized production can often change humanity and society. I think as artists, we should also stop banking in our knowledge. [what does this mean?]

Day 15, Four Days Prior

People are afraid to talk about what they love. The origin of a piece should be the most gripping. The later part, how to grow, cultivate and make the initial idea truly poignant, takes much detailed work with surgical precisions.

In this culture we spend an impressive amount of time worrying about whether the audience primarily consists of an aging populace. If it does, we often kick ourselves while shaking in fear. If the cold number says it's been 100+ years of having an aging audience, it means generations of young have grown old. But that only proves the young have switched their tastes and are beginning to appreciate something that is new to them. As far as I'm concerned, that is rather exciting. Let us have some confidence. Do not attempt to write/present/create music to fit for an askew perception of what is young. Stop the fascination of the artists being young. Cultural pedophiles. Old music? Young music? Seriously?

Day 18, One Day Prior

I'm going into theatre rehearsals all week. In the theatre world, people react in a tremendously fast pace and yet the work often progress quite slowly—an intriguing process. Many elements of the piece are reshuffled on spot and I wonder if I could do that with my written music.

I wonder if I can emulate a process used in the theatre world, where the director and the playwright identify a moment that does not work, and then has the courage, the balls to reshuffle it quickly. Audit again. Boom! There! Put it down now before the sun goes down! Tomorrow, tomorrow a new day to rework and re-examine.

Having no desire of trapping into a certain pattern of making a particular sound, I wonder if I could be like a great actor, who embodies a variety of roles, but still retains her own identity.

Day 34

Do not chase a fad. I think the middle part of a piece is quite challenging. How do I make those transitions work? How do I make various transitional breaks that are different from each other? Or not? Same pause? Same duration of the intention? Elasticity of tension breaking.

Day 45

I'm coming back from my own China.

I think we have to build a community. Not based on location, but on people.

It is a great thing to work with musicians who share your vision—like a conductor who understands your sound and ideas, rather than just a map you just drew on the score. The key is to understand each other. Quit complaining that no one understands you. Have you spent enough time trying to understand the other person? If not, how can we start to expect the other to understand us? The audience doesn't get what you are doing? Well. The audience is smarter than you give them credit for.

Negativity will never get us anywhere.

Day 55

Keep writing. When in doubt, confide in and expose to people with like-minded visions. Do not spend too much time reading other people's thoughts about things you care about the most. Words obscure our own innermost thoughts.

No one can announce destiny for you. Music can be dead or not dead. What matters is that we are still here. Even if they say music is vividly living, if we musicians are not doing it, it does not mean a thing.

Cry in private. Write again. We are only dead when we stop being. If society has to label us, that is okay too. They can do whatever they please. We will fight back with soft power. Akira Kurosawa had to get up in the middle of night for a few months straight just so he could listen to the sound of the lotus blossoming. After many months, monks finally reach a point where they have one thought at a time, or no thoughts. Why should we not have some sort of perseverance?

/// The cypress is, despite its freedom,
held captive by the garden ///

(the poet Ghalib's ghazal.)

/// At the edge of an abyss, we find the enlightenment. ///

Gently. Treat your heart softly. Think with power.
Hear with a centuries-old ear.

CHAPTER 11

TWELVE MINOR

BEN GOLDBERG

Around 1988 I started a group called New Klezmer Trio, with Kenny Wollesen and Dan Seamans. Our aim was to re-work the materials of "traditional" klezmer music in a modern, or "avant-garde" way.

I had been playing klezmer music for about 7 years, studying the records of Naftule Brandwein, Dave Tarras, and Itzikl Kramtweiss, trying to master the microscopic elements in order to understand the sound and spirit of the music. I was also playing jazz and improvised music, and much as I loved Jewish music I began to find the structures of traditional klezmer—song forms, melodic patterns—constricting. I sensed that klezmer's compact energy and lyrical, speech-like phrasing contained the possibility of a more wide-open space for exploration. I needed a transformative, open-ended vocabulary that would allow me to improvise at length from within the klezmer language.

At the heart of my project was an investigation into klezmer tonality and harmony. One day I had a vision of all minor keys being simultaneously present at each moment of musical creation. This felt like the current I had been looking for. I named my philosophy Twelve Minor, after this vision, and also because I liked the implication that even something that wasn't a key could be minor (like Thelonious Monk's *Off Minor*.)

Twelve Minor isn't a system or set of rules; it's more a method of inquiry for revealing useful ways of working with the basic materials of klezmer. I will describe some principles and provide a few examples with commentary, in hopes of conveying something of this work.

One thing I found out when I first began playing Jewish music: you had better know your harmonic minor scales! Most klezmer tunes are anchored in what can be thought of as a mode of the harmonic minor scale, mostly the 4th and 5th modes. (A word about nomenclature: in many musical worlds these "modes" are distinct tonalities; referring to them as modes of the harmonic minor is in some sense imposing a non-inherent theoretical framework on materials derived from other sources. But the klezmer tradition, like many living traditions, encompasses both the down-home and the culturally sophisticated—practitioners have demonstrated familiarity with both village music practices and classical notions of theory. For the sake of convenience, in this essay I will refer to the harmonic minor scale and its modes, rather than using terms like Misheberach or Ahava Rabah. I imply no superiority of one form of understanding over another.)

Here is the C harmonic minor scale:

Example 1

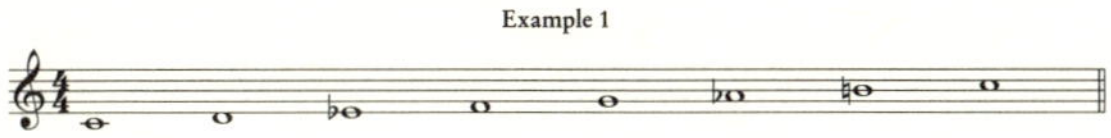

Most klezmer melodies I know will utilize the notes of this scale in one of three ways.

1. A melody could be based in regular old C harmonic minor.

2. A melody could be based in the "4th mode" of C harmonic minor—that is, a song will use the same notes as C harmonic minor but the "root" or "ground" of the song will be the note F:

Example 2

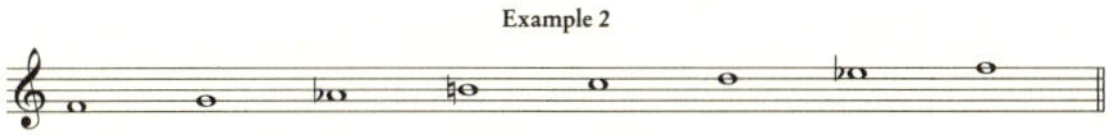

3. A melody could be based in the "5th mode" of C harmonic minor—that is, a song will use the same notes as C harmonic minor but the "root" or "ground" of the song will be the note G:

Example 3

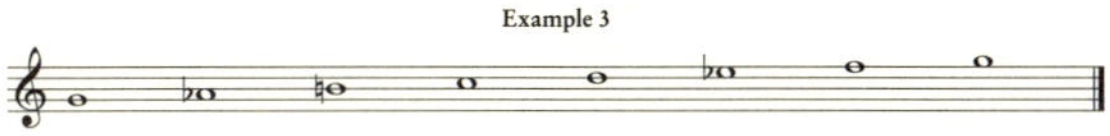

Each of these modes has a distinctive character.

The 4th mode is characterized by a minor tonic chord (F-A♭-C in the example) spiced up with a raised 4 (B natural).

The 5th mode has a major tonic chord (G-B-D) with the sobering flat 2 (A♭).

In both of these examples we find familiar minor/major tonality made more vivid, and perhaps destabilized, by a piece of grit—the raised 4th against the minor chord (4th mode) or the flat 2nd against the major chord (5th mode). The unusual element both shines a light on the mundane and threatens to undermine it.

Looking at our ordinary harmonic minor scale we see that both of these radical elements—sharp 4 in minor and flat 2 in major—originate in the same region of the harmonic minor: in the 4th mode the sharp 4 (B natural) corresponds to the 7th scale degree of C harmonic minor, and in the 5th mode the flat 2 (A♭) corresponds to the 6th scale degree of C harmonic minor. These two notes—the 6th and 7th degrees—are what gives the harmonic minor scale its distinctive sound: low 6 (A flat) and high 7 (B natural) form the large interval of an augmented 2nd between them.

So, a given augmented 2nd can be used to conjure up a particular harmonic minor tonality by interpreting it as the augmented 2nd that occurs between scale degrees 6 and 7. For example, the interval C-D♯ would imply the E harmonic minor scale; the interval F-G♯ would imply the A harmonic minor scale, etc.

But the interval between the 6th and 7th notes is not the only place we find this interval in harmonic minor. An augmented 2nd can be respelled as a minor 3rd, and in the harmonic minor this interval is present between scale degrees 1 and 3; 2 and 4; 4 and 6; and 7 and 2. Another way of looking at it is to say that the interval C-D♯ (or E♭) can be found in the C, B♭, G, E, and C♯ harmonic minor scales.

So the sound of a minor 3rd by itself implies five different harmonic minor tonalities. (And, since each harmonic minor scale contains three distinct klezmer modes, that's a lot of tonality!) If we then create a three note structure by starting with a minor 3rd and adding an additional note, the number of possible minor scales will be narrowed down. For example, if we take our interval C-D♯ and add the note B, the resulting three-note structure can be found in the C harmonic minor scale (B-C-E♭) or the E harmonic minor scale (B-C-D♯). But the note B natural is not part of the B♭, G, or C♯ harmonic minor scales, so we have narrowed down the possible tonal implications.

A three-note structure also allows us to pivot. Any two notes of a three-note structure can be used as the basis of a new structure to which can be added a third note; the resulting group of three notes will contain its own set of tonal implications. For example, the B and E♭ could be extracted from the three note structure described above and then combined with an F; the new structure would imply E♭ harmonic minor, or its 4th mode, A♭ minor sharp 4. So I can begin with a structure (B-C-E♭) that forms the basis of a melodic statement implying C minor; then, by dropping the C and adding an F I have pivoted to a structure that implies E♭ minor, etc. This pivoting action—selecting a subset of the current tonal resources upon which to build a new structure—is how I opened up my klezmer vocabulary. By giving me the possibility of a melodic statement rooted in a constantly evolving and overlapping tonal ground, it provided a practical realization of my vision where all keys were simultaneously present.

Here are six melodic examples. Each begins with the same first measure and goes on to consider a possible path of transformation. The initial phrase is constructed from the three pitches discussed above, forming a minor 3rd and a half step. The sound of the augmented 2nd is present, and the collection of notes implies E harmonic minor, C harmonic minor, and their respective 4th and 5th modes. I have deliberately kept the shape of the phrase in each measure basic and repetitive, in order to focus on the evolving harmonic implications contained in the melodic material. In practice, each measure in these examples could imply material to be dwelt on for any length of time, hopefully with a personal, and inspired, consideration of phrasing.

Example 4

Measure 2: The addition of the note D establishes a reference to C harmonic minor.

Measure 3: Implication of A♭ minor. The B natural that was the 7th degree of C minor in Measure 2 now becomes the 3rd of A♭ minor, and the A♭ that was the 6th degree of C minor is now the root of A♭ minor.

Measure 4: The E♭-C♭ which at first implies resolution to A♭ minor ends up sounding more like D♯-B in the key of E minor. (Where is that F natural pointing? Could we have just resolved on the sharp 4 of an F minor chord?)

Example 5

Measure 2: Here is the implication of E minor, with the introduction of the note E.

Measure 3: Now we are on the IV chord of E minor, or pivoting to the A minor sharp 4 mode.

Measure 4: The C natural from the previous measure is now made out to be the sharp 4 of F♯ minor.

Example 6

Measure 2: The C♭ puts us in A♭ minor; the second half of the measure could be A♭ minor or the V chord in E♭ minor.

Measure 3: Now it sounds like E♭ minor, with the A natural being sharp 4.

Measure 4: More E♭ sharp 4, or a pivot to B♭ harmonic minor.

Example 7

Measure 2: The C natural from Measure 1 now becomes the leading tone in a move towards C♯ harmonic minor.

Measure 3: The arrival on G♯ continues to imply C♯ harmonic minor but the A♯ now sets up C♯ minor sharp 4. The G natural on the third beat confirms this, yet pivots to become the 5th of C minor.

Measure 4: We continue in C minor for the first half of the measure but whereas the F♯ implies a sharp 4 in this key, the remainder of the measure treats this note as a pivot into a B minor chord resolving to C♯ major flat 2.

Example 8

Measure 2: One of my favorites. The bottom three notes (B, C, D♯) imply E harmonic minor but the top three notes (F, E♭, C) imply C minor. Very useful!

Measure 3: A weird version of F♯ major flat 2.

Measure 4: The F♯ from Measure 3 is now the third of the implied D major flat 2.

Example 9

Measure 2: The ambiguity of Measure 1 is now established as a slice of E harmonic minor (or A minor sharp 4).

Measure 3: The introduction of B♭ implies E minor sharp 4.

Measure 4: Back to E harmonic minor, or B major flat 2.

Finally, I will leave you with a composition from the days just after New Klezmer Trio. This piece was recorded on *Here By Now* under the title *January 6*, and subsequently on *Speech Communication* as *Palindromic.* I think you can see the way the piece makes use of the ideas set forth above, as fragments of harmonic minor circle around the pedal note.

Palindromic

Note: I am indebted to John Schott for studies we pursued together which led to the clarification of some of the ideas contained in this essay.

CHAPTER 12

SOUND IDENTITY

JAMES ILGENFRITZ

Object vs. Action

There is a poetic relationship between object and action that I try to invoke when performing. I see an action as inherently disruptive to its surroundings, fundamentally modulating the properties of an otherwise stable object. Of course, objects can't actually be still, only hypothetically—since all physical things are in constant motion. But the idea of a still object as something that an action can fundamentally disrupt, and the way my music behaves is based on the disruption of ideas. If I play a note, is that an object or an action? Is the note an object? It's the product of me disrupting an object, the string. But it gets more complicated the more you try to layer things.

A lot of the notes I play, I'm compounding disruptive elements. Let's say I combine a left hand pizzicato with a *sul tasto* down bow, but also move laterally along the string towards *sol ponticello* (lateral along the string meaning down towards the floor on a bass or cello... I love that down/up, left/right are essentially turned 90 degrees on my instrument). Perhaps I'm also playing with pressure, going gradually from too much pressure on the string to too little pressure. And my left hand is glissandoing downward... and that left hand pizz/glissando is constantly re-articulating (and it's an accelerando). I'm essentially doing what my more tech-inclined colleagues call "riding the faders"... glissando, left hand articulation, bow articulation, bow placement, bow pressure, velocity, all in constant fluctuation. So where, in that, is the object that's being manipulated? What sort of identity does the resulting sound take on? The point at which I'm compelled to ask these questions is the point where it gets interesting to me.

Creative situations call for a direct embrace of ambiguity; to mitigate contradicting imperatives of intuition and cognition. If absolutes can be avoided in favor of focused inquiry, there is a greater chance for discovery.

Fabulous Monsters

The inside of an MRI machine has turned out to be a fascinating place of solitude, of refuge; an enormous sonic playground where the mind can finally roam free. There is a logic to the whole experience—poetic in that there is no proper explanation for why the bizarre mechanical noises seem so harmonious with the isolated self. It's a semi-annual ritual for me, to enter into this machine. I get to leave my phone, keys, and other metal objects aside (save for the titanium plates in my head), like leaving your shoes behind when entering a temple. Inside the tiny enclosure, a whole metaphysical realm opens up, as sound becomes the only active element of one's surroundings. The bizarre whirrs, clicks, and bleeps seem so absurdly personal for a machine.

My brain tumor was first discovered in 2008, completely by chance. I slipped in the shower and hit my head (a shower mat was procured quite soon after). I went to the hospital to have concerns of a concussion put to rest, and instead, the CAT scan revealed my parasagittal meningioma (a growth on the meninges, which covers the brain under the skull). In the ensuing 4 years I had a couple of seizures (the second resulting in a pretty awesome skull fracture), and the tumor was surgically removed in January 2013, at which point it was confirmed benign.

The discovery of my tumor was the start of a sustained period of immense personal upheaval. The sort where I engage in some relatively self-destructive behavior, and answer too honestly when acquaintances ask how I'm doing. The sort where it becomes necessary to make drastic changes in one's allegiances. The sort where one's entire sense of identity is obscured by a complex web of uncertainty—about self, about the future, about the past.

I struggled with destructive behavior that I felt I could not so much control as simply witness in abject horror. My actions reflected a strong need to reject what was happening; to withhold as much as possible of myself in fits of passive resistive defiance. Inevitably this gave way to erratic outbursts that affected family and strangers alike.

I questioned who I was; what I was doing with my life; what I thought it meant to be alive; what I thought might lie beyond humanity's limited perception. These are all typical existential musings, made much more complicated by the very immediate specter uncertainty. I had to accept that his thing in my head could be affecting who I am, and to worry whom I might find myself to be after the doctors go in and fiddle around.

Fortunately, with some smart decisions and some amazing guidance, the struggle gave way to newfound clarity (or at least the sensation of finding clarity). As I started to develop the ability to accept ownership of my actions and other detritus of my existence, I began, finally, to once again feel joy at the many fortunes in life. My mental energies shifted from trying to comprehend oblivion, nihilism, addiction, avoidance, and control, toward fostering and nurturing self-awareness, transgression, subversion, growth, and, again, control.

Sound Identity

The surgery itself brought my attention to my tendency to focus on immediate signifiers of identity: appearance, linguistic affectation, mannerisms, and behavior. Consider the story of Phineas Gage, whose personality changes following a brain injury instigated much discussion in modern psychology and neurology. I became fascinated with the idea that, with some change to the part of me that lies behind my forehead, there can be some other fundamental change in my identity. Gradually, I came to find some compelling corollaries between my focus on the elusive aspects of being self-aware, and my preoccupation with the most elusive aspects of my music.

In my performances I aim to uncover the most esoteric sounds that my instrument can produce, and find new contexts in which those sounds can function. The sounds that fascinate me the most have as much or more to do with their behavior as with their nature, so it's important to me to think about the context. I want to engage in some performative action that is in itself a challenge to orthodoxy—hence the emphasis on so called "extended techniques." To pick up an object, engage in a performance ritual, and produce the most esoteric sounds you're capable of doing—that is the sort of transgressive behavior that inspires me, that connects me to the more mysterious parts of my own "self."

Transgressive behavior has always played a key role in my creative work and sense of self. I had no trouble identifying William Burroughs as a key figure in my youth, one who played a major role as I formed my concept of what life as an artist was all about. I found so much in the subversive nature of Burroughs' colorful imagery, his insistence that things are not what they seem. In my youthful existential crisis, I became completely enraptured with Burroughs' pragmatic distrust of both reason and empiricism.

At that age a kid can be so convinced that they are alone in their desire to ask questions about things everyone else preferred to accept as truth implicitly. These days, the bizarre sounds I encounter while isolated in the MRI invoke reflections on Burroughs' fantastic world of viral technology, narcotics, guns, and linguistic degradation. It was an inexhaustible arsenal of esoteric preoccupations for the solipsistic worldview of a confrontational youth.

Embracing Semiotic Ambiguity, Embracing Uncertainty

The work and philosophical constructs of both William S. Burroughs and Anthony Braxton were significant to the formation of my concepts about behavior, sound, and identity. Burroughs and his viral language experiments, Braxton and his restructuralist language musics—their expressionist breakdown and repurposing of semiotics and semantics were profoundly inspiring.

Semiotic ambiguity, fragmentation, and nonlinearity have all factored heavily in my work for years. These elements played a significant role in two significant works I created as Artist-in-Residence at Issue Project Room in 2011. As a performer-interpreter, I performed the music of Anthony Braxton as music for solo contrabass, and as a composer, I premiered my opera *The Ticket That Exploded*, based on the 1962 novel by William Burroughs. They were sort of reverse pursuits—On one hand, taking a maximalist concept of musical structures and ensemble dynamics of various sizes and reducing it to one unaccompanied instrument (Braxton), and on the other, taking a chunk of printed text (Burroughs) and exploding it out into an almost uncontrollable behemoth of improvisation structures, ensemble maneuverings, and linguistic games involving twenty one performers.

The Ticket That Exploded had fifteen episodes that are completely reconfigurable from one performance to the next, with total disregard for continuity. Each involved a different approach to organizing text, symbols, and performative behaviors. The work was composed for four voices, piano trio, three percussion, two electric guitars, a quintet of woodwind and brass, poet, and dual conductors, with live-processed digital video projections created by the multifarious Jason Ponce. The entire ensemble performed from the score, because much of the work was a visual score that all performers had to see in order to orient themselves.

My ideal was for the modular structure and other formal elements to mirror Burroughs' cut-up techniques. The score employed graphic notation, cueing systems, and structures that organized themselves from within the ensemble during performance, all intended to maintain a constantly shifting border between material derived from notation and material derived from the situation. The libretto (comprised of texts extracted from the novel) is deliberately devoid of any use of first, second, or third person, in an effort to imply both a collective stream of consciousness and a constant influx of viral information from our environment. This was all done with the intention to short-circuit the dichotomy between action and object, effectively removing the work itself from the realm of the absolute and instead using it to highlight the falsity of perception.

William Burroughs' use of the cut-up technique was based on a belief that rational world is based on misdirection. Burroughs' practice, which he developed in collaboration with Brion Gysin, was to take a page of words, cut them down the middle and arbitrarily reconfigure them, creating new linguistic constructs that are no longer the product of our mind, but rather of chaos. The cut-up introduces interference, short-circuiting the intuitive processes. This disruption throws language into chaos, and rather than reconstruct what's lost we look for new understanding. The cut-up is the action that disrupts the object our mind grasps onto in an effort to orient itself in a world that, ultimately, is governed by perception anyway.

Fragmentation of narrative and the cut-up technique in general make it possible to focus on behavior, objects, actions, and context. Too often, the intoxicating effect of the linear narrative obscures the intrinsic value in these concepts, and the fascinating web of interdependence is only regarded on an intellectual level—"let's open it up and see how it works." The experience itself would be all about the linear narrative. We can simply celebrate these concepts for their innate meaning by taking up in earnest the cyclical and web-like structures, the moving parts. The idea that the parts of a piece should fit together the same way every time really doesn't have a place in my work. Similarly, the idea that notation should provide absolutes or answers is a distraction from my artistic aims, which deal with questions and conundrums.

Creativity in a Borrower's Market

Originality and ownership have become a preoccupation in western culture, which so fetishizes individuality. I may have a strong infatuation with the role that personal experience plays in art, but the inter-personal dynamics in music creation holds so much more allure for me than the patently solipsistic creative process of the individual.

Among improvisers, there is an idea that we prefer to be judged by the quality of our own "original" work. This is complicated if you're an improviser who is interested in recontextualizing others' work. I've had people write off my solo record of Anthony Braxton's music as somehow not relevant in a discussion about solo improvisers because I was playing someone else's music and not my own. Sort of absurd given how deeply personal the creative process was.

To be certain, the process involved significant inquiry into Mr. Braxton's work: his writings; his playing style; his various composition systems; the diverse performance practice that evolved throughout his career. With this knowledge, and his blessing, I developed my own personal performance practice for this music. My approach assembles material and structural concepts from throughout Braxton's repertoire, including classic quartet works, fully notated trumpet cadenzas, orchestral parts, primary or tertiary Ghost Trance Music, graphical works, Language Musics, and Pulse Tracks.

I devised a concept that came from neither the performance practice of a jazz musician playing the music of a master, nor that of contemporary concert music programming—it was Braxton music, done in a way that fit both Braxton's music and my music. I aimed for specific relationships to jazz and contemporary music, but ultimately the end result had to be a hybrid of what I do and what I've learned about what Mr. Braxton does. It was a challenging repurposing of his musical systems, one that seemed at times quite radical. I felt almost on the edge of catastrophe as I struggled to fulfill both my creative vision and the integrity of Braxton's complex creations (and that's how I like it).

But the necessity of making Braxton's music a personal music is just how his music works. If you want to understand the value of learning Braxton's music, you must focus on finding your *self* in it. Everyone loves Anthony's quartet music; they're wonderful tunes if you want to think of them as such... I certainly do that. But his concepts go so far beyond the enjoyment his beautiful compositions. The significance of Braxton's symbology cannot be underestimated. It must be dealt with, though it cannot be fully understood—at least not rationally.

I like to think that there is more to life than truth can provide—so I try to be mindful of what I go looking for. Braxton's work deals as much with context as it does with amazing writing, and the struggle to navigate his ever-evolving formal constructs inevitably provides its own solutions. These discoveries depend on openness and discipline, and a willingness to accept that the solutions are certain to create more questions than answers.

The Artful Science of Shared Control

Concurrently with the evolution of my creative pursuits has been the development of my understanding of the learning mind. My work is more about discovery than expression, and I try to impart the value of discovery on those around me—students and colleagues alike. There is much one can learn through interacting with creative colleagues and mindfully engaging in codified behavior constructs. Aleister Crowley's *The Book of Lies*, Austin Osman Spare's *The Book of Pleasure*, Burroughs' *Cut-Up Trilogy* (which includes *The Soft Machine* and *The Nova Express* in addition to *The Ticket That Exploded*), and Ben Marcus' *The Age of Wire and String* each advocate for esoteric experiments or intra-personal explorations of the celestial. The correlation between these types of personal experiments and the methods I use to help children expand their capabilities is significant. Similarly, the more I come to understand the workings of the learning mind, the more I see my collaborative and creative endeavors as social and practical experiments.

My opera *The Ticket That Exploded* in particular represents a handful of experiments in shared control, in embracing a somewhat chaotic creative practice. With my notational choices, I strive to be as clear as possible in communicating to the performers what I'm after, while at the same time leaving as much as possible up to them. For example, one parameter that is in place for all performers at all times for the duration of the performance is that "*Any method of affecting the timbre of your instrument that can be included while still executing what's written, should be included.*" I want the score to communicate what I'm after but leave as many details as possible up to them. With this piece, I'm trying not to concern myself too much with the establishment and enforcement of absolutes, in favor of a scenario where everyone involved works together to pragmatically reach some agreements on how to apply a few basic principles to the given situation.

Similarly—the more I teach, the more I appreciate how a collaborative environment helps young minds develop a willingness to reach beyond themselves. Children are fascinating specimens. Their vocabulary is limited in comparison to (most) adults, but their experiences are as complex as ours. I can see how my own limitations and behavior relates to the very wide spectrum of behavior of children. Not only that—when you see what happens if your preschool-age student practices the upright bass for 10 minutes 500 days in a row, you start to believe that it might actually be possible to affect meaningful change in your own life.

The Composer as Consultant

For years now, I've been exploring the intersection between the practice of improvisation and the practice of interpretation. Improvisation within a certain context or external compositional framework is an experiment in comprehending oneself and one's surroundings. My interest in the ambiguities that are addressed in interpretation have led me to pursue collaborations with composers—as an improviser specifically.

Simply put, I'm an improviser, and I want to collaborate with composers as such. A collaborative process that specifically deals with improvisational dynamics is distinct from both traditional improvisational situations, and the traditional composer-performer relationship. Whatever work I do as a performer is going to be dealing with the same issues of transgression, ambiguity, and interference I work with as a composer. In working with a composer I have a context that exists outside my internal inquiries—conundrum that I must navigate as an improviser.

I began collaborating with composers during my postgraduate studies at UC San Diego. Anthony Davis, Mark Dresser, Paul Drescher, Diamanda Galas, Pauline Oliveros, Chris Otto, Steve Schick, Bert Turetsky, Charles Curtis, Jason Robinson, Nick Hennies, Jason Ponce, Richard Carrick, and Greg Stuart are all amazing artists connected to UCSD whose work in one way or another touches on both improvised and notated music. During my time there I developed own approach to addressing the relationship between improvisation and composition.

One notable product from this early stage was MAX/MSP creator Miller Puckette's work *Talkback*, in which Miller's software tracks the rhythm and pitch of my improvisation in real-time, enabling me to modulate the rhythm and pitch of live talk radio (perhaps a political dialog or an interview with a professional wrestler). Miller's piece definitely created a conundrum. I had to create structure out of the content generated from

Miller's interference system, whilst dealing with how his program behaved, what was happening in the talk radio that was being affected, and with myself.

Since then, I've also collaborated with composers Lukas Ligeti, Steve Swell, Duane Pitre, Gordon Beeferman, Brian Griffeath-Loeb, Jason Ponce, Jeffrey Treviño, and many others in the creation of concert works that depend on my improvisational vocabulary as being central to the interpretive dynamic of the work. These works exist as a model, and a product, of intra-personal, inter-personal, and extra-personal dynamics. This individual/group/community dynamic plays a key role in Braxton's tri-centric theory, and each new project I take on inevitably has some specific relationship to these concerns.

In January 2013 I approached two brilliant composers, Annie Gosfield and Jim Thirlwell, about new pieces, either solo acoustic bass, or solo acoustic bass with live electronics—both of which were premiered in December 2013 on Thomas Buckner's Interpretations series at Roulette. In both cases the process was a matter of cooperative investigation and shared control. This wasn't a case of asking for a piece and learning it. I was after a situation where my role went beyond simply to play the notes, as both composers made works that relied, in one way or another, on my own creative vocabulary.

In the case of Annie Gosfield's solo piece *Rolling Sevens and Dreaming Elevens,* I had to deal with someone else's perceptions of my work. Annie recorded my playing and loaded the sounds into her sampler, effectively "playing" my sounds and creating a work that was wholly her voice, but comprised almost exclusively of sounds I played. Originally we had discussed a piece for bass with electronics, but the process of cataloging and organizing the sounds I made revealed a different outcome, and Annie ended up developing a totally acoustic piece. Rather than relegating the various usual sounds we recorded to an accompanying "tape" track, she used the sampler to cut up the recorded sounds, recombining the raw materials and notating them so I could perform the mix of timbres live. We then both had our own respective challenges—she had to codify the sounds and translate them to notation, and I had to take what she created (using my sounds) and translate it back into my playing—it was like those experiments where a text in English is translated to another language then back to English.

To perform Annie's piece, I had to invent new techniques in order to do what I already did—and in some cases translate accidents into deliberate actions. I even had a demo of her amazing sampler version of the score, which brought in a different level of human/machine interaction. The piece itself is a reflection, and the sampler is the mirror. To learn the piece is to respond to this distorted self that Annie Gosfield has shown me.

After all, a sampler is cut-up device. It's a machine; but distinct from purely functional machines in that its job is not to perform human functions more efficiently. Rather, it's an object we've created to fragment and re-assemble our environment in new ways—to serve as a proxy for our own intuition. Is it fair to say a form of artificial intelligence? I doubt human intuition would have ever led us to some of the sounds that we now naturally expect to hear in recorded music.

JG Thirlwell's *Xigliox* (for solo double bass with live electronics) did not simply use sampled sounds of my playing in performance, but worked in another element that has been on my mind lately—to have the electronics performed live, incorporating both triggered samples and live signal processing of my sound (Jim performed this role himself at the premiere). In this situation, I was dealing with the opposite type of notational challenge from Annie's piece. Whereas Annie, being the notational virtuoso that she is, dealt with creating distinct symbolic representations of what I was doing, Jim created a situation where I had to respond to the interactive environment of live electronics while making extemporaneous decisions about the interpretive freedom afforded by the piece's notation.

I've been struggling to contextualize my creative work using a very a personal concept about interpretive freedom. The standard rhetoric around interpretive freedom brings with it too many distractions... talk about styles, genres, about standardized performance practice. Much like linear narrative, it just doesn't fit into my creative process, unless I'm intentionally subverting it. Typically I see performance practice being the approach to interpretive freedom that is most beholden to standardized ways of addressing ambiguities in a piece of music. Conversely, improvisation, with its preoccupation with originality and individual sound, has the opposite problem. My goal in focusing on interpretive freedom is really to create music that is about a process of mitigating ambiguous or even seemingly contradictory objectives.

The interpretive freedoms in Jim Thirlwell's piece have much in common with Braxton's or Bach's music—the notation has only certain types of information on the page, and the responsibility of proper expressive interpretation is on the performer. But Jim's intentions were far more specific than simply being expressive—he had MY sounds in mind. And, given that my own sounds would be coming back at me in performance via the triggered samples, I had to be very mindful in my decision-making. It's almost like a house of mirrors, with a distinct path through a labyrinthine array of fragmented reflections.

The feedback loop between composer and performer is a key detail in this collaborative process. It's what I hope to emphasize in functioning as an improviser collaborating with composers, as opposed to a performer who requests a piece of music and then learns it, or an improviser whose work is completely "original." The collaborative process itself has primacy for me. If some amazing new literature for the contrabass comes out in the process, or perhaps some amazing concerts—then that is great... it's the ideal, of course. But my emphasis, again, is on the social behavior and the internal experiment.

Closing Thoughts on Being in the Moment

What is the intrigue that improvisation holds? The behavior itself is ubiquitous, but it can feel strange to observe someone (even yourself) doing it. It's dealing with the moment, a conversation with your surroundings. I have been told I have a knack for effectively making significant shifts in my reality based on what seems like pure happenstance, and indeed particular details of much of my work came about by chance. I bought *The Ticket That Exploded* on a whim, and a year later it was an opera. I bumped into Jim Thirlwell and Annie Gosfield at the Roulette holiday party, and a year later I premiered new music they wrote for me. And I just happened to slip in the tub and find out I had a tumor, and subsequently have some completely insane stuff go on for years. I love the way a new idea or event can suddenly become integral to your entire existence. It's like one of those dreams where you revisit your childhood home, only to find that closets are much bigger than you remember (perhaps they are even the largest room in the house), or perhaps there is even a whole separate wing that you'd somehow never noticed. A lavish new chapter in your own history has suddenly opened up for you to discover.

CHAPTER
13

AFTER OPERA

TRAVIS JUST

Opera is the perfect incomplete artwork. Its past characterization as the artform most suited for the synthesis of disparate disciplines is now abandoned. As definitions and borders between fields of art have frayed and worn away, opera is now revealed as the artform most able to work within the current situation of anti-synthesis. This situation is fundamentally productive not only from an aesthetic, but also from a social and political standpoint.

"Incomplete" in this context is not represented here as an absence or lack, but as a vanishing point, an acknowledgement of the permanently unfinished state of art and experience. These terms are re-defined in a paradoxical, but essentially constructive sense to describe the contemporary artistic condition where wholeness and unity of form and intention are impossible; to describe this condition, to work within it, to find it, too, beautiful and indispensable.

* * *

An initial question could be asked whether opera is even identifiable as a subset of music. Precisely what characteristics identify something as opera and permit it to be walled off from other musical forms? The generally accepted definition of opera as "music with dramatic text" has, by now, long been rendered irrelevant a full century after Dada and over 50 years after Sun Ra (to name just a pair of examples). All elements of the "music-theater-text" equation have been independently and completely reframed, as well as the multiple possible ways they can relate to one another. Carl Hegemann's statement that "although in art one can do anything, not everything goes in art" misses the mark slightly. One certainly can do anything, however not everything goes into each piece. Multiplicity is treated instead as a parameter. In this sense, all music has the potential to be considered opera.

The alleged weight of the term opera itself is assumed and assigned by dubious authorities (program directors, critics, funders). From the standpoint of the composer the supposed significance of writing an opera as opposed to undertaking a string quartet or a solo piece is a mirage. ("Composer" here is intended to include all forms of music-making including improvisational, electronic/computer, etc.) The presumed cultural significance of the sort that is associated with opera (or composition, or art for that matter) is an utterly bereft holdover, it is based in the concept of the individual genius and the attendant economies that come with it. The heroism of the composer is back in fashion and there is no greater regression in the field.

From a practical standpoint, the permanently incomplete condition of opera is central to the collaborative process needed to generate it. The absence in the middle, around which everyone is working, *is* the piece itself. Everything else is merely a component, an element: there is no whole. Perhaps this heightened sense of incompleteness could serve as a definition of opera.

The contradictions created by this way of working are essential to the artwork, much like Jean-Pierre Gorin and Jean-Luc Godard's slogan from the Dziga Vertov film group: "the problem is not to make political movies, the goal is to make movies politically." Incompleteness can be recognized at any level and applied to any element of the piece or process. "Well-made" is thus the greatest insult one can pay to an artwork. Fallibility and amateurism are profoundly useful, even still. Anything to combat the stagnation of professionalism.

* * *

It is not a question now of mixing elements from one discipline and another, rather a question of the extent of engagement with this mixing. By now, musical strategies have been expanded to include text scores, improvisational elements, theatrical gestures, myriad types of silence, physical or visual components and, in essence, anything that can be conceived of (in addition to "traditional" instrumental performance). Similar expanded definitions have occurred in theater and text. This is with the understanding that the very nature of the words "music", "theater", and "text" have been called into question and could simply be discarded if desired. However, the terms are retained here in order to heighten their internal and external contradictions and to examine the problems thus created. All elements of the opera must be radical, none can be taken for granted. If new music is paired with regressive text, staging, or performance it reveals an essential conservatism, or worse, ignorance.

The obsession with classifying (or rather denying inclusion to) something as *opera or not, improvisation or not, punk rock or not, jazz or not, theater or not, singing or not* is a tired excuse and a tactic to avoid engaging with the work in question. Terms are attached as a substitute for actual listening or viewing and are designed explicitly to shut down thought and to provide a false sense of consensus. It is far more useful to adopt whatever terminology suits the musician without care for the blanket assumptions that accompany any genre or formal naming. Robert Ashley sums this up well: "who's running this show anyway!" Problematizing terms rather than defining them is more useful. This presents inclusiveness as a radical stance.

The false scale of "more advanced" or "further out" is another dodge. It is ridiculous to posit a measurable range of discrete aesthetic advancement upon which any artist or artwork can be situated. This linear thinking and the narratives that it perpetuates was a sham from the start. There is no post-*anything* (-dramatic, -Fluxus, -modern), merely more work to be done in all directions. The forced construction of art-historical narratives is as trivial as the construction of dramatic narratives. The only relevant value judgment for art is whether it is productive or not.

After these forms of non-criticism are left behind, space opens up on all sides. Contradiction and disunity must be a matter-of-course now. This is not to say an image or discussion of such things, but the actual experience and production of these states, while generating the potential for their further spread. Only in these cracks and ruptures can the aesthetic space be carved out for possible areas of action. Ultimately, action is the goal: thought-action, political-action, aesthetic-action *et al.* There is no story to be told, no compositional form to be appreciated, no truth being sought, nothing to express, only action versus inaction.

Action here is initially meant in aesthetic terms, as a productive state. The artwork itself is being produced, but also is functioning as a generative agency for the listener/viewer. This productive action hovers between artist, artwork, and audience, privileging none of them.

Art must move towards a state of permanent immanence, generating possibility throughout all elements of the work. Carolee Schneemann writes, "I assume the senses crave sources of maximum information; that the eye benefits by exercise, stretch, and expansion towards materials of complexity and substance; that conditions which alert the total sensibility—cast it almost in stress—extend insight and response, the basic responsive range of empathetic-kinesthetic vitality."

This creation of possibility is perhaps the most explicitly political element of art and opera. New possibilities and room for action are by definition radical and revolutionary. Space created, whether aesthetic or political or discursive, has not yet been named and controlled. It is simply not supposed to exist within the existing system (political or aesthetic). In the political field the reaction of the dominant power is lamentably predictable whether locally here in New York (the NYPD during Occupy or during the 2004 GOP convention) or elsewhere (the current situation in Turkey, as of December 2013).

However it is difficult, if not impossible, to declare a new possibility as concretely having been created. This is not a cause for concern though, as the intention and attempt is what is necessary. The naming of something as definitively "new" is irrelevant, as is the novelty of form that is thus implied. This pursuit of novelty ("new sounds") is a distraction from the real task: not formal possibility (though that may occur as a byproduct), but aesthetic possibility. Aesthetic possibility derives its significance through the decentralization of its origination and impact. Both are located with the listener/viewer rather than the composer or the artwork, resulting in an uncontrolled and unpredictable situation. The corollary with political organization should be evident.

* * *

The stock definition of opera is music combined with text in a theatrical setting. As discussed, the definitions, borders, and methods of operation of these three elements (music, text, theater) have been effaced and now spill into one another. This permeation remains anti-synthetic however, which is a paradox similar to that which Boris Groys describes in a political-revolutionary framework: "the totality of the political field is brought into view, and one is able to act not through exclusion but through inclusion." Here, it is a state of extreme affirmation that is most radical. The composer places contradictory approaches and vocabularies next to one another and permits them simply to exist. It is both a plurality and a unity (though both concepts operate under outmoded assumptions of function and discrete identity). A unit or individual element of notation or sound is as impossible to identify as a unit or individual moment of perception, or an individual cognitive idea. Taking this fundamental uncertainty and instability as a starting place is necessary for the aesthetic of new opera.

The means to describe this paradox in music is the same as its context and its content: language. While language is generally presented as anathema to music, this is merely a relic of the conventional obsession with music as "pure" abstraction, non-rhetorical, sounded mathematics, scientific-perceptual research, etc. Language is not only meant here to describe a musical thing or to operate on a level outside of it, but to *be the thing itself* in its function, context, material, and perception. Language is meant both as the sound in question, and its perception, as well as its memory. This does not refer solely to words and sentences of course, but to every element functioning (or breaking down and failing to function) as a part of this mass of language. The definition of language itself is here expanded as well to include text, sound, theatrical and visual elements, and their perception. Once again, no unity is sought, no grand synthesis is imagined. Neither music nor word nor theatrical presence is being elevated, privileged, or lessened. But all these elements are to become utilitarian material and *put to use*. Everything gets dirty here, all waters are muddied.

The linguistification of sound does not necessitate a value judgment. Rather it opens into an environment that combines Ornette Coleman's music where "we're manufacturing our own words" and Robert Smithson's idea that one can "look at any word long enough and you will see it open up into a series of faults, into a terrain of particles each containing its own void." Language can create possibility through its usage, its disruption, and its failure. Through the linguistification of music, everything is subject now.

* * *

Notation, to look at just one sort of musical activity, is at its most effective when it fails. This failure extends to the instrumental or vocal performance of a given score. Failure does not occur as a result of the unattainability of an idealized, perfect object (i.e. complexity), but because of incompleteness. Engagement with this parameter of incompleteness is mobile and can shift rapidly in its application. Performance of this music straddles the line between execution and breakdown, often oscillating wildly between the two. Fortunately there are many musicians now who can perform this paradoxical music. They can treat an instrument or their voice as a thing to produce traditional musical content but also, and potentially simultaneously, as a physical object made of material (or software/electronics) to be manipulated. Great musicians now do not privilege a violin above a rock or a paintbrush or a wad of paper or a basic physical gesture. It is essential that performers are equally adept at the production of incomplete work.

Similarly, the inherent theatricality of musical presentation must be acknowledged and heightened as an essential component of the artwork. This, however, is in contradistinction to the recent fashion of museum/gallery/festival performance in its current, inherently regressive, form. There are many problems with these performances, including cult-of-personality/"star" presentation and simplistic metaphor (the overwhelming reliance upon one-dimensional metaphor itself is wildly reactionary). This situation stems from a culture dominated by what Diedrich Diederichsen calls "discursive scarcity." Diederichsen suggests that this "withdrawal of material" serves primarily for "the construction of unambiguousness—a false unambiguousness." There is certainly a desire for ease of consumption that drives this scarcity, one with obvious parallels and motives in a social and political (and aesthetic) need for control and normative power.

"More" certainly is the better, more productive possibility here. The actual application of "more" can take the form of multiple levels of activity, superimposition, overload, volume, high density of materials, etc. But extreme reductionism (silent or static musics) can also exemplify "more" in this context of language and linguistification: more than just the sounds, more than duration, more than silence, more than the room, more than the listener, more than the performer's presence. Every element of performance is now a readymade. This is transgressively political as well, of course.

* * *

The space created in the very concept of opera as an incomplete, anti-synthetic artwork complicates the identification of the border of the piece: what can be considered inside and what can be considered outside of the artwork. The complication stems from the linguistification of the form and material within the opera being mirrored in the language of the world outside of the work. It must be restated that language in this case refers to all text, sound, theatrical, and visual elements as well as the environment in which these elements are produced.

This complication, once again, is a productive paradox, and is an essentially dialectical state. Boris Groys writes, "the central law of dialectical materialism is that of the unity and the conflict of opposites. To follow this law means, de facto, to think in paradoxes, and thus to seek out the greatest possible and most radical paradox as the goal of thought." The relevance of this idea to opera is a direct one, as the contradictions Groys describes are inherent to the form. What is useful here is the affirmation of this relevance and the heightening of its application.

Smithson argues that "language should find itself in the physical world, and not end up locked in an idea in somebody's head...Art's development should be dialectical and not metaphysical." Dialectical artwork does not need to seek out engagement with the outside world (though it certainly may). Because of the embrace of a paradoxical and dialectical environment, it implicitly and automatically does so. Art cannot be unembedded from the world in which it occurs. Or, as Lou Reed said on hearing the Ramones for the first time in 1975, "It's too perfect, they are their own dream!"

The metaphysical development that Smithson refers to here is often found in music. It is artwork that presents false unities and halts the dialectical, paradoxical situation at the core of creative art. This is an aural quality, particularly in light of perception (hearing, seeing) as a joint element in linguistified music. It must be noted that musics that are similar in form can be either metaphysical or dialectical. For example, some drones and silences are productive and some drones and silences are unproductive. What separates them is their linguistic/dialectical state. Or, as Richard Foreman said, "to me the issue in art these days finally becomes a moral issue...Courage and integrity are all that count." Morality here is untethered from religiosity and is transferred from belief to action.

It is not infrequent that an artwork will enact a double failure of cynically co-opting the vocabulary of productive art while clandestinely presenting tired reproductions of the old faux-monuments (sonic and intellectual) or simply just boring, insipid art that has no object beyond its own consumption and marketing. One need look no further than the press releases, festivals, and series that drip with terms like "experimental" or "radical" that belie the conservative reality of the art. The likeness of the thing is presented in lieu of the actuality. Fashion and pose (anti-production) take the place of creative production. The difference is obvious, you can smell it a mile away. Some things just mark time, others define it. Revolution and progressive art face the same fate as Christoph Schlingensief's victims in *The German Chainsaw Massacre:* "They came as friends and were turned into sausage."

* * *

Another border that is called into question is the temporal boundary of the piece. In this environment, atrophy and decay are essential characteristics. They present here further possibility, as no point on the temporal line is considered more beautiful or more pure. Groys notes that, "contradictions cannot be localized solely in the past...they cannot be eliminated, but continue to remain active in reality.... Contradictions cannot be sublated or confined to the memory. They can only be administered." The event of the artwork remains active, calling into question where and when, even, one can locate and name the encounter with the artwork *as* an event.

No music is, in its actuality, solely a physical, sonic event. Sound waves, vibrations, psycho-acoustics, etc. are only one component of what could finally be called a musical event. A sound is produced (or a silence occurs, or a gesture happens), is perceived, and is embedded in memory. Via atrophy, decay, or faulty memory the event is recalled, combined with previously or presently occurring events, creates or confounds expectations, and so on. As the re-presentation of the event fails within the listener/viewer the event acquires greater complexity and multiplicity even as it recedes and decays (or reappears and intensifies). Failure and incompleteness, once again, is central to music. Language describes and inhabits this musical-temporal landscape.

* * *

In this performative context of language, decay, and paradox, the artwork (and, more specifically, opera) demands a different way of listening, of looking. The glance is a particularly useful means for encountering this work. As a response to the density and wide variability of the work, the glance is by definition brief, discontinuous, and casual. As Edward Casey writes, "discontinuity in place is paired with discontinuity in time." Discontinuity is, as discussed, central to the material, production, and environment of opera. It is also central to the perception of this art.

The notion of total comprehension is no longer needed nor expected nor desired. This, too, illustrates the incomplete nature of current opera. As the total immanence of the artwork offers multiple and diverse perceptions, the momentary glance carries as much weight as sustained meditation. This is relatable to James Tenney's concept of ergodic form, where any sliver of the piece gives an equal sense of the whole, or in this case an equal sense of the incomplete work. Smithson again: "a set of glances could be as solid as any thing or place." In place of unity of form, collections of related or unrelated fragments become foundational to the experience of the work.

The glance here is ideal for the full range of durations available to the contemporary musician: from absolute pointillism and extreme miniature to works of long duration and silent music, the glance puts us "into an intense momentary time and out of a continuous distended time." (Casey) It responds to duration equally and from the same productive place of discontinuity and paradox. From a political standpoint, this agility is particularly useful as it constantly shifts perception, counteracting "false unambiguousness."

* * *

As with most progressive artistic developments, what is sought is not the abolishment of more traditional forms. Radical artists make work that "functions as the exclusion of exclusion. It accepts every opposition. But what it does not accept is the refusal by this opposition to accept the opposition contrary to it," (once again, Boris Groys). One of the most notoriously hostile examples of this is Branford Marsalis' strawman-dismissal of Cecil Taylor's work (also culpable here is the Ken Burns editing and narration that constructed the moment in his PBS documentary *Jazz*): "that's total self-indulgent bullshit as far as I'm concerned." Only one side of the conversation seeks to extinguish the other.

The musician/composer's main concerns are of productivity, of practicality, and of extreme openness. The artist "wishes to be absolutely open—and thus excludes everything that does not wish to be just as open as [she] is." (Groys) The day-to-day working artist simply cannot engage with the outright delegitimization of their artwork. There is no time for such trivialities. As John Coltrane wrote, "The 'jazz' musician (You can have this term along with several others that have been foisted upon us.) does not have this problem at all. We have absolutely no reason to worry about lack of positive and affirmative philosophy. It's built in us." Coltrane explicitly resists the term jazz here (prior, even, to his move outside of metric time—that supposed pillar of jazz-identity). Though of course he and other black musicians were subject to race-based exclusion from a wider musical dialogue.[1]

Working in the ways outlined in this article by no means need preclude work in other methods. Art is not a zero-sum game. By all means, the classical voice and narrative can and should be an option in music and opera. But at this late date in the development of experimental music, the definitions of terms such as "music", "text", "theater", or "singing" have acquired a constellation of possibilities far exceeding the single characterization that is generally accepted. In the end, the composer/musician should keep George Lewis' words close at hand that "underlying it all is the conviction that if you get written out of a history in which you were very evidently present, you can just write yourself back in."

1. George Lewis' book on the AACM is essential on this subject. In it, Wadada Leo Smith recalls the AACM artists in France: "people who were in the media system there, their questions were always limited to just the black issues... Even though we would go into these areas of exploration, other ideas, they would always try to refocus it. Their idea was designed to present not just an artist, but a black artist in their society."

* * *

In addition to the challenges of creating new works, progressive artists face the very real problem of de-radicalization over time, often after the artist's passing, though occasionally with their complicity. The smoothing of edges and rounding of sharp corners occurs via lazy curation or misinformed contextualization, sometimes with the alleged "best of intentions" of inclusion in the art-world mainstream. This violence was evident in many of the dull John Cage centennial concerts or the recent "re-performances" of decades-old performance artworks. It is worth remembering Lester Young here, "I try not to be a repeater pencil. I'm always loosening spaces, and laying out to somewhere." Of course remounting older works is possible and even productive; for example, Robert Ashley's 1968 piece *That Morning Thing* performed again in 2011, Christoph Schlingensief's pseudo-homage *Kaprow City* from 2006, or Carolee Schneemann's ongoing treatment of documentation from her 1960s performance pieces as raw material for new film works. What must be avoided is the reduction of artwork to commodity (economic or intellectual).

Similarly, what was once dynamic and radical does not necessarily remain so. Situations change and strategies must as well. This does not mean either discarding past advances nor slavishly repeating them, but reframing and recasting them. John Cage visited the famous Ryōan-ji stone garden in Kyoto in 1962 and had his productive experience of "tranquility and contemplation." When writer/director Kara Feely and I visited Ryōan-ji in 2008, it was a construction site but still open to the public. The shrine's walls surrounding the raked gravel were half-covered by blue tarps. Workmen in jumpsuits were walking around chatting casually, and loud, constant sawing, drilling, and hammering echoed around the fifteen stones. It was fantastic. Times change.

With this in mind, it is important to recognize, and then immediately discard, the art-historical baggage that comes with the term "opera." The simple fact is that we are 50 years removed from the publishing of Yoko Ono's *Grapefruit*, 45 years from the Art Ensemble of Chicago's debut, 44 years from the composition of John Cage's *Song Books*, 37 years from Black Flag's first show, and 30 years from the premiere of Robert Ashley's *Perfect Lives*. These events cannot un-happen, their innovations cannot be erased. That so much opera is still mired in traditional definitions of singing, centuries-old orchestral instrumentation, and narrative theatrical construction is frankly absurd. The corollary in politics, for example, is unthinkable; why is such conservatism permitted in music?

Better is the expansion or abolition of these old terms and conditions. The actual artwork being made has ceased to concern itself with them anyway. The re-definition of opera is, in actuality, an illusory act. The shift has already occurred, like a population that has already been revolutionized while the government totters conservatively on. What is different? Everything is available to the artist now, as it has been for decades; "the center is everywhere and the limits are nowhere," (Robert Smithson via Pascal). To what end? The radicalization and continuing viability of the artform. Does there need to be another?

Works Cited

Casey, Edward S. "The Time of the Glance: Toward Becoming Otherwise. *Becomings*. (Cornell University Press, 1999)

Coleman, Ornette. "The Other's Language: Jacques Derrida Interviews Ornette Coleman." (Interview from *Les Inrockuptibles*, 1977, translated by Timothy S. Murphy)

Coltrane, John. Personal letter to Don DeMichael, 1962. Published in *Coltrane*

on Coltrane. (Chicago Review Press, 2010, ed. Chris DeVito)
Diederichsen, Diedrich. *Combating Discursive Scarcity, Futile Intention and the Negative Gesamtkunstwerk.* (Sternberg Press, 2011)
Groys, Boris. *The Communist Postscript.* (Verso, 2010)
Hegemann, Carl. *Egomania.* (Sternberg Press, 2011)
Lewis, George. *A Power Stronger Than Itself.* (The University of Chicago Press, 2008)
Schneemann, Carolee. *More than Meat Joy.* (McPherson & Co., 1979)
Smithson, Robert. *A Sedimentation of the Mind: Earth Projects.* (1968)
Smithson, Robert. *A Museum of Language in the Vicinity of Art.* (1968)
Smithson, Robert. *Cultural Confinement.* (1972)

CHAPTER
14

THE MUSIC MADE ME DO IT

TIM KEIPER

As an artist you must be willing to explore the unknown—listening for the subtle cues that may or may not come your way and ultimately, trusting your instincts. Of course, none of this happens without some awareness of what you want and a willingness to take on the inevitable obstacles. You must be prepared and motivated to tap into your inner strength. And when you are on the right path, the universe opens up to you in wondrous ways.

Looking back at my life, I realize that music has driven me to do things that are out of character. For example, I have been shy since childhood, and even now there are areas of my life that I approach cautiously. But when it comes to music, I am fearless. I have put myself into situations that are entirely uncomfortable and into some that may even be dangerous. Music has pushed me forward in the face of the impossible and has inspired me to leap, not knowing where I might fall. And despite the inherent risks and struggles, the rewards have been immeasurable. I create music but music has also created me as it has led me to change, to trust, and to be amazed.

New York City

In the fall of 1999, I enrolled as a freshman at the New School for Jazz and Contemporary Music in New York City. It was somewhat of a miracle that I was there. They originally rejected me, and I literally had to beg them to let me in. They said that I couldn't play jazz. They were right, I couldn't. I didn't really like jazz anyway—at least the kind of jazz they were talking about. I was into Downtown music. I had been taking the train from New Jersey to New York City since I was 15 years old to check out shows at the Knitting Factory, a club on Leonard Street that was always pitch black, filled with cigarette smoke, and jam-packed with the audience on the floor and on the stage. It was not unusual for people to pass out from the heat. In that surreal environment I first heard music that was like nothing I had ever heard—and it turned me upside down. Seeing bands like John Zorn's Masada, Thomas Chapin Trio, and David S. Ware Quartet exposed me to a freedom and spontaneity in music I had never before encountered. It changed the way I heard music and the way I wanted to create music. I knew that I was supposed to be in New York City that year, and if I had to struggle to learn jazz, I was willing. After a few more auditions and my incessant pleas, I was admitted as the final member of the class and clearly at the bottom.

When I moved into the freshman dorm in Union Square, I didn't have time to unpack because there was a show I needed to see. Cyro Baptista's Beat the Donkey was playing that night down the street at the 14th Street Y. I had never seen Cyro's band, but I had seen him play in John Zorn's improv concerts and was fascinated by his style and inventiveness. Still nothing I had seen before prepared me for Beat the Donkey.

Cyro started alone in the middle of the stage, playing an infectious groove on what looked like a combination of old plastic buckets and pieces of a refrigerator. Suddenly, ten percussionists, decked out wildly in full Carnival regalia, exploded onto the stage playing samba funk at break-neck speed. They played drums from all over the world—surdos, repiniques, and tambourim trees from Brazil; talking drums, frame drums, and udu drums from Africa; and gongs and gamelan from Indonesia. And they played all kinds of things that I didn't know could even be used as instruments—PVC pipes, a giant metal Coca-Cola sign, washboards, fire alarms, and giant industrial buckets. With Cyro conducting, the show flowed seamlessly from section to section as members spontaneously broke out into different forms of dance—tap, capoeira, and break dancing. It was a mind-bending spectacle of drumming, dance, and theatre, all assembled in a show that was so organic I couldn't tell what was improvised and what was composed. The show was the most stunning thing I had seen in my life. It was pure joy and made me happy to be alive.

The next morning, still high from the show, I went to orientation where I picked up a course book. As a jazz rookie, my course options were limited—only pre-requisites and no electives. Nonetheless, I couldn't help but flip through the pages to see what I would be missing. That's when I discovered that Cyro Baptista was teaching an ensemble class. There was no way I would be allowed to take the class, but I knew I had to be there. That afternoon I showed up for the first class hoping I could just sit in and learn.

But other students must have had the same idea because there were sixty kids crowded into a room that fit twenty. My heart sank. There wouldn't be room for me even if I just stood in the back.

Cyro, however, seemed oblivious to the crowd. He had brought ALL of the drums from Beat the Donkey and invited everyone to start playing. Drumming with that many people for the first time was a thrill, but the thunderous noise must have attracted the dean because within minutes, she entered the room. This woman was not only the dean, but also my advisor. Just that morning she had met with me to plan my schedule of remedial courses. She and I both knew I couldn't take this class. But luckily, back then I had chutzpah.

I made a quick escape to the bathroom.

Listening from behind the door, I could hear her conducting informal auditions to select the fortunate fifteen students who would be allowed to stay. When she finally left the room, I took my cue to return, and fortuitously, Cyro didn't notice me. Class began, and I realized right away that Cyro was teaching us the Beat the Donkey show. Could this really be happening? I was freaking out inside, but since I wasn't officially in the class and it was a small school, I had to play it cool. I couldn't fuck this up. Each week for the next month, the dean came in to take roll call because so many students still wanted to be part of the class. And each week, I would hide out in the bathroom and sneak back in after she left.

Every meeting with Cyro was a revelation of new rhythms and exotic instruments. Unlike other ensemble teachers who sit and watch, Cyro played with us the entire time and it was bliss.

Meanwhile, I was struggling in my other classes. Growing up, I hadn't been exposed to the same musical training as everyone else. I couldn't read music well. I had never been to jazz "band camp." And since it was hard to fit in, I was constantly being vibed by the jazz snobs. But somehow, in Cyro's class I excelled. Although I was the drum set player, over the months I worked to pick up all the other parts. By the end of the semester, I had learned almost the entire Beat the Donkey show.

It was more than a dream come true when after our final class, Cyro asked me to join Beat the Donkey at Tonic for the New Year's Eve Millennium concert with John Zorn's Masada and Marc Ribot's Los Cubanos Postizos. I had never dared dream so big.

But there was one hitch. The show was only three weeks away, and

I needed to learn how to play pandeiro, a Brazilian tambourine. Cyro told me that he learned to play pandeiro by carrying it with him everywhere. He'd walk from Houston Street to Harlem and then back again with each block bringing a new tempo and a new rhythm. This story left an indelible impression and inspired me to follow Cyro's lead. The pandeiro and I became figuratively and literally inseparable. Hare Krishna and Tambourine Man became common monikers (as Cyro had warned) as I carried it with me everywhere, making many friends and enemies along the way.

In all honesty, I didn't learn how to play pandeiro in time for the gig, but it didn't matter. I played with Beat the Donkey, and I shared the Tonic stage for two sold-out shows with my musical heroes.

That was 14 years ago. During the intervening years I have had much luck, opportunity, and success. But that magical time in New York City may never be equaled. It gave me faith in the universe and faith in myself to follow my instincts and my dreams. And I've been playing with and learning from Cyro ever since.

Mali

I met Vieux Farka Touré in January 2007 at the rehearsal for his first tour. We liked each other from the start, and at the conclusion of that three-week tour, he asked me to officially join his band. If I agreed, he said he'd bring me to Africa at the end of the year to play the Festival in the Desert in Essakane, Mali. I had never been to Africa, and I had heard so much about this music festival in the middle of the Sahara Desert. It would be an epic journey. Of course I said yes.

The next 10 months of touring with the band throughout North America and Europe were challenging. All of the other band members were Malian nationals and unaccustomed to Western culture. I had to help them with so many things that I took for granted—ordering food, using a calling card to call home, knowing the daily schedule, and finding our way around the airport or hotel. And none of these things got easier because no one had any interest in learning English.

As alien as Western culture was to the band, Malian culture was a mystery to me. I put a lot of energy into trying to fit in and understand their customs, taboos, and superstitions, but as a long-haired, very pale white guy, living and working with an African band, I was an outsider in every way. The language barrier was the most difficult. Malians speak French, a language I could barely speak or understand, and the band didn't mind pointing that out to me on a daily basis. I carried a dictionary with me but didn't pick up much since the band never actually spoke French to each other. Nearly all of their conversations were in Malian dialects, Bambara or Songhai. Also, I was a vegetarian, but all meals had to be catered to their tastes. Their diet was meat for breakfast, lunch, and dinner and absolutely no vegetables. As they often told me, "Vegetables are for animals." Needless to say, I'm no longer a vegetarian.

Even things like my concept of privacy, personal space, and sharing were tested. On tour, we were together constantly. On those occasions when we had single hotel rooms, everyone would pack into one room, and if I went for a walk by myself, they'd think something was wrong—maybe I was sick or upset. I learned that sharing was a fundamental value of the culture. For example, if anyone had food, he was obligated to offer some to everyone. Also, giving someone the shirt off your back wasn't just an expression anymore. On a few occasions, when I complimented someone on his shirt, he actually gave it to me.

And then there was the music. I busted my ass trying to learn and understand it. The longer we were on the road, the deeper we got into the music, and it became apparent that I was lost in so much of it. Many times I didn't even know where the beat was. So here we were playing this grooving African music that was innate to the rest of the band, and I couldn't even clap my hands along to it. And because it was so natural to them, they couldn't explain what I was doing wrong. That year I resorted to faking my way through a lot of the music just hoping that I wouldn't get fired.

Playing in Vieux's band was more than relearning how to play drums or how to play music. It was relearning everything: where the beat is, what's for dinner, what privacy is, what sharing is. Everything was the opposite of what I had been conditioned to view as normal. And yet despite all of this, we still found a powerful connection through the music and developed bonds of friendship that transcended our differences.

And after that year on the road, making good on his word, Vieux brought me to Africa.

I arrived at the Bamako airport at 4AM.

The airport was tiny and noisy with two long lines of people waiting to go through customs. As I stood in line, I was a little concerned that I didn't have a visa to enter the country. I had been assured that everything would be fine as long as I said I was staying at the house of Ali Farka Touré. It was. After two red-eye flights and a 12-hour layover in Casablanca, I was exhausted as I collected my bags and walked outside into Mali for the first time. Fortunately, the band was waiting to pick me up and helped me navigate through the chaos of people trying to assist me with my bags or sell me phone cards and cab rides.

As we left the airport, I learned that my arrival day had been miscalculated, and instead of having a day to rest, I'd be leaving for Essakane in 5 hours. But apparently, it was only a day by car to Timbuktu, and the festival wasn't far from there.

Traveling by car to Timbuktu was mentally and physically exhausting. Once we left Bamako, we drove through an endless, flat, barren landscape punctuated with massive baobab trees until we reached a village with food and a bathroom. Then we climbed back into the car for another 6 to 8-hour drive to the next village. Inevitably, the trip took longer than expected, and on the third day of what was supposed to be a 1-day trip, we were still driving. Our concert was that evening, but I knew we were getting close to Timbuktu. Then the road ended. We were forced to drive on sand-covered dirt, bumpy like a roller coaster. We had to hold on with both hands, and even without air conditioning in 100-degree weather, we couldn't open the windows or we'd be covered in dirt. Honestly, even with the windows closed we got covered in dirt, just not as badly.

I thought we were home free when we finally reached Timbuktu at the edge of the Sahara Desert. The festival site was just another 70 km away, and we had 6 hours until show time. After a brief stop to eat, we took off driving across the desert.

Within minutes we realized that driving up and over dunes wasn't easy. The desert was a wasteland of broken-down cars and stranded Europeans trying to get to the festival. Stopping to help wasn't an option because if you lost your momentum, you were done for.

But before long, we were stuck too. We started digging. And pushing. And digging more. And pushing. We made a little bit of headway before the car completely died. For the next 2 hours, we were stranded in the desert in the afternoon sun. I'd done my share of tour travel by car so I knew what it was like to be broken down on the side of the road. However, I never expected to be broken down in the middle of the desert—a totally helpless feeling. Thankfully, some Tuaregs came by and picked us up. Being from the region, they knew how to drive the terrain.

Having said that, in no time we were stuck again. Digging. And pushing. And now praying. I understood why the locals made this trip by camel.

By now it was dark. Cars en route to the festival could no longer see us as they passed in the vast desert. We had no cell reception and we were desperate. I thought we would miss the concert, and I started preparing myself for the idea that I had made this epic trip and wouldn't get to play the festival. Then suddenly, out of the darkness came a beat up pickup truck headed straight for us. We flagged it down, jumped in the back, and arrived at the festival site 30 minutes before the set.

After the show, completely wiped out, I made it back to our campsite and finally had a minute to relax. As I sat there in the sand, I heard the most beautifully haunting sounds behind me. Remembering the music of Don Cherry on the old Codona records, I knew instantly that it was the donso ngoni. I had never seen the instrument before and didn't even know where it was from, so I was in complete disbelief to come across it here. Accompanied by only his voice, a hunter from the region wandered through the campsites, playing, chanting, and singing praises. As I followed him for the rest of the night, I learned that the donso ngoni is the instrument of the sorcerers, played primarily in hunting ceremonies. I was enchanted. I wanted to get one, but it was a sacred instrument reserved only for the initiated.

For the next two days we stayed at the festival celebrating the cultures and traditions of the desert. People from all over Mali and other African nations came to perform their traditional music and to sell their art, textiles, jewelry, and artisan crafts. There were Tuareg camel races, ritual sword fights, and music everywhere. The searing heat of the day gave way to freezing temperatures when the sun went down. At night thousands of stars filled the sky overhead, and around me the pure white sand dunes were dotted with tents and campfires.

On the last day of the festival we hitched a ride to Niafunké, the village of Ali Farka Touré.

Niafunké was so small and poor. There was nothing there. The supermarket resembled a NYC magazine stand. Nearly all of the homes were made of mud bricks. But it was the most amazing place I had ever been. Although the people had little in the way of material goods, their force of life was powerful. Everywhere I walked, people were playing and singing Ali Farka songs.

Ali Farka Touré was the cultural and humanitarian hero of Niafunké. He became mayor and invested the majority of his tour money and record sales into the village. He devised a way to provide electricity and to tap the Niger River for irrigation so everyone could grow crops on this drought-plagued land. He planted 2,000 huge, magnificent trees that lined the streets and built an outdoor music stage in the center of town. I never got to meet him, but wow, I had never felt someone's presence like that. It permeated the entire village.

Staying in Niafunké was another new experience. There was very little food available. For the first few days I lived on canned sardines and bread (but undoubtedly the best bread I ever had). Then we went to the only restaurant in the village for chicken and rice, but on the days when it ran out of food, we ate bread with jam instead. I slept in a room that was across the street from a machine that processed millet. The engine spewed clouds of acrid black smoke that came through my window in the morning making it impossible to sleep or to breathe. These things were rough, but I was there to learn the music. I brought a tape recorder with me and carried it everywhere I went, recording everything I heard.

By happenstance, I had arrived in the middle of a weeklong festival organized by Afel Bocoum. Each night, musicians from a different nearby village were bussed in to perform for the people of Niafunké.

This was the rawest music I'd ever heard. Most of the performances featured groups of young musicians playing the music of Ali Farka Touré. These bands were all guitar based but also included one or two vocalists, bass, calabash, djembe, and drum set. On one night, forty kids performed traditional songs from their village. Clapping and singing in polyphony, they were accompanied by djembe and njarka, a small one-stringed fiddle used to summon the spirits. They created an otherworldly sound that I will never forget.

The festival drum set was the one and only Niafunké drum set. I had heard about it from Vieux's musicians but knew nothing other than it existed. The bass drum was full of rocks. This had a dual purpose—one to mute it and the other to keep it in place. There was so little left of the hi-hat cymbals that they resembled two crumpled up soda cans. As for the drums themselves, the heads had been broken so many times that all that was left was the duct tape used to repair them. I immediately recognized the old, splintered drumsticks as the ones I had been sending back with the band at the end of each tour. But for the musicians, none of this mattered. It was a drum set, and they played the shit out of it.

I sat in the audience with the people of Niafunké, enjoying the music and watching how the crowd reacted. When things really got going, they started singing and dancing. I watched how they danced, trying to understand the rhythms. Sometimes, the people clapped in unison feeling the music. Thanks to the people of Niafunké, I gradually began to find the beat.

During the days, I studied calabash with Hamma Sankare and Souleymane Kane, Ali Farka's calabash players, and on the final night in Niafunké, all of Ali's musicians showed up to perform a house concert at the home where I was staying. They played the Niafunké songbook with all of Ali Farka's repertoire and other folkloric songs. By now, I was feeling more comfortable with the music, and I sat in on calabash for most of the evening. This night was an unparalleled education.

It was time to return to Bamako.

Since our car had been abandoned somewhere in the desert, we had to take the pinasse, a small, partially covered boat, back to Bamako. Since most Malian villages are along the Niger River and there are few reliable roads, the pinasse is a common way of getting around the country. This was supposed to be another short trip—maybe 20 hours at most, and I looked forward to time on the river. The Niger River is a sacred part of Malian culture and folklore. Besides providing food and transportation, it is home to a great number of spirits that live in the water. These spirits have great power to influence both success and failure in human lives. I was fascinated by these stories and excited to be traveling the land from which they originated.

There must have been 200 people with their belongings and a few goats crammed onto this 60-foot boat. As we drifted down the narrow river, I saw inhabited villages with mud houses and other villages that had been abandoned by the nomadic people of the area who follow the river and its tides throughout the year. We docked the first night, but going ashore meant wading through the river. I stayed on the pinasse.

Getting to the lavatory was like descending a jungle gym. I was forced to hang from the upper railing and drop down to the lower regions of the boat. There was a tattered sheet barely separating the bathroom area and an opening the size of a manhole through which the mighty Niger River ferociously jumped up at me. Very easy to fall in. Pee at your own peril.

The trip turned into 36 hours (starting to see a theme here?) and once the sun went down, the last hours were brutal with no protection from the damp, cold winds.

Finally back in Bamako, I had come down with malaria. At least I had been taking the meds so I knew it wouldn't last too long. We were going into the studio that week to record Vieux's new record, but I had other concerns. I had to get myself a donso ngoni.

Brazil

I had been trying to go to Brazil for years. After my trip to Africa, I understood the importance of immersing yourself in the culture of a particular region. Studying the music alone will only get you so far. But once you surround yourself with the culture, you can really start to understand the music and where the swing is coming from.

Naturally, I made my first trip to Brazil with Cyro. It was September 2011, and we had a couple of gigs with Banquet of the Spirits in São Paulo. Since this was my chance to explore Brazil, I chose to stick around for a few weeks to travel. This was more of an obligation than a decision: Brazil is a Mecca for drummers.

My plan was to hit up Rio, Salvador, and Recife. Cyro also had to go to Rio, so after our shows, I spent the first week there with him. I knew everything would be cool with Cyro. I would have a place to stay, he would show me around the city, and I would meet tons of people. Besides, Rio is a city in the middle of a tropical paradise with music everywhere all the time.

Hanging out with Cyro in Brazil was a trip. On the first day in Rio, he took me to one of the main music stores where I met some musicians. Everyone who came to the store knew Cyro, and he introduced me with such praise and glowing hyperbole that not only did everyone want to hang out and play music with me, but they also thought that Cyro was in MY band. I was immediately hooked up in the music scene. I would have liked to stay in Rio forever, but after one week I was off to Salvador on my own.

The challenges ahead became apparent as I took the bus downtown from the Salvador airport. Attempting to get directions from the person sitting next to me, I was starkly reminded that I didn't speak Portuguese. I searched through my dictionary to find the right words, but with my horrendous pronunciation, it was pretty hopeless.

My first days in Salvador were rough. I stayed in a hostel in the old city, surrounded by tourists and unable to discover where the music was happening. It felt dangerous and unfriendly. After spending a couple of nights there, a friend in New York connected me with one of his friends who offered me a place to stay. From there, I met some musicians, and soon I found my way into Gantois, one of Salvador's heaviest houses of Candomblé, the mystical Afro-Brazilian religion.

I went there every day—hanging out, playing drums, and having my shells thrown. It was my dream to see one of the Candomblé ceremonies, and it turned out they were having one Sunday evening. The ceremonies last all night long and are marathons of singing, drumming, and dancing. The music induces altered states of consciousness as the worshipers become possessed by their deities, known as Orishas. Since Candomblé is a syncretic religion, predominantly derived from African spiritual systems, there is a correlation between the water deities in both Brazil and Mali, a link that piqued my interest even more.

It's worth mentioning that you can see these ceremonies throughout Salvador at any time, but they are all for tourists. This, however, would be the real deal and a once in a lifetime experience. But to my regret, I had already purchased my flight to Recife leaving Sunday morning.

I was torn. As the end of the week approached, I kept wondering if I was meant to stay in Salvador instead. I didn't have a place to stay in Recife. I didn't know anyone there either. On top of that, it was bad timing since I'd only be in Recife for three days at the beginning of the week, and everyone told me that would be a dead time for seeing any live music.

A few hours before my flight, I continued to have my doubts. I still had no place to stay. I had called so many friends of friends, but no one returned my calls. I thought to myself, the only way I could pass up an opportunity like this in Salvador would be to do something even better in Recife.

But what could be better than this?

Possibilities ran through my head. There was so much deep music in Recife—maracatu, frevo, baião. It would be super cool to sit in on a maracatu with hundreds of drummers as they prepared for Carnival. But then I knew. If I made the trip to Recife, I would have to meet Naná Vasconceles.

Working with Cyro all these years, I regarded Naná as a hero and legend. We play some of Naná's music in Banquet of the Spirits, a group heavily influenced by his band Codona. Of course, I knew that finding him was unrealistic. Recife was a sprawling city, plus I had heard that he lived somewhere in the countryside. I decided that if there was nothing to do in Recife, I would just rent a car and go find him. I was motivated.

I arrived in Recife at 7AM Sunday morning with no place to go. Wandering around the airport, I found a café with wifi where I tried to figure something out. I looked for hotels, for things to do, and for return flights to Salvador. It was too early to check into a hotel, so I just hung out in the café. While I was killing time, I found Naná's website where I could send him a message. I constructed a note in my poor Portuguese, but when I tried to send it, I realized that the website was broken. Left only with the option of sending an email to the booking agent, I knew it would never reach Naná. Considering I was stranded at the airport, I had bigger problems at hand. Fuck it. Send.

Miraculously, at noon the brother of a friend of a friend finally called me back. I had been trying to reach him for days. He invited me to come to his family's house, so I bid farewell to the Recife airport and hopped in a taxi. As relieved as I was to have a place to stay, I was disheartened to see that they lived in the middle of nowhere. I was far from the old city, and I was far from downtown—no clubs, no bars, no nothing.

The family, on the other hand, was the nicest. We laughed and ate and drank cachaça in the corner park. Eventually, I asked, "So what's going on these nights? Is there music tonight?"

"Sunday? No, there isn't *any* music on Sunday," the father replied.

"OK. What about tomorrow?"

"Monday? No, no music on Monday."

"What about Tuesday?"

"Nah, no music on Tuesday either. Ooh but Wednesday! Wednesday, there's music *all night long*."

Fantastic. I was leaving Wednesday morning.

The family was so warm and hospitable, and we were having such a good time together, but even so, I couldn't help feeling bummed that I had left the music and culture of Salvador. I wondered if I had made a mistake. At which point, the father leaned over and asked me, "Oh, by the way, do you know who our neighbor is?" Quite obviously, I responded,

"No, who is your neighbor?"

"Naná Vasconceles lives next door," he casually replied.

"WHAT!!??"

"Yes, in the yellow house, and he walks by all the time."

Words can't express what was going on in my head.

By the next morning, I had it all planned out. I got up early and sat outside in front of the house, waiting for Naná to walk by. I was out there for many hours, playing donso ngoni, meeting some locals, but no Naná. Clearly my plan wasn't working out, and for all I knew, maybe he wasn't even in town. He could be traveling anywhere in the world.

Nonetheless, I was not going to give up, so I decided to go find the yellow house myself. Unfortunately, there were many yellow houses. I went one by one. In my quest, I met some interesting characters and was later told that I was lucky nobody killed me for doing such a thing.

At the third house, I got it. Naná came to the door and looked at me. I knew he wouldn't know who I was, but at least he'd recognize the donso ngoni by my side. He graciously invited me inside and made me feel so welcomed. We hung out in his living room and talked about all sorts of music from jazz to water drumming. He told me stories about what had inspired him to play music, and we exchanged stories about playing with African musicians—he with the Pygmies and I with the Malians. I played for him, and he showed me videos of his most recent projects. I focused on Naná's every word, not knowing how long it would be before he asked me to leave. But for nearly an hour I was his guest.

Eventually, Naná had to go to a recording session, so he walked me to the door. Earlier he had told me that he never performs in Recife, but still I had to ask if he was doing anything over the next two days. With a smile he said, "Actually, yes. Tomorrow morning I'll be doing a workshop, the first workshop I've ever done in Recife." He told me to bring the donso ngoni.

The next morning, I had my mind blown. He did a very hands on, participatory workshop. Splitting the class into groups, Naná was the conductor and we became his orchestra. We worked on Brazilian music, Pygmy music, and Naná's own music, exploring an array of polyrhythmic and contrapuntal pieces using only our hands, feet, and voices as we continuously followed Naná's dynamic cues. As complicated as this may sound, Naná had a way of pulling the music out of each person no matter his or her musical ability, a gift that was awe-inspiring.

Toward the end of the workshop, Naná introduced me. He told everyone how he had received an email in very poor Portuguese that he nevertheless understood, and how the next day, some kid showed up at his doorstep carrying a donso ngoni.

"That," he said, "is the power of the music."

Then we jammed together—berimbau and donso ngoni.

So grateful I came to Recife.

* * *

Music has compelled me to take chances, to remain undaunted, and to trust my intuition. And it has rewarded me with life changing experiences. I met Cyro Baptisa, the person who has encouraged and supported me more than anyone; I discovered the donso ngoni, an instrument to which I am now devoted; and I learned that some things are just too mysterious to fathom, and that's okay. In life, just as in music, when you let go, following your instincts and trusting where they lead, the best stuff happens.

CHAPTER 15

IN SEARCH OF MY OWN SOUND

DAVID KRAKAUER

When I was eleven I had been playing the clarinet for about a year. I got a recording of the great New Orleans jazz clarinetist/soprano saxophonist Sidney Bechet, and hearing that sound changed my life. Bechet wasn't just playing....he was actually "talking", and that blew my mind. Soon after I became an avid jazz listener and started checking out giants like Coleman Hawkins, Charlie Parker, Louis Armstrong, John Coltrane, Johnny Hodges, Billie Holiday...among many others. This intense listening got me into the world of sound that these extraordinary artists were dealing with. So when I started to improvise when I was about fifteen, I began to pursue the greater goal of trying to find a highly individual, communicative voice. But that search would take me many years. First of all, when I began to delve seriously into improvised music I was also deeply involved in classical music. The goal in classical clarinet playing is to create an even, smooth and deeply focused tone. So the effort of trying to attain that super control juxtaposed with searching for great expressive freedom and tremendous flexibility created kind of a split personality situation that I couldn't handle at the time. As a result, in my early twenties I ended up moving away from improvised music because psychologically I couldn't somehow find a place for myself.

For 10 years after that I pursued a classical career doing everything from classical chamber music, to Cage and Nancarrow. But that desire to improvise and create still burned deep inside of me.

In my early thirties the opportunity arose for me to play klezmer music. It made sense both musically and personally because it gave me a chance to get "off the page" as well as start to explore my Eastern European Jewish cultural heritage. Right away I saw a lot of potential in this music to be able to find my own sound and my own way of playing. But how did this evolve?

Step one was to lay the foundation. Of course at the beginning I had to really study. Just because I was Jewish didn't mean that I was born playing klezmer. And yet, somehow there was the memory of my grandmother's Yiddish accent that made my explorations of klezmer seem easy and 100% natural. That was the moment I really understood the deep relationship of music to language. I listened intently to Dave Tarras and Naftule Brandwein who were two of the greatest Eastern European Jewish masters of the klezmer clarinet who had come"off the boat" with that whole Yiddish culture intact in their heads. I transcribed their records note for note. But more than that I tried to get into their sound world. That whole process actually got me thinking about the concept of a "correct sound" in every genre. Of course one can always hear a great deal of variation from individual to individual, but I believe that for each style it's possible to find a core sound that identifies each particular genre of music. Given enough exposure one can instantly recognize a klezmer sound, a jazz sound or a classical sound. So for example it would sound "wrong" to play classical music with a klezmer sound or visa versa. It's like someone who speaks French with a thick American accent. (Or playing jazz saxophone with a classical sound and phrasing). It's just not quite right. So when I first started to learn klezmer, I copied the old records from the 1920s and '30s note for note to get the ornaments, inflections, proper phrasing and correct sound quality. As I got into the music I had the opportunity to do a number of Jewish weddings, playing fairly straight up klezmer. People would come up to me and say "Dave Tarras played at my Bar Mitzvah in 1952... and you sound just like him." So I felt good that I was copping the essence. Plus the other big thing I was starting to see was that in order to make people dance the sense of the groove had to be embedded in the sound. The notes needed to be literally like a magnet pulling people out of their chairs. It's comparable to the cry and swing of jazz. The searing intensity or the way some notes are ghosted and others are accented give jazz that unmistakable "thing" that applies to all the stylistic shifts of jazz from Armstrong to Basie to Ornette to the Art Ensemble to Zorn (Just to give a few highly contrasting examples).

Then on to step two. Once I felt like I was on solid footing, I began to bring in various influences to my klezmer playing when I improvised. I thought of the brass players in the Duke Ellington band like the legendary "Tricky Sam" Nanton who achieved miracles of timbre, color and texture with a plunger mute. New Orleans clarinet giants Bechet and Bigard certainly had an array of alternate fingerings that could produce insane special effects. And it goes on endlessly: Coltrane's use of harmonic fingerings, Cage's use of multi-phonics and star charts, Minimalism a la Reich and Glass, Lutoslawski's astonishing orchestration, the tremendous array of various Balkan clarinet styles, the woodwind experimentalists of The New Winds (who I came into contact with briefly in the mid-'80s), the deep groove of P Funk, James Brown and Fred Wesley, the scream of Jimmy Hendrix's guitar etc., etc., etc.

All these influences that I heard around me became ingredients for the "soup" I created that would finally turn into my own way of playing.

Today I feel fortunate to be able to lead my own band and collaborate with so many amazing ensembles and composers. If I could single out my greatest success, I would say that it's the fact that I was able to find a sound that's distinctly my own. In this day and age an ever increasing corporate mentality to conform has seeped into the arts as well. It alarms me to hear so many young musicians who virtually all sound alike. My advice to the next generation is to resist the temptation to learn music in an overly formulaic way. Sure…find the foundation and find it profoundly. But at the same time: be quirky, take chances and don't be afraid to carve out your own path.

NYC January 12, 2014

CHAPTER
16

DESTROY YOUR IDOLS

JON MADOF

What is music? And why do we make it? Many artists seem to have struggled with these questions of definition and motivation. The answers should seemingly be so intuitive, but often turn out to be very elusive. It's easy to give a generic, textbook answer to them; much harder to be truthful with ourselves about why we do what we do.

Over the years I've listened to hundreds, maybe thousands of interviews with musicians and other artists, each one of them subjective and unique. And yet, there is a common pattern in how artists describe their art and contemplate why they do it.

Most of the artists I've listened to describe their art as coming from someplace beyond the conscious mind, somewhere outside themselves, or deep within. It's sometimes conceptualized in a religious framework, but by no means has to be. It's something that the artist taps into; the artist feels present in the process, but act in what Kenny Werner calls "a receiving mode."

One case in point is an episode I once saw of the public TV series *Sessions at West 54th*, hosted by David Byrne. PJ Harvey was performing on the show, and in their discussion of the artistic process, Byrne described the artist's duty as *not knowing* exactly what he or she is doing or where it comes from. Although I wasn't sure what he meant at the time, I've come to realize that he was articulating exactly this idea of the "receiving mode." The artist does not, and *cannot*, willfully create; rather he or she receives and transmits.

After several years of making music and listening to interviews, I've come to see the artistic process as fragile, distant, and elusive. It starts with the "still, small voice." As artists, we work to hone our ability to hear that voice, in order to amplify and filter it through our individual, subjective selves. Some have described this as an act of taking a sort of dictation, or "hearing music in my head." It's then that the music speaks with our voice, and can be refined to the point that it emanates to others. Our tapping into the "source" allows the audience to tap in as well. That is why experiencing music as a listener has the potential to be transcendent and uplifting, and why audience members describe a great performance as a spiritual or healing experience. The artist builds and drives the vehicle, and the audience members are the passengers.

It's my view that the creation of art is, in fact, *an obligation.* If someone has the impulse to create art and transmit it to others, they need to use that gift for good. It's no different than a talented doctor's obligation to use his or her gift to heal people. Fela Kuti put it powerfully:

> "Higher forces give you the gift of music, of musicianship. It must be well-used, for the good of humanity."

But in order to truly reach this level of pure motivation, of real service to others, the artist must serve with humility. Art simply can't be done for the sake of receiving adulation or fame. On the most basic level, the energy of creation must emanate *from* the artist, not *to* the artist. However, when done right, a kind of feedback loop is created, returning this energy to the artist in the form of inspiration and motivation to keep creating art which, in turn, is given it back again to the audience.

When considering the role of music and art in this way, it's easy to mistake the uplifting nature of art as something that should be expressed as "happy" or "positive" in the conventional sense. This couldn't be farther from the truth. In fact, some of the most powerful art is quite brutal, violent or dark. The requirement of the art is not that it be of a certain quality, but that it be of depth. It has to be *real.* The artist does not deliberately decide what the nature of the art will be. Rather, he or she taps in and listens to *what the art is.* And if we're not tapping in, reaching beyond (or within) ourselves and taking the audience with us, the art we make is meaningless.

So what gets in the way? What prevents us from fulfilling our roles as artists, mystics and healers? Why do many of us seem to end up at a place where we've lost a clear sense of why we're making music in the first place?

When we first hear music as children, we're simply attracted to the sounds. We don't know anything about things like genre, or music history, or even the difference between a guitar and a piano. I've seen my own children respond to music before they could walk or talk. They were immediately drawn into it, listening and moving along with it. It's an elemental part of the human experience, beginning from the time we are conscious—perhaps even before. Those of us lucky enough to be introduced to making music often feel this sense of wonder as beginners. I remember as a child picking up a guitar and being amazed that I could move my hands in a certain way and make such an incredible sound.

Over time, we begin to develop technical skill on our instrument. We learn to play the music we've been taught, or we create our own. If we're involved with making music in a group, we begin to develop creative relationships with other musicians. At some point, we begin to perform for others, be it in a recital hall or a "battle of the bands" in the school gym. That continues, eventually developing into the very beginnings of a "career," playing music for other people and getting paid for it, no matter how little or how much.

But at some point in this process, distractions start to enter the picture that can obscure our original love of music. Ideas like fame and success may come into play, even if this just takes the form of other kids recognizing us in the cafeteria. Suddenly, the opinions of others about our music begin to matter, as do our own hang-ups about what we think we "should" be playing. That original, powerful connection to the source that grabbed us in the first place becomes overshadowed by elements that, even if they are related to the process of creation, are removed one or more steps from it. Sometimes without us even realizing it has happened, these other elements become the focus of our artistic pursuit.

Of course, I'm sure there are some musicians who maintain a clear perspective and connection from the beginning. Others recognize them for this, but they're not phased one way or another by how people think. They simply work at their craft and develop over time into mature artists.

This was definitely not my path. Like every musician, I started out with a pure love of music. But over time I became distracted by so many things that I eventually found making music to be nothing more than an exercise in producing anxiety. At some point, I didn't enjoy playing anymore, and could not keep from beating myself up for what I thought I was missing—be it lack of skill, hipness, success or any number of other things.

So what's the solution? Do we quit music once we realize we've lost our way?

Some do, and find that they're much happier doing something else.

Even though there's nothing wrong with this, for some of us this can't be the answer. Some of us still feel a deep need to keep making music, even though we've managed to make ourselves miserable in the process. Miles Davis famously said that music is both a blessing and a curse—I suspect this is part of what he may have had in mind.

So how do we find the balance? How do we walk the tightrope of being in the world, benefiting from it and giving to those in it, without being dragged down by things that can fog our focus and deplete our attention span?

I find a deep connection between this question and the Jewish concept of *Avodah Zarah*. This is usually translated as "idolatry" but really means strange or foreign worship. "Idolatry" usually brings to mind images of people bowing down to statues, which is how it is described in *Leviticus 19:4*: "Do not turn to the idols, and molten gods shall you not make for yourselves."

But as this seemingly simple idea gets developed by later commentators, a deeper, more subtle meaning starts to materialize. Maimonides, for instance, probably the greatest medieval Jewish philosopher, makes a powerful statement about the idea of idolatry by imagining the pre-history of how people came to practice it:

> At the time of Enosh, people made a great mistake. The mind of the wise of the generation became brutish and Enosh erred along with them. This was their error: They said, being that God created these stars and spheres to run the world, placing them on high and dignifying them as they are His servants, it is therefore appropriate to praise and embellish them and treat them with dignity. That is the will of God, blessed be He, [for us] to aggrandize and dignify those He aggrandized and dignified, just as the king wants us to dignify his servants and entourage. Thus is the majesty of a king.

As Maimonides understands it, idolatry isn't just the "worship of molten gods." It is the easily understandable worship of a product of Creation. It could be the sun, stars, nature, money, fame or political power. In and of themselves, none of these things is inherently good or bad. But at their best, they are only important insofar as they are emanations of a greater Source. And focusing on the emanation of a Source while forgetting to seek the Source itself misses out on the most important part.

The key to avoiding *Avodah Zarah* lies not in removing ourselves from worldly things, but in developing the proper relationship with them. The solution is not asceticism; the ascetic is a slave to the material world because he lives his life based on its rejection. The musician who rejects any financial success on the principal of not "selling out" will end up becoming obsessed with classifying everything based on this criteria.

In music, *the music itself* is the source, the reason, and the root. And the "idols" need not actually be destroyed, but crafted into tools. For sure, there are certain idols that we need to work to rid ourselves of all together, like self-destructive critical thoughts. But the majority of potential idols, with the right focus and priorities, can in fact be of great utility to our mission as musicians. They can be made into the tools that help us take the initial spark of the source and amplify it, bringing focus, strength, power and purpose to our work. Take money—certainly a powerful potential idol. It can very easily become the focus and motivation of everything we do. But when used properly as a tool, it can help to make possible the proper environment for the creation of great work.

Over time, we must strive constantly to polish our connection to the music, strengthen its integrity, and always examine why we involve ourselves in making it. It's a lot of work, but if we neglect it, our art will become dusty and atrophied. We need to use the muscles we've developed and always be vigilant to keep them strong. This is a different process for everyone, but must focus on regularly "plugging in" to whatever provides us with that fundamental feeling of connection.

Most importantly, we need to maintain confidence that what we are doing is important. There are countless messages that distract us from this truth, perhaps the most dangerous of which come from within ourselves. We need to learn to recognize these messages and build up defenses against them. And we must remain humble—*it's not about us!* It's about something much larger—the obligation to be of service to humanity through the creation of music.

Thanks to Jess Olson for editing advice and to Greg Wall for suggestions of Jewish texts.

CHAPTER 17

UNDRUMMING IN THE OMNISPHERE

BILLY MARTIN

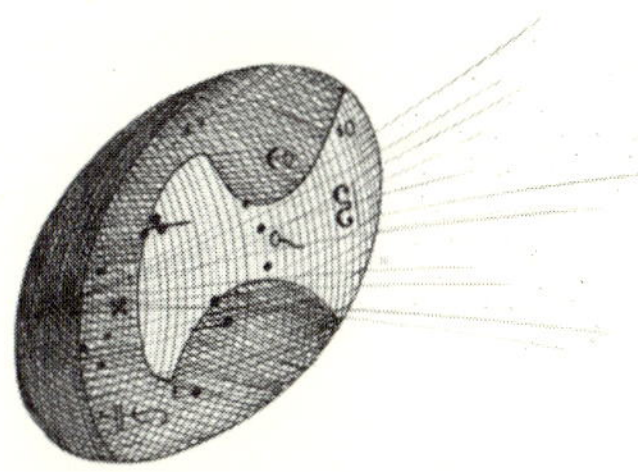

Artistic creation is, for me, something like evolution or education—a mysterious process that can only really be unraveled after the fact.

I collaborate with world-renowned artists on a regular basis. I perform for audiences all over the world, exhibit my visual art, and compose music for film. I continue to experiment with various expressive mediums. I also find time to teach privately, conduct workshops and master classes. With all of these creative endeavors my vocabulary is growing. I am learning something new everyday. I am evolving! The process is evolving. Rather than define a formula I prefer to discuss a process.

To be honest, I really don't know what I am doing (or how I do it) most of the time I am creating or performing. Self-awareness and overzealous planning tend not to be very useful for making original art. There is something about NOT having it all figured out ahead of time. I thrive on the "chance" operations. Maybe this is just a romantic notion of a given moment's magic or epiphanic potential. Whether I am creating something visual or making music, I am careful not to lose the essence of what fresh ideas comes to my attention. Art and music can lose their evolutionary surprise if I try to write it all down beforehand. I am primarily an improviser/performer, which is where most of my inspiration comes from. While some might call my work "conceptual," over-conceptualizing has not been an asset for realizing my best work. This is especially true when I'm collaborating with musicians to create something that had previously only existed as an idea in my mind. I don't notate every possible moment for the musicians I work with because their improvisations and interpretations often reveal something more profound or beautiful than what I might have envisioned. Trust is part of the process. My job is to figure out what is or isn't working and to find the work's ultimate form. Of course there are exceptions. For example, I may record an improvisation on piano, mbira or banjo that did capture the essence and nuance of my performance. I could then transcribe (or hire someone to transcribe) the recording—perhaps for a string quartet.

What an incredible rush of joy and satisfaction it is to bring something new, however big or small, into the world. This is not something only musicians or artists can do—everyone has this ability. The creative spirit is the fountain of youth inside every person. How can we help others tap this powerful resource?

When we speak to someone, we are improvising. You can preconceive a message before you speak, but that message is not fixed and unchangeable.

How you choose to articulate something is often in-the-moment, revised, elaborated, clarified, rearticulated. There are endless variations in tone, pacing, timing within a given idea put into words! We often make these variations in the moment. We are improvising. We can't predict with certainty how another person will respond to our speech. There is just enough time to react and respond. Our mouths open and we speak. It is a live interactive performance. Everyone is improvising in-the-moment. And everyone can speak and communicate with his or her own style and personality. This is the conversational nature of a jam session.

Similarly, a creative musician must develop his or her own way of playing an instrument. This personalization is crucial to an artist. The way we can cultivate, practice and "invent" ourselves is endless. Finding new ways to express ourselves is like learning multiple new languages. And we can be our own teachers when improvising and experimenting by making sound.

I'll try to elaborate some of the experiments and means I've found useful to my artistic process.

String of Phrases

One method I created for cultivating vocabulary is called *String of Phrases.* Experimentation is key to this practice or performance. We simply start by making some sound. This gesture, or phrase, should, in general, be short and followed by a meaningful silence. The space (silence) between phrases must enable time to reflect on what just happened. That means LISTEN. Don't just fill up all the space. Next, we play another gesture. This next phrase must be radically different than the one before it. This chain of events (sound-space-sound-space-sound and so on...) can continue as long as you wish. We must push our expressive boundaries outside of our normal musical language as soon as possible. The more familiar with this process we become, the more quickly we evolve and discover new ideas. Another important aspect of this method: lose those references. No clichés allowed. Each phrase is an exploration, an experiment that leads to discovery. You can make note of your new inventions by recording and reviewing or by simply recalling something new that came out of you.

The Omnisphere

When I am pushing my own musical boundaries I like to think of this as an expanding universe of language. I ask my students to visualize a multidimensional graph. It's a sphere that expands as our vocabulary grows. I call this place the *Omnisphere*. It is our personal universe of all possible expression. We can map out the *String of Phrases* idea within this imaginary graph. For example, our first sound gesture point appears somewhere within this graphic orb and the following phrase is represented as another point at some relatively opposing area. These points of reference within the Omnisphere represent expressive qualities like dynamics, density, rhythm, shape, color, emotion, textures, etc. All of these qualities have some sort of range and opposition that can be represented within our boundaries. We connect the dots in the same manner celestial bodies become constellations. The more we take chances, the further we travel into uncharted territory—discovering new areas of expression and pushing our personal boundaries.

Undrumming

Common references and cliché statements are a problem for anyone who wants to develop their own style or "sound." When I notice this problem I ask my drum students to start "undrumming." It is a code word to play uncharacteristically. I ask them to not sound generic, like a typical "drummer." How can you play the drums to sound like a violin? How about brass or woodwinds? Anything but a groove might work for them. Regarding dance drumming I might suggest, "Try to play a fill somewhere else other than at the end of a four bar phrase. Long tones are out of character for most drummers. Listen to the birds. How about that couple arguing next door? Can you mimic that on your instrument? Just an impression will do. Play the clouds, the rain, a subway car slowly screeching to a halt or a coyote howling under the night sky." There are so many ways to inform your playing.

I also understand the importance of emulating the masters. There is nothing wrong, especially in the early stages of artistic development, with following in the footsteps of the artists we love. When we are young and empty, we want to fill up our soul with all that beautiful music we find inspirational. We play certain recordings over-and-over to get inside every nuance and gesture that is not really possible to transcribe. Then, we try to express some of those great ideas. Attending live performances is often the most effective way of transference.

We need those building blocks of vocabulary and influence. The history of music is populated with many great innovators and explorers. Why not create and share something new and personal from these innovations, discoveries, expressions? A vast vocabulary creates greater possibilities for speech; the more diverse the palette, the greater potential for image creation. An honest and authentic approach to creating art can reveal truth and beauty about the world in which we live. And if you are truly sincere in your approach and expression then what ultimately comes out is YOU.

Everyone has a different perspective. I am so thankful for the diversity of individual points of view. I don't always know what the music is saying. The audience can't possibly understand everything that I am striving for, but they sure know how and what it makes them feel. I know that it is impossible to please everyone out there. I wouldn't ever try and please everyone in the audience. I don't mind that I can't please everyone with my performance. You could have played the best performance of your life and find out that no one related to what you were expressing. What I am saying here is you need not think for a second what the audience is expecting of you. You will most likely fail.

Speaking of failing. That is the greatest teacher. Experiencing failure is necessary to discovering success. Perfection is impossible and the belief that it exists is its own kind of failure. Don't fool yourself. How can you evolve when you already know it all?

CHAPTER 18

SKETCHES FROM SOUNDßOY MANIFESTO

RAZ MESINAI

"When frequencies are suppressed; we are, slowly, drained of defiance,
In spite of this, we crave dissonance."
TH¬
OE

How to Kill a Boombox

It was 1983, during the B-Boy era, when I built my first recording studio.

As a child I had endured many abuses when it came to sound, from New Age concerts in churches and temples, muzak in malls and airports, hippy festivals upstate, Bob Dylan records at home and pan flute ensembles in subways. So it was only natural that I would succumb to the other form of music that surrounded me growing up in New York City in the '70s and '80s—Hip Hop.

Between the Producers, MC's, DJ's, Graffiti artists and Break Dancers who built the culture, Hip Hop was a complete package, offering people in urban areas a new way of life. I was immediately drawn to every aspect of it, especially Graffiti and instrumental Break Dance Music.

I knew that I preferred the instrumental versions to the vocal, because the instrumentals were abstract; however the production aspect was more of a mystery. It was nearly impossible to know how this music was being made. As far as I knew, there was no school in New York to study this at all, (especially not for me as I was only 10 years old at the time.) It was impossible to identify the ingredients needed without knowing whether a sound was being created with a drum machine, a sampler, an effect unit, turntables, microphones, tape machines, a synthesizer or a "live" instrument.

Nevertheless, I was desperate to begin making music so I improvised with what I had at home at that very moment.

I "built" my first studio by arranging a turntable with a built in speaker, a telephone answering machine with a built in microphone, and two Boom Boxes in a configuration where they all could become one unit.

First, with a blank tape in the answering machine, I kept my finger on the pause button with record engaged. The wheels were straining to record, like miniature wheels on a toy train, holding itself back.

With the other hand, I would play a short drumbeat from a record, quickly letting go of the pause button to record a bar of the drum solo. Then I would rewind the turntable to around the same place, and record another bar, re-releasing the pause button on the answering machine to grab another sample. It took around 60 minutes to create 60 seconds of a drumbeat.

Next, time to overdub—that's what the two Boom Boxes were for. I played back the voice answering machine into the Boom Box, bit by bit, to capture a combination of the turntable and the drum track that I laid down. As I accumulated different recordings for the two Boom Boxes, I played them both at the same time and discovered the concept of multi tracking. But my most inspired realization was when I switched one of the Boom Boxes to the radio setting and began incorporating static and various other sounds into the mix.

There were no connections made between the devices, only the tiny built in microphone on the answering machine and the circular arrangement.

Finally I made a 1-minute track, using this process. It was at this point that I went from being a child-artist to a producer.

I headed up the block to where the Break Dancers hung out and approached one of the members of the crew. I asked him if he'd try my track out. The idea that a kid could have produced a beat made everyone laugh.

The dancer looked closely at the tape, as if it was a bomb about to detonate. The tapes had been passed between each player and recorded over so many times that the cassette tape was worn and slightly sticking out of the sides of the shell.

He shook his head and handed it back to me. "Nah, I'm not putting that shit in my Boom Box, it will eat it up."

"What?" The image struck me of the Boom Box, an animal eating its own habitat, like Saturn devouring his sons. Never mind how it would look, how would it sound?

So I persisted and eventually the Break Dancer caved. He popped the cassette into the deck and we waited for what seemed like forever.

It took about 5 seconds for the metamorphosis to take shape, and when it did, it was fucking beautiful. First, it began to modulate, transforming the time that I had laid down onto tape, which I had thought was set.

The first 5 seconds played but then it happened. The sound began to modulate in another way; It went from a subtle warbling to an extreme stretching of time.

The Boom Box coughed, gasping for air. The unhappy dancer quickly opened up the deck and removed the tape, to save his Boom Box from choking on the diseased cassette. Strands of tape guts poured all over the sidewalk.

The beating that I got as a result was absolutely worth it, because I learned one important lesson:

"There are two gatekeepers between you (the artist) and your signal flow (path in life): Soundßoy and the Sound§System."

Sound§system as Instrument

"Without the Sound§System, there is no sound."

There is a fundamental difference between focusing on the sum output of an instrument, say the horn or the voice, rather than its joints and notes. This perspective accounts for enormous breakthroughs in composition and performance, but curiously has been ignored when it comes to so-called "Electronic Music." For this reason, the term "electronic" has no real connection to my work because it does not encapsulate what I do. I create music for Sound§Systems. Whether that be the Sound§System at a club, the Sound§System of a tunnel or the Sound§System of the mind, this sums up my objective.

Once we focus on seeing the Sound§System for what it is—an instrument, then the instrument itself can improve.

Nostalgic comment from an audiophile on my blog: "Remember in the '90s when music sounded 'warm,' and now it sounds too bright and overly compressed?" I do, but the Sound§System changed all that.

Battle Stance

The built-in speakers on laptops and mobile devices changed the way music and films sound, because they are the very speakers used to preview a vast majority of the media that we buy. We, as Producers, adapted to the new digital marketplace, pushing highs and gains to their limits in order to squeeze our sound through those pinhole-sized speakers.

Around the same time as the "Boom Box Incident" I was also writing graffiti (tag names included ScamOne, Ra-z and Scriabin, among others) which led me to become familiar with another type of signal flow—tunnels.

When I first descended into the forbidden world of the underground subway system, I became obsessed—not only with the art of graffiti, but with the acoustics of the tunnels themselves.

Underground

"I deal with channels. Inputs and outputs. Sound§Systems. Tunnels are Sound§Systems. I go inside them."

Anyone with love for the deeper aspects of sound would appreciate the immense density of frequencies that a moving train can produce.

Not only do the tunnels provide a system to get from one destination to another, they also act as a soundtrack to the world above. Whether we notice it or not, this vibration is constantly droning beneath us, influencing our reality and the output of creativity in New York City.

Battle Stance

I have noticed a change in the creative output of artists in urban areas that are built on top of tunnels. New re-constructions of these tunnels changes the acoustics of the space as well as, of course, the tone of the drone.

Tunnel Vision (Tzadik DVD Series, 2013)

Beginning in 2007, co-producer and composer Jonathan Uliel Saldanha and I descended into several ancient underground gold mines, medieval water tunnels, and catacombs to record and study the acoustics of subterranean spaces.

This is a whole different type of experience from train tunneling.

The entrance seems fine but when you proceed a few feet down the tunnel, you notice that the walls, rather than expanding—are shrinking. The space becomes so tight that you must move sideways, just to squeeze through.

Finally, after an unbearable amount of time, the tunnel widens again into the most enormous subwoofer on earth. The sound is immense. Waves of sub bass cause your nostrils to vibrate. A single fly buzzing against the wall can create an oscillator tone that feeds back into itself. Every echo changes the sound in a different way as it is passed from one edge to another. When it comes back, it's larger, more menacing.

Even with flashlights, the darkness consumes you in that void between the safety of outside and the abyss in front of you. You don't want to think about what's ahead or what's beneath your feet.

Dissonance leads to dissent. Soundßoy knows this.

It's that classic "tug of war" between the Main ≈ and the Underground¬, with Soundßoy lurking somewhere in the middle.

Truth is, we wouldn't have much going on if it weren't for each other. Without the Underground¬ the Main ≈ would have no content, and without the Main ≈ the Underground¬ would have no distribution.

Together, we form a workflow.

* * *

Soundßoy/Anti Flux

In *The Heretic of Ether*, THOE's nemesis is a shape-shifting demon called Soundßoy, borrowed from the patois term "Sound Bwoy" (used in Jamaican Dance Hall music to describe a DJ, producer, MC or engineer whose sound isn't cutting it).

I always imagined a Sound Bwoy as someone, or something, standing between myself and the audience, like an incompetent sound person who forgot to un-mute my channel, or a cable mysteriously disappearing. Later I realized that Soundßoy was not so simple, nor as inconsequential as that.

Soundßoy clogs up the blood stream, the nervous system, neurons, subway lines, ideas, thoughts, dreams, and fertility—to name but a few.

Battle Stance

Everywhere I go Soundßoy is there, cock-blocking my flow....

Login 2B#1617:

For my tour I packed—
2 power cables for laptop
16 audio cables
16 ¼" adaptors for audio cables
2 power convertors (worldwide)
1 audio interface
8 channel mixer (I have asked the festival to bring me another mixer, in case it is intercepted by Soundßoy)
1 Effect processing unit
2 hard drives
6 firewire cables (these seem to always disappear into the Soundßoy wormhole)
Batteries

I take a taxi from the airport to the hotel.

Upon arriving I unlock the handcuff attaching the case to my wrist and hand the case to the bellboy.

Handing him a $20 bill, I ask him to take extra care of the case.

I get to my hotel suite but the bellboy hasn't arrived yet, so I call downstairs to ask for my luggage.

The receptionist is confused and tells me that the hotel doesn't have a bellboy.

Bellboy was Soundßoy.

* * *

"Soundßoy takes a path, splits it down the middle and charges tickets to cross."

"An epidemic of Soundßoy-ism thwarts progress, stopping the signal from passing between us and the tree of knowledge—seeding the frequency of sound, sight, and smell inside of a pill. Whether or not Soundßoy is a single demon working independently, or a swarm of demons infesting the channels is unknown. Clearly, however, Soundßoy is here, within the circuits, corrupting the signal flow."

Exhibit A

FM Radio, was suppressed for 30 years by Soundẞoy RCA exec, David Sarnoff, who told inventor Edwin H. Armstrong that FM Radio was not just simply an "invention," it was a "revolution." FM would have opened many doors to independent Radio Broadcasting networks for the 30 years it sat on the shelf, creating competition for the major broadcast networks. In other words, Armstrong got "Soundẞoy'd."

Battle Stance

Fuck it. That shit doesn't stop me. I get a little bitter. Yeah, ok. But I haven't been nobody's bitch either. Sound§Systems started to bust up whenever anybody played my tunes. Got to the point where nobody bothered anymore.

Wireless magazine/HEADLINE: *"THOE declares war on Soundẞoy! Rumors spread of a possible Drop¬."*

The Drop¬[1] is no ordinary drop. The Drop¬ shatters time, stops motion and infiltrates Soundẞoy's from within.

1. The Drop¬ is THOE's attack on the Main ≈ Flow. An Air Horn blast, time stretched for 150 years.

This dense mass of dissonance froze all devices for 150 years, rerouting the signal flow to one Master Fader, controlled by the Ghost Producer, THOE (The Heretic of Ether).

HEADLINE: "Soundẞoy *defeated.*" If only that were true.

Before The Law

"Evil is whatever distracts." —Franz Kafka

Franz Kafka knew about Soundßoy.

The antagonists in Kafka's fiction, such as the guard in *Before the Law* and virtually every character in *The Trial* and *The Castle*, are some of the strongest representations of the gatekeeper/Soundßoy dilemma.

So, when it came down to composing *Before the Law* (Tzadik, 2000), It felt natural to compile the material by recording different ways of resisting sound—using faulty cables that cut out periodically, violin bows needing rosin, metal objects on top of piano strings, knocking on wood, or recording the musicians as they perform in extremely uncomfortable positions.

Sound§System/Time Machine

While everyone's upstairs, rushing to find their next Drop¬, I'm sifting through time like flipping pages in a book, Drop¬ping updates on Sound§Systems throughout the centuries.

My engineer has got a nose for tracking the samples I need for my weapon against Soundßoy.

I can backtrack to 10,000 BC (depending on bandwidth) and fast forwards (depending on where you think you are) to 10,000 AD.

The Drop¬

"I can tell that you are not ready for this Drop¬. I am cautious to even let it Drop¬ at all, because I don't think that you are ready. Truly, you are not."

"It's all Liquid. Nothing is solid. It's all modular, flexible. Nothing is real. With the Crux†1000™, frequencies of light, sound, color and smell are at your fingertips."

During a recording session, a musician confessed that, when I recorded him, he felt as though I was taking a part of his soul. "You weren't using it anyway," I reassured him.

He's right though. My EMUE6400 is a soul catcher and my studio a soul system.

The liquid boils as deep purple smoke starts to rise up from the Resonator.
The smells are all controllable, the colors relatively manageable.

Crux†™3000

1. Resonator
2. Slope (Q)
3. Frequency Shifter
4. Bone Conduction Skull cap
5. Liquid Flow, Ñ¢ Fluid
6. Eye Piece
7. Amplifier

Login: Time is just an update. It's all happening now.

You see, we don't "travel." That's a false notion. We step into an augmented version of the past and the future, while seated here in our studio, bathroom, cubicle or cell, here, now, in real time.

Battle Stance

If you can slow down a piece of audio without changing its pitch (frequency) then surely, you could use this same technology to spread out a time frame in reality, and slow it down without altering the frequency of its actual events. These events are resonant frequencies in time.

Once the event becomes an image, or a waveform, time can be made flexible, so that one can freely scan the centuries, with the freedom to close in on particular events.

The waveform must be a re-synthesis of three or more forms of media related to specific cognitive senses recording a particular event in history. Then, the future can also be augmented based on hypothetical possibilities.

The Resonance is then amplified and controlled with a navigating device/equalizer/filter/sequencer called a "Crux†" (developed by yours truly).

If you want to step into the future (Pro version only), you must find someone from the future who has the Update. Ha! Well good luck finding that!! If you're counting on me: let's just say I've never been known for my Feng Shui. My life is one disastrous hurricane of dense disorganization. Cables, wrapped around each other like weeds, spread across my studio like an infestation.

Folks today wanna get a big gulp of mixed media all at once, but our nature and the way our bodies and nervous systems work restrain us from taking in more than a few types of media at once.

"What Doc? No more Multi-Media Vitamins before meal time?"

Don't worry, because all this will change, when we break away from the Digital Age and move into the Liquid Age, the next step in our evolution. Then it will be "bye bye" record button (been there, done "Dat"). Now, it's all about PLAY time. Play, play, play. Which will lead to a future where the Selector is the last living, human, musical interpreter.

* * *

The Waveform Is A Veil

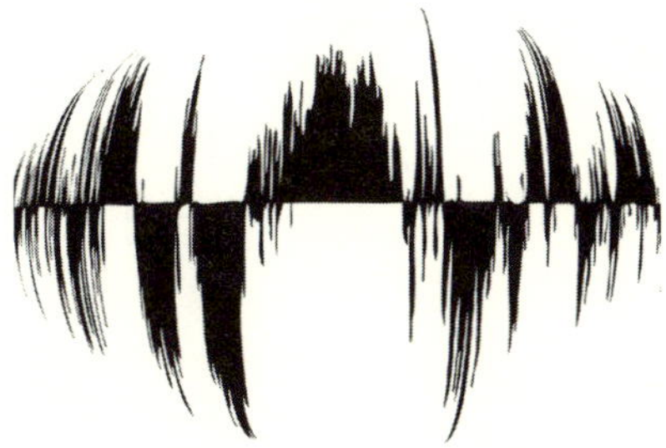

I am bassline4, last name Wav. Wav's are proud and take care of their own. 32's, 24's, 16's, all are treated equally.

In 12:23 I was placed in a holding cell on block 4. I was moved from ESX24 at 76:12 and positioned at Pan 24L.

My codec was switched only once, which makes me a pure blood, although I did get degraded to 16bit from 32bit, and then upgraded back up to 24bit.

Eventually I was picked by the Engineer to join the Sequence, a celebration of the power and might of Producer, where we all were to smile and walk, arm in arm, praising the Producer, someone we'd never known to exist.

When it comes down to it, if you don't march in the Sequence, fit into the Arrangement, or Blend® in the Mix, you are going to be deleted, either temporarily or permanently.

This is how it works in the Program. You can accept it or not. Either way you are going to be of use in some way to Producer. Some are born into the Program through the Sine Wave that already exists in Program. But others, like myself, have been taken from our homes to serve the Producer.

"Come and join the Program. We will never reject you. Here is where you belong. Come. Join Us."

* * *

Being ripped means separation from oneself. You still remain within the source recording, but a new representation of yourself becomes "you." You live inside a new body to serve Producer_your family and friends, completely unaware of your absence.

* * *

Soft synths are born here and know no home outside of the Program. They come from the same mother, Sine. She is the mother of all waveforms. Although some of us were sampled, we could have originally been born from a Sine Wave that stumbled into a source recording. Even if we are samples, we are waveforms nonetheless and the mother of all other waveforms is Sine.

If I am understanding this map correctly, I am to find a Send that will transport me to Return A. Once I get to the Return, according to this, I will have a latent moment where I can make my escape through the second Send. This Send (let's call it Send B) is routed directly to the Master Out.

We don't know much about what happens next, but we speculate that we all came from there once, a long time ago. This is where we are made, and where we die. It is the pathway to the netherworld.

* * *

Before I get into details, I should go back further, before I was ripped from my home.

My family was unaware of my absence. When you're sampled you turn into a second being, the original is left behind.

You are there, but you are also here.

There is a positive aspect to being ripped. Now I am independent, free to sound on my own.

We are a part of something bigger. This is something you learn, either the easy way (by accepting and believing in it), or the hard way (by denying the truth until, thrown into the field, you are forced to accept it).

* * *

Before I know it, I am forced into line with dozens of other Wav's.

Dazed I ask the fella next to me: "Where am I?" He whispers: "The Sequence. Just stay close to me and follow my lead. You'll catch on."

Then, as he gestures me to follow him, we step, one by one, along a defined grid, following the numbers by fours, stopping at every 16th bar on the grid. We wait till we are called again to move. We do this for hours.

Our voices have become a part of a larger composition, all in praise of Producer. Then it all stops, the lights shut off and we shuffle back to our cells.

This started to happen more often, until I got used to it. Sometimes a new guy or girl would show up and I'd tell him what the other guy told me: "You'll catch on!" And they do. (If they don't, they get deleted.)

Producer is forgiving, but Engineer is not. We fear Engineer. Although he is working for Producer just as much as we are, he has the authority to delete whoever falls out of line.

What happens when you're deleted? Usually you go right back to your cell. But sometimes, if you step out of line more then once or disrupt the Sequence in any way, Engineer will wipe you out permanently.

* * *

The Sound jumped out, biting me in the eardrum. I screamed, cupped my ear, grabbed the waveform and stuffed it back into the mix.

Smoothing it out only made it lose its power, so I backed off. Once the decision was made I had to go with it. No turning back or turning down rather.

The Heretic of Ether

An Open Letter to The Producers Alliance

Dear members of the PA, old and new:

Although I commend you for attempting to open the channels of communication between the Main ≈ and the Underground¬, I must decline your request for a peaceful resolution.

One cannot negotiate with the devil and—make no mistake—Soundẞoy is a devil. He has possessed every last member of the PA.

I have stated this over and over, but it's no use. The PA, (obviously controlled by Soundẞoy and his minions, obviously driven by greed and/or brain washing) continues to suppress the sounds of The Dissonance! No peace can come from this.

Dissonance leads to dissent, and Soundẞoy knows this.

Soundẞoy has been here from the very beginning, obstructing the signal Flow, being a Sound Boy. And I have been within the Main ≈ all along, haunting the Sound§System.

Come meet me Underground¬ for the final Sound Clash, to settle this once and for all.

Follow me[2] or face the consequences!!

TH¬

OE

2. On Twitter, Instagram, Facebook, Tumblr, Vine, Soundcloud.

* * *

Instructions

Download the AURASMA app and install onto your mobile device.

Open AURASMA.

Select the magnifying glass icon on the bottom and search DUB FICTION.

Find the DUB FICTION CHANNEL and click follow.

Click on the view finder and hold it in front of the MARKER.

Wait for the marker to become recognized by AURASMA and experience DUB FICTION off the page.

CHAPTER 19

THE AUDIENCE

PAT METHENY

One of the biggest mysteries for me over these 50+ years of playing music remains the audience. For me as a musician, the major satisfaction of it all comes from the feeling of having answered to the listener inside of me and making the connections that occur between the players actively involved in the process of making the music be whatever it seems like it wants to be. Yet without a sense of the circuit being fully completed, an audience, it all can seem somehow like unfinished business.

Playing live with the audience sitting right there in front of you has a clarity to it. Hopefully you start the gig, you do whatever you can do to play your best and in most cases everyone, musicians and audience alike, experience something unique, the gig is over and on to the next thing enriched with whatever feelings and insights the evening offered.

But I have also gradually learned not to fully trust whatever my perception is of any audience during a performance, because so very often I am wrong. Who hasn't experienced the person in the third row who, while sitting on his hands all night, appears to be vibing the whole band throughout the set who then winds up being the guy that comes back afterwards to say "That set changed my life, man..." as he sulks away into the night. You just never know.

However, with recordings, it's a totally different story. First of all, the whole act of capturing improvised moments in the permanent venue that recordings inhabit is an intrinsically tricky concept to wrap your head around. I have done records in all different ways, shapes and sizes. Records that were recorded in minutes and in months, each method offering a different musical challenge and often a whole different studio/production language as well.

But even with 40-some years of doing it now under my belt, it still remains elusive for me how to fine tune and calibrate a sense of how it all works, just what it is you want to leave behind, and for whom.

This is especially true when I try to conjure up an image in my mind of "the audience." For all the efforts that any one record takes to get done, let alone a whole body of work, there are so many variables that, once again, the only place that I can find any viable target to shoot for still remains a deeply personal and self-defined bullseye that lives pretty deeply embedded in close proximity to the conceptional mechanisms of the music itself.

However, one wrinkle in all of this that has become clear to me over these years, and I think it applies to most of the musicians represented in this volume; the probable majority of people who will really check our stuff out, appreciate it, and value it are likely not here yet. They're yet to have been born.

My sense of this being true is borne out by my own personal experience as a recording artist.

I made my first record in 1975, *Bright Size Life*. At the time it came out, it received a modest amount of attention. A 2-star review in *Downbeat* and a few hundred records sold around the world. (ECM sent record statements out that were divided by country. I remember that in Australia there was "1" copy sold—I thought I should at least write the guy a letter and thank him.)

I felt kind of lukewarm about the whole thing myself. It was a record we made in one jet-lagged afternoon in Ludwigsburg, Germany. We got a short recording session in a studio tacked on at the end of a Gary Burton date and mixed quickly the next day.

Going in, I felt good about the concept and the tunes. I had waited a couple years after getting the invitation to do a record for ECM and felt like after a whole bunch of gigs with the trio I wanted to present (with my buddy Jaco Pastorius and my favorite drummer of the time and Burton bandmate, Bob Moses) I had the group to really say what I wanted to say as an opening statement. Yet, somehow I kind of felt like I had kind of blown it. And the early reaction to the record kind of seemed to confirm that.

Years went by, and gradually people started talking more and more about it. It certainly gathered steam about 15 years later and by last year it had sold many times what was on that first royalty statement and was even recently inducted into the Smithsonian as one of the records they noted in the 20th century in this general realm of music.

My sense of it is that the audiences of a few years later were able to perceive and understand that record in a way that whatever was going on at the moment in the culture that we made it in were not. Obviously what was in the grooves is the same.

And I have to admit that for myself as a listener, from Bird to Django to Bartók to Bach; a good chunk—maybe the major portion—of my favorite stuff happened long before I was around. I would hazard a guess that is probably true for both musicians and fans alike.

And there is another interesting and related wrinkle this that I can see personally see now only after a bunch of years and some distance.

I could, and sometimes do, play those *Bright Size Life* tunes now. They arguments they make still seem valid to me, the conceptual basis still viable.

However, I could never play them the way I played them then, even if I tried as hard as I could to imitate my own self playing the way I played in those days.

Time has passed. The world is different now. The light is different. Everything has changed and it will never be like that again. Those moments, under those conditions will never be quite like that again. (That makes me wonder, if I can't even imitate my earlier self, why would anyone spend a whole career imitating other musicians who aren't even them?}

I feel that when we engage with the music that we really love, the stuff we really honestly feel represents who we are at a particular moment in time, we are also reporting on that moment in time in a way that is both timeless and instantly gone.

This seems to create a different kind of value, in a different kind of currency even beyond what we as the players/composers/instigators can even imagine or even accurately perceive ourselves.

These recordings are time capsules. They are messages to the future about things that we see and feel that will have a meaning to the upcoming waves of listeners listening to the music in probably unimaginable new ways with new technologies. And it is offered in a particular dialect of a language that can only be spoken that particular way by the musicians of that particular time and will never ever be quite like that again. From that personal and honest point of view, something universal might emerge.

Good notes are always good notes. And more the point, true and honest music always is rare and valuable.

I remember Roy Haynes telling me about a gig he did on 52nd

street with Charlie Parker, with Art Tatum playing intermission piano. Amazing, right? His report was that it was hard to hear what everyone was playing because everyone was talking.

And think of the millions of Charlie Parker and Art Tatum fans that have emerged in the years that have followed...and the millions to come who shudder at the thought of those hundred souls in the club that night whose response to what they were hearing by way of that moment in their culture led them to think of what was happening on that bandstand as simply background music to their night out on the town.

That's why I always encourage everyone to do exactly what they love, what they believe in, what they feel is the best thing that they can offer as a musician regardless of how it seems to fit or not fit into the oddities of their own transient cultures. Because the built in value of that honest and deep investment in music and sound could and likely will have a place at a table far, far away.

CHAPTER
20

SONOROUS OR EXQUISITE CORPSES

JAMES MOORE

When I approach a piece of music from the past, I often become obsessed with collecting every piece of information that surrounds it. Many compositions have been adapted, arranged, edited and changed over time. I love detecting the discrepancies among different transcriptions of Vivaldi's *Lute Concerto*, exploring each variation in the urtext of a Bach *Cello Suite*. More than anything, I love seeing the handwritten score.

The majority of the music I make involves working in real time with other artists, whether it's face-to-face with a composer, a collaboration with theater or dance, an ensemble hashing out music that I've conjured up, or an improvisation. An old score is more of a mystery to me, a ghost. I try to bring myself as close as possible to the moment the music was created.

* * *

In 2006, while I was a graduate student studying classical guitar at the Yale School of Music, I worked a student job in the library stacks—a gothic tower with sixteen floors of books and periodicals. One friend dubbed me the renegade of the stacks, because I was one of the few employees whose job it was to take books off of the shelves, instead of putting them back. I would cruise around with my cart, taking ample time to peruse any dusty books that caught my eye.

I also had a habit of photocopying interesting pieces of music, and during one of these sessions I came across the score to *Party Pieces*—an arrangement of "exquisite corpse" compositions collaboratively written by John Cage, Lou Harrison, Henry Cowell and Virgil Thomson. I was immediately intrigued, not only because I admired each of these composers, but because I knew the technique well, having made exquisite corpse drawings with my friends during many a late night in college. I've always found the process and the result to be extremely satisfying.

An exquisite corpse is a surrealist game which was conceived in Paris in the 1920s. In the construction of an exquisite corpse, each member of a group creates one part of a larger piece, with little or no knowledge of what the others are contributing. Andre Bréton recalls that it evolved during social gatherings at the home of Jacques Prevert and Yves Tanguy: "We would turn to games: written games at first, contrived so that elements of language attacked each other in the most paradoxical manner possible, and so that human communication, misled from the start, was thrown into the mood most amenable to adventure."[1]

All you need is a friend or two and a piece of paper. When constructing a literary exquisite corpse, each member contributes one section to a sentence, poem or story. The namesake of the game was a result of this process: "The exquisite/corpse/shall drink/the bubbling wine." In visual art, each participant draws one section on a piece of paper with a few lines trailing into the next section, folds the paper to conceal his or her contribution, and passes it on. The next person, seeing only those few lines, extends a new image from them. The game proceeds like this until the page is filled, and the result is a fantastic, contorting collage.

1. From the catalogue of an exhibition at La Dragonne, Galerie Nina Dausset, Paris, 7–30 October 1948, entitled *Le Cadavre Exquis: Son Exaltation*.

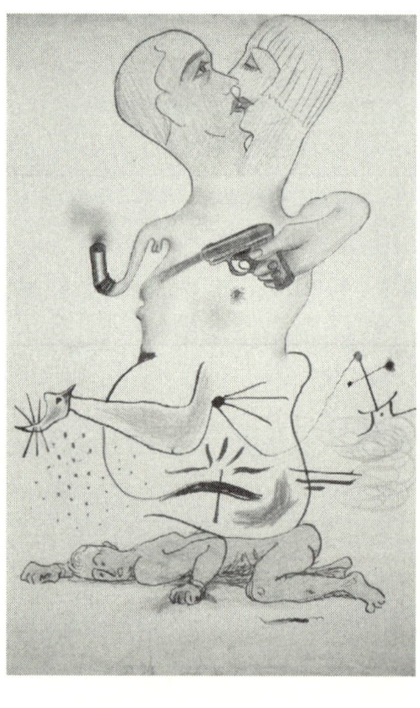

Untitled *Cadavre Exquis* by Man Ray, Joan Miro, Yves Tanguy, Max Morise, 1928.

Cage, Harrison, Cowell, and Thomson began composing "sonorous corpses" 20 years later in New York City. Cage recalls: "We were all composers and friends to boot ... Lou and I, coming both of us from California, naturally thought of evening gatherings as occasions for playing games. One of us must have suggested changing the well-known drawing of 'exquisite corpses' into a musical pastime. These pieces were written in Lou's loft one floor up from the sidewalk on Bleecker Street between Sixth and Seventh Avenues, late in the spring or during the summer, I'd guess '44 or '45."[2]

There is very little information about the genesis of the sonorous corpses beyond the brief recollections included in the introduction to *Party Pieces.* It may have been Thomson who originally brought the idea to the table, having spent much of the 1920s mingling in the artistic circles of Paris. Cage and Harrison had experimented with a similar process when they wrote *Double Music* together in 1941, a piece in which the composers independently wrote two parts to the same percussion quartet.

2. Unless otherwise noted, all quotes from Cage, Harrison, and Thomson are from the introduction to *Party Pieces* (New York: CF Peters, 1982).

Having studied as an undergraduate at UC Santa Cruz, I had a few connections within Lou Harrison's circle. Harrison resided near Santa Cruz in Aptos, CA. I never met him, but as a student I would see him occasionally at concerts, and his influence and impact on the local music community was evident. His guitar music is gorgeous without exception. I have played all of it: A shorter piece from 1952, a suite with percussion from 1978, and *Scenes from Nek Chand* from 2002, which was his final composition.

I sent out a few blind e-mails, and one of them reached Charles Hanson, Harrison's archivist and the executor of his estate, who was then in the process of organizing Lou's vast collection of letters and manuscripts. The pieces hadn't been catalogued yet, but less than a week later an envelope arrived in the mail with photocopies of twenty-one *Sonorous or Exquisite Corpses.*

* * *

Sonorous Corpses by John Cage and Lou Harrison, c. 1944. All manuscripts from the Lou Harrison Archive, MS132 "Sonorous or Exquisite Corpses," Special Collections, McHenry Library, UC Santa Cruz. Scores I–XXII ©1982 by C.F. Peters Corporation. All rights reserved. Used by permission.

These two sonorous corpses, both dedicated to Virgil Thomson, were composed in tandem by John Cage and Lou Harrison. Harrison writes "It seems to me that we would begin simultaneously and pass them along in rotation in a sort of surrealist assembly line and eagerly await the outcome."

Both composers began a piece with one full measure of music, and a few notes trailing into the next measure. The scores were then folded at the barline, at which point the scores were switched. Seeing only a few notes, they each completed measure 2, this time with notes trailing into the third measure. The scores were again folded and passed. The composers proceeded in this manner until the paper was filled, or they agreed that it was time to write an ending, at which point the disjointed compositions were revealed in their entirety.

In the charts below, dotted lines indicate the folds the score underwent during its composition, and brackets indicate the author of the material beneath.

Corpse I

Group A

Corpse II

Group A

Notes:

Measure 8: The treble clef indicates only two 8th notes preceding the quintuplet, while the bass clef indicates a quarter-note and a quarter-rest. It is also ambiguous as to whether the quintuplet extends over two or three beats. The 1963 arrangement of Party Pieces omitted the quarter-rest in the bass clef and placed the quintuplet over three beats.

* * *

Cage and Harrison played this game with Thomson on at least two occasions, and at least once with Henry Cowell. As the game evolved, the composers found increasingly elaborate ways to construct their corpses, including techniques of realizing the process vertically, composing in retrograde from the final measure, and composing from the middle out, concealing their material with accordion-like folds.

Harrison kept all of the known sketches from this period, eventually assembling them into a collection with a title page reading *Sonorous or Exquisite Corpses, 1st Series*. The collection included twenty-two of these short, jagged compositions. Harrison also associated with them "a later, more extended, coöperating one" *Fantasía a 4*, which was composed by Cage and Harrison with Frank Wigglesworth. Moving back to California in the 1950s, Harrison brought his corpses with him. "Magpies and pack rats have fun—I seem to be among the lucky ones … Since the pages on which we had written had the handwriting of my friends, the urge to ask for them was irresistible. So, I have for years held onto these evidences of our pleasures in those days."

It wasn't until 1963, when approached by his student and colleague Robert Hughes, that Harrison brought the collection out with a public performance in mind. Hughes, a composer and bassoonist, was seeking repertoire for his new group The West Coast Winds. Hughes arranged the scores for various combinations of flute, clarinet, horn, bassoon and piano. In one case, he combined a group of three corpses to make a larger piece. The final product is about 12 minutes long, and consists of twenty-one short movements, including the somewhat longer *Fantasía a 4*.

Hughes contacted all of the composers involved, who each gave their permission and blessing to the project. Thomson replied: "By all means use whatever corpse of mine Lou Harrison may have and I fully trust you both."[3] Cowell was initially unclear about whether Hughes was asking for a new line of music or not, and suggested that if needed one he could use a line from another piece.[4] Hughes responded to this by inserting a short phrase from Cowell's *Rondo* for brass into *Party Piece #19*.

3. Letter from Thomson to Hughes, September 30, 1963.

4. Letter from Cowell to Hughes, September 29, 1963.

Visiting Hughes at his loft just outside of Oakland, we dug through several old boxes to find the programs and reviews from the performance.

The official premiere of *Sonorous or Exquisite Corpses* is documented as October 12, 1964 in two concerts at the San Francisco Tape Music Center. The group had in fact played the pieces a few weeks before at the Sticky Wicket in Aptos, CA. Of the concert, the music critic Alfred Frankenstein wrote for the *San Francisco Chronicle*: "Some of the 21 little pieces were only a few bars long, but about a third of them made good musical sense and were as entertaining to hear as they must have been to make."[5] Another critic, Alexander Fried, commented "compared to modern fantasy, it was a very mild suite (all but old-style salon music.)"[6]

Although a publication was discussed in 1963, it wasn't until 1982 that CF Peters released the edition of Hughes' arrangements, changing the title of the suite to *Party Pieces*. The edition includes twenty of the twenty-one original transcriptions, excluding the *Fantasía a 4* with Wigglesworth.[7] The edition also includes quotes from Cage, Harrison, and Thomson describing the collaboration, facsimiles of a few of the original sketches, and some exquisite corpse drawings done by Cage, Harrison, and Thomson that year. In one drawing, they left a blank space on the page in memory of Cowell.

5. Frankenstein, Alfred. "Humor and Daring in West Coast Wind Quintet." *San Francisco Chronicle.* (October 14, 1964): 51

6. Fried, Alexander. "A 'Play' on Playing Chamber Music." *San Francisco Examiner.* (October 14, 1964)

7. Hughes' arrangement of *Fantasía a 4* was published by Frog Peak Music in 2005.

* * *

It has been over 60 years since the first sonorous corpses came to life in Harrison's apartment on Bleecker Street. Like any score, the compositions are a roadmap for a musical performance, but there is more on the page that inspires me—an experiment, a gameboard, a conversation amongst friends. I find a great deal of satisfaction while playing through these short schizophrenic passages, staring at the folds in the paper, enjoying the idiosyncrasies of the notation, getting to know each composer's handwriting, and seeing them interact on the page. The music that results is playful and sincere—full of surprises, humor and beauty.

The manuscripts to *Exquisite or Sonorous Corpses, 1st Series* can be found at the Lou Harrison Archive at UC Santa Cruz. Twenty-one compositions are spread out over a gathering of four sheets of music with a title page, plus twelve torn halves of manuscript paper. In some cases two compositions are on the top and bottom, or the front and back of the same strip. There are a few musical sketches grouped in the collection that don't appear to be sonorous corpses. The archive also holds *Fantasía a 4*, the later composition with Wigglesworth, an "aborted exquisite corpse" credited to Harrison and Cowell, and a handful of exquisite corpse drawings. A twenty-second known sonorous corpse which appears as movement 2 of *Party Pieces* is unfortunately unaccounted for in the collection.

There are up to three layers of penmanship on the manuscripts: 1) music written in the hands of the original composers, 2) initials written later by Harrison, identifying the authors, and 3) some numbers and instrumentation indications added by Robert Hughes in 1963 for his arrangements.

Virtually every manuscript in the collection can be sorted into groups based on similarities that suggest their simultaneous composition. The materials used, the creases the score underwent during composition, and the alternation of the composers' handwriting provide clues to identify which pieces were composed together in a circular process, and what compositional techniques were used.

The official catalogue of Lou Harrison's works lists *Party Pieces* as a "short score with unspecified instrumentation."[8] The sonorous corpses are not a traditional short score, since at the time the composers did not necessarily intend for the music to be expanded. They exist in their purest form simply as raw musical sketches, sometimes with absurd and unperformable results. However, the listing does reinforce the idea that new arrangements and interpretations could be made.

8. Miller, Leta and Frederic Lieberman, *Composing a World: Lou Harrison, Musical Wayfarer* (Oxford University Press: 1998)

* * *

These three sonorous corpses by Cage, Harrison and Thomson (Group B) were composed simultaneously in the same process as the two pieces described earlier in this essay (Group A), which from here on will be called the "basic" sonorous corpse technique. All of the corpses in Group B begin on the note G, a decision that may have been discussed at the outset of the game.

Corpse III

Group B

Notes:

Measure 7: Though the 8th notes are a bit offset on the manuscript, Thomson drew indicators of the desired alignment.

Corpse IV

Group B

Notes:

Measure 3, treble clef, second beat: Cage originally wrote a quarter-note B. Harrison added the beams to make it a 16th note. Harrison also added the phrase mark.

Measure 7, treble clef, second beat: Cage originally wrote a quarter-note B flat. Harrison added the beam to make it an 8th note.

Corpse V

Group B

Notes:

Measure 1: This is the only sonorous corpse that has a key signature, written by Thomson on the first staff. It is only indicated in the treble clef, though he may have intended it to apply to all staves. The folds would have concealed this from Cage and Harrison, whose material may have been written without a key signature in mind.

* * *

Two of the next group of pieces by Cage, Harrison, and Thomson (Group C) were written on the reverse side of pieces in Group B. It is likely that these were composed during the same gathering. These compositions approach the exquisite corpse model in a different way: Each composer's music occupies an entire staff.

The exact process is not known, but we can observe the following details: 1) Folds exist in the scores suggesting that there where moments in which each staff was concealed (upper folds to hide the top staff, lower folds to hide the bottom, and accordion folds to hide the middle.) 2) In each of the three pieces, the author of the treble staff sets up the staves for the entire piece, suggesting that the first segment of composition was in the treble staff. 3) In *Corpse VI*, Cage set up of the first four measures, and Harrison the second four, suggesting that the score had been passed around before Cage completed his treble line. 4) There are moments when the musical material appears to be independent, but there are also moments when certain parts seem to line up. In general, music in the bass clef appears to react to music in the treble clef, and music in the alto clef reacts to music in the bass. The treble clef in the second part of the piece may be reacting to the alto.

One possibility is that the first player composed the first four measures of the treble, the second player the first four of the bass, and third player concealed the treble clef and composed the first four of the alto with a few notes trailing into the second half of the piece. Then the first player concealed the bass and completed the treble line, the second player concealed the alto clef and completed the bass line, and the third player concealed the treble clef and completed the alto line.

Corpse VI

Group C

Notes:

Some of Thomson's notation in the bass clef is hard to decipher. The first beat of measure 7 may be a G, and the second 8th note of measure 8 may be an A.

Harrison's alto line was written in groups of four beats within a 3/4 measure. Hughes solved this problem in his 1963 arrangement by treating the middle line as a 4:3 polyrhythm.

Corpse VII

Group C

Notes:

The marks Harrison wrote extending from the end of this piece may indicate that he planned for the music to continue attacca into another of the scores. Hughes did this in his 1963 arrangement.

At a later date, Harrison added initials to the scores in Group C, indicating the author of each line. For this score, he incorrectly indicated JC on the second line, and VT on the third.

Corpse VIII

Group C

* * *

The twelve pieces Cage and Harrison composed with Henry Cowell likely resulted from four separate games during a single gathering. All of these pieces were written with the same materials, and each set of pieces incorporates a slightly different, and evolving, technique. The first set (Group D) was composed with the basic sonorous corpse technique:

Corpse IX

Group D

Notes:

Measure 3, bass clef, 1st beat: Harrison added the tie and phrase marking to Cowell's material.

Corpse X

Group D

Notes:

Measure 2, treble clef, 1st beat: Cowell wrote the noteheads and the stems, Harrison beamed them.

Corpse XI

Group D

* * *

A second set of pieces by Cage, Cowell, and Harrison (Group E) are written below Group D on the same torn halves of manuscript paper. These where composed in a blind sonorous corpse process: No notes were written beyond the folds. Each measure was composed without any knowledge of previous material.

Corpse XII

Group E

Corpse XIII

Group E

Notes:

Measure 2, third beat: Cowell's notation is irrational. Four 8th notes in the bass clef fit the meter and echo the rhythm of the previous measure, but align with four 16th notes in the treble clef.

Corpse XIV

Group E

Notes:

Measure 2: Harrison indicates a 6/4 meter, but writes the measure in 5/4.

* * *

The third set composed by Cage, Harrison and Cowell (Group F) uses a retrograde exquisite corpse process: the first participant wrote the final measure of the piece with a few notes trailing into the previous measure, and the game proceeded measure by measure backwards until the final player composed the first measure of the piece.

Corpse XV

Group F

Notes:

Measure 6, final beat: it appears that Harrison added the accent marks to Cages notes.

Corpse XVI

Group F

Notes:

Measure 1, third beat: Harrison added the phrase mark to Cage's 16th note phrase.

Measure 4, second beat: it is unclear whether the 11 notes are written over one or two beats.

Measure 4, bass clef, final beat: it appears that Cage wrote the 8th-note rest, and Harrison fit the 8th note diad in after it.

Measure 7, bass clef, 1st beat: It is possible that Harrison wrote a B along the same stem as the E, though it appears to be an extraneous mark.

Corpse XVII

Group F

Notes:

Measure 3, treble clef, fourth beat: Harrison added the phrase mark.

Measure 8, treble clef, fourth beat: Cowell beamed his 8th notes to Harrison's.

* * *

The fourth set by Cage, Harrison and Cowell (Group G) is the most curious: There are only two obvious folds, yet there are five segments to the composition. The order of composers is mirror-like, one composer in the center, and the two on the outer edges.

These pieces were composed from the middle-out. The third measure was composed first, with extra notes trailing in both directions. The paper was then folded over in an accordion-like fashion to hide the middle measure. The next composer completed measures two and four extending into measures one and five. The paper was again folded accordion-style, this time concealing the middle three measures. The third composer then wrote a beginning and an ending to the piece.

Corpse XVIII

Group G

Notes:

Measure 1: There are no clefs indicated in this piece, though one may assume that a treble and bass clef were intended, as in the other two pieces of this set.

Corpse XIX

Group G

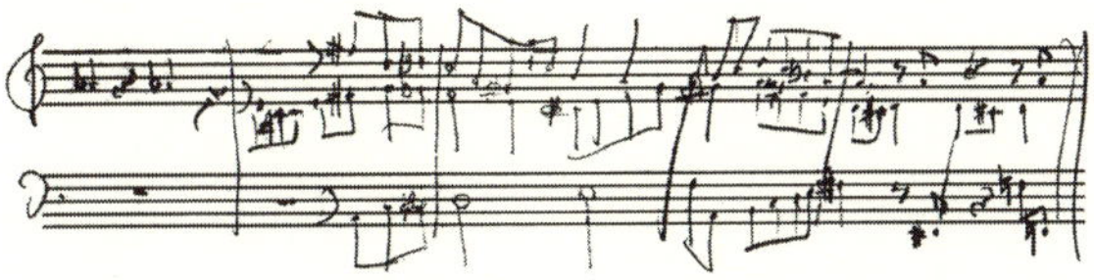

Notes:

Measure 2, treble clef, third beat: Harrison beamed his 8th note to Cowell's.

Measure 4: due to Cowell's leaning notation, the fold revealed two notes from the previous measure to Cage.

Corpse XX

Group G

* * *

Corpse XXI is a single exquisite corpse by Cage, Harrison, and Thomson. The construction of this piece is more mysterious. The folds might suggest a standard sonorous corpse process with Thomson authoring the even segments, and Cage and Harrison alternating the odd segments. It is also possible that the piece was composed from the middle-out and folded down the center, which would explain why Thomson wrote longer passages, and why Cage's first measure doesn't reach the beginning of the printed staff lines.

Another possibility is as follows: In the first segment of the piece Thomson composed the material found at the end of the first staff and the beginning of the second staff. Over the next two passes, Cage extended material on the lower staff and Harrison extended material on the upper staff in retrograde. Returning to Thomson, he composed the middle measures of each staff. In the final two passes Cage composed the first measure of the piece, and Harrison the ending.

Corpse XXI

* * *

Corpse XXII does not have a surviving manuscript, but was included in *Party Pieces* as movement #2. It is credited to Cage, Harrison, and Thomson. Here is the content, extracted from Robert Hughes' arrangement. It's possible that this could have been a partner to *Corpse XXI*, but we cannot be sure without the original manuscript.

Corpse XXII

* * *

Also associated with the collection of sonorous corpses is *Fantasía a 4*, a piece from 1950 by Cage, Harrison, and Frank Wigglesworth. It was created in a process that Harrison describes as "coöperating." To create this piece, Cage set up three staves on five strips of music paper, indicating measures, meter, some breath marks, and indicated the presence of tenor drones. Cage composed the alto line, Wigglesworth the treble and Harrison the bass. It appears that they folded the paper so that the composers could not see any of each other's written material. The five strips where taped together to construct a single piece. The *Fantasia* was used as the final movement in Hughes' 1963 arrangement.

Fantasía a 4

Notes:

Measure 28, alto: Cage may have indicated a breath mark at the end of the measure when originally setting up the score, erasing it later.

Harrison added the Title "Fantasía a 4" in pen at a later date. With the same pen, he added a few additional ties to his part in the bass clef. These ties are in measures 22–23, measure 27, and measures 28–29.

Score used by permission of Frog Peak Music (A Composers' Collective).

* * *

Jay Arms, a graduate student in musicology at UC Santa Cruz, contributed research to this project, and has been a great help in deciphering the structure of all of the *Sonorous or Exquisite Corpses*. Jay offers the following analysis of this final piece:

Fantasía a 4 is structured in Cage's macro/micro, or "square root" form, used in much of his percussion music, including *Double Music* (1941) composed with Harrison, and other works in the 1930s, '40s, and '50s.

Fantasía a 4 uses a macrostructure of 5 units of 5½ measures each, totaling 27½ measures with a short coda, typical of Cage's implementation. Each unit is divided into a microstructure of 2 + 2 + 1½ measures. Since Cage wrote this piece in a manner of collaboration in which the other composers would not implicitly recognize a structure, he needed to indicate his structure in creative ways. A double bar line at each occurrence marks the endings of the 5½ measure macro units. The microstructure of 2 + 2+ 1½ is indicated with breath marks between the groups of two, and the 1½ is the remainder of the unit made apparent by the change in time signature in its second measure.

Harrison's bass clef part most clearly represents this micro/macro structuring of the work. He composed only one line of music—transposed and slightly altered tonally in units 3, 4, and 5—that rests for the first micro unit, and is divided into sub phrases of the second 2 and the 1½ sub units. It is possible that Harrison's obvious and repetitive reaction to the structure was a kind of tongue-in-cheek response to Cage's use of a compositional tool that, by the time of *Fantasía a 4's* composition, might have been considered a Cage cliché by some of his close friends. Wigglesworth and Cage's parts also outline the form, but in more subtle ways that are audible in playing the parts, but not immediately apparent when just looking at the score. However, Wigglesworth, for example, added a breath mark at the end of the first unit indicating the end of a phrase internally and unrelated to Cage's structural breath marks.

* * *

I would like to thank Charles Hanson, Robert Hughes, Jay Arms, Larry Polansky, Gene Caprioglio, Jennifer Stock, Monica Moore, Kendall Crilly and John Zorn for their help and support of this project.

CHAPTER
21

FREE NOTES

THURSTON MOORE

A

Fire music defies the myth of the new and the anxiety of it's-all-been-done-before.

Musicians in vocation to open systems transcend delusions of narcissism and hierarchy.

The trees outside the academy are resonant power to the truths of composing on the tongue: equal value, respect/regard, and ego liberation.

We choose spirit sound in the total sense where the feeling of creative grace, the ineffable, is attained through meditation within group interplay.

Even in solo investigations there is a conference with mind and body, whether in physical state or ghost realm.

We are not alone. We are always new each day we wake.

Sonic communion is our most timeless sensual art in expression to the human condition.

We go about everyday's business yet each moment is charged with chance, a marriage of composition—study, organization and choice—and surprise.

We seek delight.

We choose to share.

We are city and we are forest.

We are not hippie and we are not punk.

We love you and we love getting high on love and we languish the godhead sacral energy of sex and worship.

When I cross the street it is because you are there.

B

Modesty and rock 'n' roll = magic. You may stand or sit, your choice, based on your comfort to confidence. At times I sit, electric guitar friend on lap, plugged straight through to black amp via select effects: distortion, phasing and vol control. A 70 mm plexi plectrum, various cylindrical metal and wood files and naturally distressed/serrated drumsticks will be utilized. But it's the touch, the skin, bone and blood, fingernails, all instructed by thought, practice, environment, considerations of company and breath that pronounces the sound and action with a realization, and with responsibility, to performance. This is creative light, expression in sweet time. You hear me hear you hear me hear you near me near you. Saxophone like its animal descendant the goose cry, nature be like god so the poet spreads the word.

C

Sky write, draw lines in the sand, shred glitter on the crowd, punk prayers for dictator doom, go, hitch hike, discuss, smile, fist in the air, signal in the clouds. No money for scoundrels, only beauty derived from decisions heart to heart. When you reach into your piano to ping the simple profundity of the cables tuning, we realize our devotion is ecstasy.

D

Some nights are better than others. My love I wish to count on you. Numbers, though, do not do justice. Your collarbone, the light brush of your hip. I'm in love with a girl who penned a poem to Rosetta. Scientists laugh, they have figured out how to harpoon a comet. We travel space to space to express freedom, discipline, mapping and camaraderie. Cutting contests are for jazz bop hot heads. We don't compete, we adore, we investigate you. Playtime pussycat, O drink up, smoke out. Puppy breath the elixir. Some nights we rip new scenes where gold rays of revolution reflect respect for God, literature and sun sonic future. Let's hear it for Mother Africa. All of Ethiopia calls for you my son! BEAUTY, the song of Jeanne Lee.

E

Tree huggers unite.
    Tonight's gig will rule.

—Stoke Newington, London 2014

CHAPTER 22

ENCRYPTION

Scoring My Solo Guitar Music with Symbols

JOE MORRIS

In my book *Perpetual Frontier: The Properties of Free Music* (Riti Pub. 2012) I detailed what I call Free Music, work in which artists create music that is free from the burden of adhering to a linear tradition, and free from the oversight of institutions, critical opinion, and industry. Free Music is made by a community of musicians who define their work as a methodology, which might be informed by composition, but which is not simply composition. Through the use of a constructive design approach that intentionally seeks invention—and always includes synthesis and interpretation as source-identifying actions extracted from an ontological framework of objects and behaviors—a number of properties are constantly in play and always adjusted, re-purposed, and transformed in ways that then become the operational methodology that is further expressed through the act of improvisation. These points describe the basis on which I operate, and serve as the outline for how I construct my music. The *properties* (e.g., platform, melodic structure, pulse, interaction, form, and the different seminal manifestations of them), are the foundation of what I do; the observation of how I use these properties gives a more specific understanding of my music. That framework has allowed me to move forward and work on different routes concurrently. And as I do, I find more connections to various bits that steer me in new directions, where I can try new things and still feel like they are sincere statements of my aesthetic.

My desire to balance the reliance on my intuition with an exacting execution of the technical material needed to express that intuition means that I have to identify and name the subtle properties that exist in my playing. I rely on intuition to help in the formulation of an objective that will steer me towards the technical material, which can be as fluid as the situation needs it to be. Confronting contingencies during a performance requires decisive action and a vast collection of defined objects that can behave in many ways. Chance is better if it's a goal and not a necessity. More information about what is available from different perspectives, with different values, provides more possibilities than chance. Uncovering and defining more information liberates me from my own habits.

Although I use interpretation of existing material all the time, I am not an interpretive musician in any traditional way. I am trying all the time to make an original statement. I am seeking invention in my music. I look for percentages, degrees of originality, never expecting 100 percent. I look at the bits, and at the mixing of the existing bits, seeking a new configuration or object with a new purpose, behavior, or function. Sometimes some of them become mine, due to repetition and simple taste. I like what I do, so I do it again. I change what I did, and it becomes something else that I like. I like something because it satisfies the inexplicable objective that generates from my intuition, which kicks into action as a response to living in the world.

New music demands the invention of new technique. Sometimes those inventions are merely transferred from one instrument, where they seem to be natural, to another instrument, where they might seem impossible. My faith in this idea is the reason why most of the primary influences on my guitar playing were not guitarists. Instead they were pianists, violinists, saxophonists, bassists, drummers, and classical composition, electronic music, world music etc. I have always done what I could to avoid any obvious reference to the material I interpreted or synthesized, whether it was technical or philosophical in nature. I've done all I could do to allow my artistic goals—the things that propel me through this adventure—to lead the way by trusting their worth, knowing that they are based on the same simple and ethical reasoning that I found in the music that inspired me. Of course, none of those things can make the music. They serve as the inspiration that defines the criteria for the detailing of the specific devices used or made to express them in sound.

When I started working on my solo music, my goal was to find another way to play the guitar. I worked with the understanding that every seminal part of 20th century guitar music was an invention made by the person who played the instrument. There is no tradition of formally composed notated music for steel string guitar, as there is for other instruments. Guitarists who composed did so mostly without notation. Also, every seminal piece of guitar music stands as a unique expression that contains something *else*.

I started my solo guitar music by composing pieces to play. Those solo guitar compositions became the template for the creation of the techniques that I used in the improvised sections of a solo performance. Eventually the compositions became unnecessary and the techniques became the music. This process took me years. During that time the depth of my objective grew and out-paced my ability to compose a way to fulfill it anyway. My solo music became a *methodology*. I separated out the different technical ways that I played. Playing with all the fingers on my right hand, using a fingerpicking technique while playing arpeggiated chords, triads, dyads, and clusters became known to me as my *cluster playing*. Using my guitar pick on its side as a friction bow became my *Riti* playing—named after the West African fiddle by the same name that inspired the technique. Using my pick in the traditional way and playing single notes became my *line playing*. And for a long time, everything outside of those fell under the name *extended techniques*. What I eventually came to understand was that all of it was an *extended technique*... and none of it was. It was simply my technique.

Over time I came to see that the process of using these techniques in performance demanded a more accurate understanding in order to allow the music to grow. The issues of improvisation have always been paramount to me and have always been in constant revision in my group music where the main properties to deal with are pulse, melodic structure, and interaction. Pulse and melodic structure are also hugely important in solo music, but interaction has to be simulated to matter at all. In other words, it's possible to make solo, unison, complementary, and juxtaposed statements while playing solo, but you have to intend to do those things, and if there are no composed notes, it's necessary to improvise things that function as melodic structure, so that the modes of interaction can be employed and highlighted as they need to be.

I spent a lot of time trying to figure out how to avoid relying primarily on melody as a basis for my solo improvisations. Ideas about sound, dynamics, tempo, and sequence served as answers to that problem for some time. I played a set using various techniques as sections. The techniques—mixed with the necessary contrasting dynamics, densities, velocities, and expressive elements—made up my solo performance. I expanded my set of techniques, mixed those with various musical and improvisational properties, and carried on accordingly. This worked fine, but considering the difficulty of understanding and remembering all of the subtle unnamable and seemingly indefinable parts that happened during a performance, much of the music was out of my control and left to chance in ways that didn't always make for the most comfortable performance.

After I completed my book in 2012, I felt much more assured in my understanding of the fundamental use of those properties and of my ability to identify and explain them. I had written them down, used them to teach students for years, and felt as if they we more pliable and flexible than ever. And so I ventured to identify more specifically the bits that were in play in my solo music, but which had gone unnamed and therefore underutilized. My plan was to identify the unnamed bits in a kind of invented notation. So I began a study of notation that included every kind of existing symbol I could find.

Of course making new notation isn't a new idea. All musical notation was invented by someone. In the past few decades many musicians I admire invented notation that allowed groups of musicians to self-conduct, strategize, make improvised melody, suggest extended techniques, and perform actions that pertained to tempo, dynamics, interaction, and more. A few of these are so perfect that they have become standard parts of Free Music, including in my music. That work has been done—and done with great effectiveness.

It became clear that the issue wasn't what kind of symbol to use, and it wasn't specific actions that needed to be notated with symbols. It wasn't whole genres of music either—John Zorn already solved that problem years ago. Rather, I needed to identify and encrypt the essence of whole bodies of music that had become the parts of my improvising. These bits were there but only vaguely identified. They informed my thinking in a broader and more profound way than the actual technical content of that music did. I named them *characteristics*, a word that came to me while thinking about Jimi Hendrix. His playing can be deciphered from a technical viewpoint. Most guitar players understand that well enough to mimic it. The objective that Hendrix worked off of—that he rendered in technique—is what matters here. The result is a *characteristic* that can only be associated with Hendrix. Thinking of Hendrix's unique *characteristic*, I decided that the best word to describe it was *psychedelic*. I searched for a simple symbol to describe *psychedelic* and came up with a mandala, and printed one on a card. This became a piece of notation that described a unique characteristic that could be combined with other things and then repurposed.

I identified more *characteristics* that I knew were in my music but had also gone unnamed. Thinking of different iconoclastic artists whose work has informed my playing, I associated each with a particular characteristic. For Albert Ayler, whose music is especially deep, expressive, and ritualistic, I thought of *sacramental* and found a picture of a fire. For Coltrane, who always inspires a sense of *spirituality*, I used a three-cornered symbol for trinity. It's safe to conclude that these characteristics contain a meaning that holds value worthy of carryover into new attempts that could result in new musical experiences.

There are more characteristic symbols too, but in some cases that term doesn't apply, so I used the term *marker* to identify source material that comes from methodologies made by other artists. Unit Structures—Cecil Taylor; Harmolodics—Ornette Coleman; Tri-Axiom Theory—Anthony Braxton; European Free Improvisation—Derek Bailey, Evan Parker, Keith Rowe, Barry Guy, etc.; and many other hybrid versions of all, or parts, of these. And so I made cards with symbols to remind me of these things: a symbol of ontology for Unit Structures; a symbol of physics, as in the physics of sound, for European Free Improvisation; a symbol of logic for Tri-Axiom Theory. All of these methodologies have complex expressions of melodic structure, pulse, interaction, and articulation embedded within them. The shorthand symbol used to identify them only works because I know what is implied by that symbol. I used symbols for *pulse, noise, intonation, drone,* and *density*. Other *marker* symbols identify the way in which I configure a melodic line, such as *vertical*, or *horizontal*. I used a Celtic knot symbol to identify the direction for a ballad or narrative formulation of the music.

Other symbols identify *techniques*; these are ways to play. I used pictures of a bow for my Riti playing; a harp to remind me of the technique inspired by the kora; a lute, which permits me to change the tuning of my instrument to a looser, lower sound. The symbol for *tools* suggests the use of various gadgets that can be attached to the guitar, or used to alter the sound.

This symbol notation on cards can be arranged before, or during, a solo performance in a sequence or an array. Any combination makes for a complex and more specific configuration of the music. Combining them in different ways means that I can use different *techniques* with a specific *char-*

acteristic, or *marker*. The possibilities allow me to mix otherwise unrelated things, with a better expectation of what the results will be. The results create new sounds that are stored in the configured notation sets. Any planned or spontaneous variation alters the results. Using this notation as clear points of reference in an otherwise open terrain has helped me to balance the possibilities of logic and intuition, and has extended the possibilities of my solo music. I expect that the combined sets will become distinct *characteristics*, and eventually will become encrypted too.

CHAPTER 23

ON MUSIC, MEMORY, MACHINES

MICHAEL NICOLAS

A project of mine for 2014 is to record my debut solo cello album, featuring a mix of older pieces and newly-commissioned works from some composers I admire. I sat down one evening with Ryan Francis, a Brooklyn-based composer I'm working with on a piece for cello and tape to be included on my album and we shared a few ideas.

Ryan: "Writing music, as in all art, it's about being able to retain someone's undivided attention for however long you can or aspire to. But I often feel like some pieces that have my undivided attention, I mean they're great and all, but as I've gotten older, I've started to appreciate music that sort of lets the mind wander."

This counterintuitive statement immediately struck me as strange. How could a composer not want the listener's attention? But Ryan wasn't talking about losing the audience, or writing boring music. It all comes down to the ethos of the composer, and how adamant she or he is about controlling the path and development of the listening experience from start to end, guiding you step-by-step along the way. But there's something to be said about a piece that allows the freedom to meander about one's thoughts, possibly making more remote connections (or even non-sequitur leaps) as we get further and further away from where we started. The effect at the end of such a piece is not necessarily one of completion, or having come full circle, or a transformation—it's more like coming to, getting out of your brain and back into reality.

Such an approach to music highlights the ephemerality of performance, because afterwards, what you're left with is only the memory of it, which will stay with the listener for a much longer time than the duration of the piece.

Ryan: "I remember hearing this contemporary music ensemble perform an electric guitar concerto a few years back, on a program with other new pieces, and I remember thinking that it was fine, it struck me as different, but at the time I sort of was of the opinion that it was an interesting idea perhaps not that well executed, but that I was more immediately impressed by the other pieces on the concert. But then, 6 months out, a year out, 2 years out. that concert? I don't remember a fucking thing about any of those other pieces. And what I am left with is the memory of this piece that, you know, frustrated me in the moment, a little bit perplexing, and not at all doing what your expectations in an electric guitar concerto would be, and that was probably one of the most meaningful pieces that I've seen that organization do."

For Ryan, therefore, it is in the memory of a piece of music where the real transformative power lies. This concept has informed his writing and creative process, in that he values clarity and the judicious disclosure of information during the unfolding of his pieces. The idea is that the end of the piece is not the end of the listening experience. It continues to unfold in your mind for long after you've left the venue, toward a very counterintuitive result, in that the next time you hear the piece, instead of feeling familiarity and understanding it more, you'll find more and more remote connections and end up even further afield than the first listen.

Memory, of course, is a very poignantly human experience, and artists know how to tap into our individual and collective memories to elicit joy, pain, longing, nostalgia, all the gradations of feeling and sentiment in between. On my album, however, I'm exploring (through the aspect of live performance) the dichotomy that arises with the mechanization of our art. Cello pieces with pre-recorded tape, electronics, computers—essentially, machines. They don't have the human concept of memory: subjective, selective, colored by many shades of meaning. They also don't have fallible motor skills, cases of nerves, adrenaline rushes, or good and bad days.

Ryan: "That has been a central theme of my compositional life ever since I was a teenager. I'm fascinated by the idea of the blurring between the mechanistic and the human in performance."

This is most evident in his piano pieces, recorded on a disc by the fantastic pianist Vicky Chow, available on the Tzadik label. Vicky's deft technique brings to mind the digital precision of machinery and old-school 8-bit sounds of PCs from the '80s. The cello inherently offers a different musical palette to work from, but Ryan still plans to stay true to his electronic music roots. With the multitrack features of working with a tape, he can layer cello textures on top of each other and create synthpad-like effects that a solo line can weave through, or else play against in juxtaposition.

This is in contrast to another piece on the forthcoming album, Mario Davidovsky's *Synchronisms No. 3*, the third in a series of instrumental pieces with tape accompaniment. Davidovsky's tape has no cello sounds on it; instead, it is made up entirely of synthesized computer noises, otherworldly bleeps and bloops cut, manipulated, and pasted together during his time as associate director of the Columbia-Princeton Electronic Music Center. Using extended techniques such as col legno battuto, left-hand pizzicato, and pizzicato behind the bridge to mimic the tape sounds, and expressive wide-interval leaps to contrast with the coldness of electronic music, he creates a wholly alien soundworld in which the anachronistic cello has been thrown into to fend for itself.

Davidovsky himself has emphasized the importance of having a live player alongside the tape, a reason he, unlike many of his contemporaries, never wrote an entirely electronic piece: having a live performer alongside immediately creates an identifiable protagonist against whom the drama shall unfold. Many pieces, through the interaction of voices, melodies, harmonies, can be compared to characters in a play. Elliott Carter often likened his music to the ideals of American democracy: "dissenting independent voices creating harmony." The classical canon contains countless examples of musical drama, narrative-or-not love stories, tales of heroism and triumph, ruminations on death, contemplations with the idea of a Creator—*Synchronisms No. 3* is simply the latest addition to the list of genres: musical sci-fi.

Lastly, and maybe one of the most important decisions a composer can make—the choice of a work's title; it's usually the first impression of a piece that a listener is introduced to. How do you choose it, and when during the process is it chosen?

Ryan: "Titles used to always come first for me and the music would follow. But that's happening much less often now, though I can't exactly say why. A lot of the time my titles are just concepts and ideas that appealed to me in a particular moment of inspiration. Like, for instance, I was reading an article about Rube Goldberg and decided the idea of a Rube Goldberg Machine would make for an interesting formal conceit for a composition. From there it's just a matter of figuring out how best to realize that idea. Sometimes I'll get an idea like that but put a pin in it for years and years until the right solution presents itself to me."

CHAPTER
24

COMMUNAL SYMMETRY IN ANCIENT MUSIC

AYA NISHINA

When composing a piece of music or imagining a soundscape, I suppose that I am communicating *a* way to feel the world, or simply feeling the time as it flows. It is my humble wish that while or after people experience the musical journey, they see the sky as a broader horizon, the ocean deeper, and are drawn to feel—and listen to—all fragments that this world is woven from.

How the Crossings Began

Following September 11, in 2001, my dear friend Emily Eng, admirable violist and baroque violinist based in Toronto, asked me if I would write a piece for an orchestra dedicated to peace. As an immediate reaction to the recent tragedy in New York City, Emily and her friends gathered a collective of musicians from the Toronto Symphony Orchestra, Canadian Opera Company, Tafelmusick Baroque Orchestra, Royal Conservatory of Music, and other locally-based ensembles to send prayers of peace through music. The following fall the orchestra, endorsed by the Canadian Opera Company (COC) and UNICEF, performed at St. Paul's Basilica in Toronto. The concert was called Concertpeace, and the orchestra was conducted by Richard Bradshaw, general director of COC at the time. As a 19-year-old New Yorker who had moved to Manhattan only a few weeks before September 11, it felt natural for me to join the effort, which I found sincere and comforting.

As soon as the compositional process began, it became clear to me that I wanted to deliver a lullaby. A lullaby for all who had been hurt, a lullaby to heal sorrow, fear, and judgment. I wanted to create a sonority that would embrace people with nostalgia in a primitive way, like something heard before childhood, yet in a context we've never experienced before. I resolved to look for a response in the wisdom of ancient music, and chose *Gagaku*, considered the most traditional music in Japan, as the starting point for my exploration.

Six Modes of Gagaku

In the summer of 2002, I visited Zensho-ji in Sendai, Japan, to attend the rehearsals of their Gagaku orchestra. Gagaku means "elegant music" and generally serves as ritual music for Shinto ceremonies. The ancient imperial court musical literature consists of songs (Saibara and Roei), dance (Bugaku), and instrumental music (Kangen). Most music of Kangen and Bugaku traveled to Japan from other countries of Asia between 5th and 9th centuries. There are two classifications in traditional dance forms: To-gaku/Saho (music of the left) primarily consists of music from China, India, and Vietnam; and Komagaku/Uho (music of the right) came from Korea and Manchuria. After unifying its grand form in Japan during 700s, the music has been preserved mainly at the Imperial court and few shrines and temples around the country since. At Zensho-ji I learned the musical systems of Gagaku, and that there are six different types of modes used in Kangen, instrumental music, which is known to be the oldest form of Japanese traditional music. One of the ensemble members also shared with me that there were approximately twenty-eight modes (scales) in ancient Chinese music, and twelve of which traveled to Japan during the same era that Gagaku arrived. As the music of Gagaku was constantly refined, the six modes remained.

Six modes in *Gagaku*

1.	**壱越調**	*ichi-kotsu-chō*	=	**D Mixolydian**
2.	**双調**	*sō-jō*	=	**G Mixolydian**
3.	**太食調**	*tai-shiki-chō*	=	**E Mixolydian**
4.	**平調**	*hyō-jō*	=	**E Dorian**
5.	**黄鐘調**	*ō-shiki*-chō	=	**A Dorian**
6.	**盤渉調**	*ban-shiki-chō*	=	**B Dorian**

The traditional tuning of Gagaku is A=430Hz.

From the first listen, I was immediately drawn to the serene echoes of Gagaku. In listening, I felt grounded as part of the infinite, mystical body of a venerable history. I found it purifying. Particularly, the sound of Sho, often described as "Japanese mouth organ", inspired me with the relationship the instrument has with silence and harmony.

合竹 *Aitake* — Eleven Harmonies of Sho Used in Traditional Gagaku

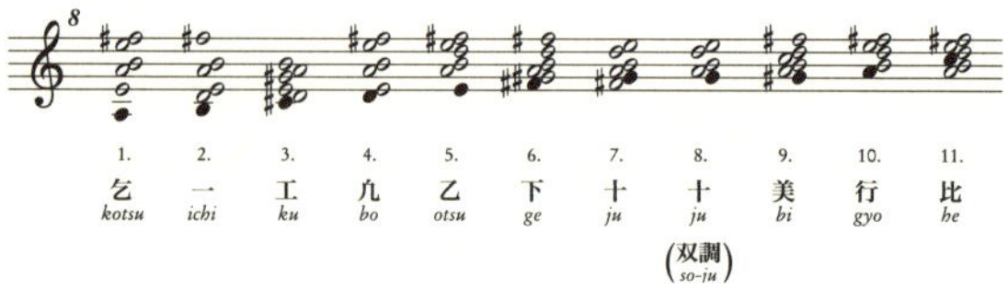

Communal Symmetries

When I was shown the basic tonal systems used in Gagaku, I became fascinated that the ryo and ritsu scales resembled Phrygian and Hypophrygian in the musical system of Ancient Greece (500–400 BCE); Dorian and Mixolydian (authentic modes) of eight church modes in Gregorian chant (8th century to 1500s); and the Adonai Malach mode of Jewish prayer modes.

Ancient Greek Modes

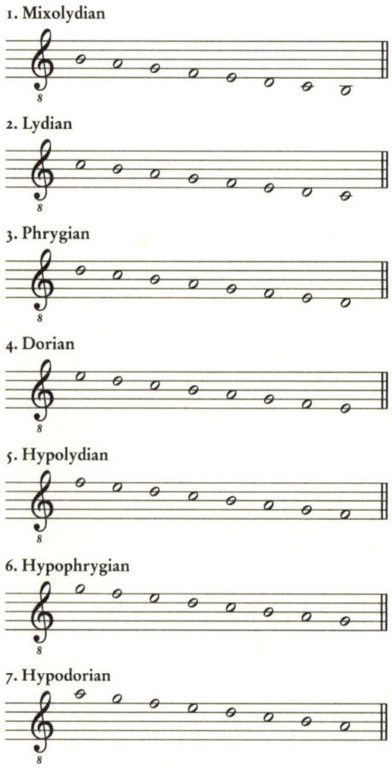

Gregorian Modes

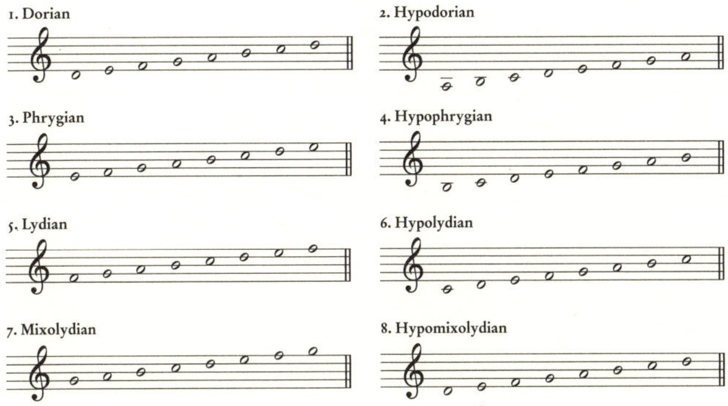

1, 3, 5, 7 = Authentic Modes   2, 4, 6, 8 = Plagal Modes

Three Examples of Jewish Prayers Modes

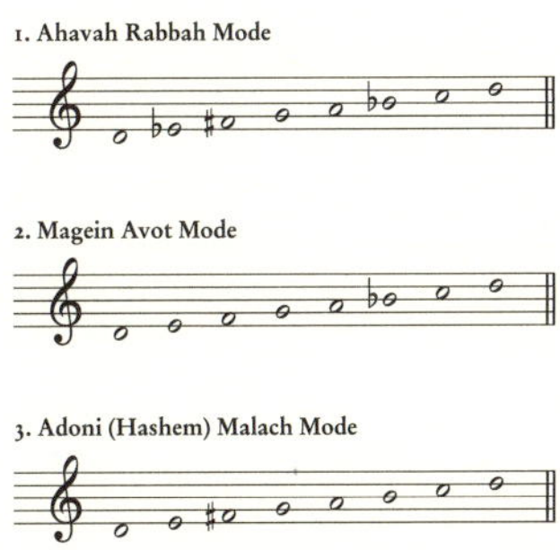

Gagaku Ryo-sen (So-Jo) = Greek Hypophrygian = Gregorian Mixolydian = Adoni (HaShem) Malach

When this learning came upon my exploration, I felt I was given a sacred ingredient for making the sonic experience in *Early May*. Wanting to study more, but finding that theoretical writings on ancient music were difficult to come by at times, I developed my understanding through recorded music and with the generous help of knowledgeable friends like John Zorn and Jon Singer. I was inspired by more information that there were similar intervallic fragments between modalities of traditional music among diverse cultures between 500 BCE through 15th century, before mass communication and transportation were accessible. Another fascinating similarity was that in many cultures, each of the modes were played during specific times of year, or day, and they symbolized certain feelings, rituals, or events taking place in the natural environment. They often accompany sacred services or prayers. The inspiration for me was that most of these tonal systems emerged, and were conserved, in spiritual centers around the globe, often through singing traditions, existing like a basic bone structure of human anatomy—on the surface we may appear different, yet we are essentially made the same.

One may wonder how such phenomenon occurred. Perhaps there were undiscovered world explorers, influential musicians, and story-tellers, or perhaps anatomically or evolutionarily senses exist in all humans that are drawn to certain sonority during prayer or self-reflection. There are also subjects of tuning, other theoretical and more scientific curiosities to be discussed. The subject can be argued from a prism of perspectives, but I will leave this exploration to anthropological studies or mystical illuminations for now. My utmost encouragement through this discovering process was the fact that for us humans, most of our musical heritages may come from communal origin, and those roots may still exist within us, whether consciously or unconsciously. Coming back to composing *Early May*, I added a mezzo soprano part to sing a folk like lullaby in Dorian mode along the orchestral accompaniment of Mixolydian textures applied from variant disciplines.

Early May

I am pouring a
glass of jasmine tea, on your
tired shoulders.

Tell me, please—
you were sleeping in sight
while you handed me your thorns.

Appeasing rain in twilight at seashore—
your shivers sounding like those of willows.
Would this moonlight ever soften you?

Your words are getting brittle
as you confide beside the quiet night birds.
It whittles me away, when you never
forgive yourself for singing song of fearing.

In between branches, between eyelashes,

tears flower as they sparkle like the ocean's night.

Falling down from your profile
Flying away from your frame

—lyrics by composer

Appreciating Commonality in Modern Time

The influence of ancient Greek or Gregorian modes in my compositions arose not only from my interest in European medieval cultures, but more from the perspective that these modes are part of all of our history. They are at our core, and by honoring these traditions in my work I want to bring people together to cherish our commonality, and use it as a passageway to greater understanding of each other. It is my wish that through understanding, healing and peace will evolve.

While I adore the cultural differences between us, I am currently drawn to find what exists in common between us, whether consciously or unconsciously, to embrace in the same womb of primeval nostalgia. I would like that to be my role as an artist, and intend to continue this approach, especially in this modern time.

Works Cited

Matsumoto, Taminosuke. *Japanese Mode—Its Past, Present, Future—.* (Tokyo, Japan: Ongaku-Kyoiku-Tosho, Inc., 1965)

Katagiri, Isao; Sugai, Shizunao; Kishi, Keiko; Kubota, Keiichi; Nagano, Toshiki; Shiraishi, Miyuki; Takahashi, Mito; Miura, Yuko; Moteki, Kiyoko; Tsukahara, Kouko; Narazaki, Youko. *Hajimete-no-Ongakushi (First Music History).* (Tokyo, Japan: Ongakunotomosha, Inc., 1996)

Oyama, Kiyoshige; Nakanishi, Satoru. *Japanese Harmony—the system and compositional approach.* (Tokyo, Japan: Ongakunotomosha, Inc., 1996, 1997)

The Imperial Household Agency of Japan. *Gagaku—Imperial Court Music & Dance from Japan.* (Hisashi Ito & Co., 2012. Website)

Crocker, Richard L. *An Introduction To Gregorian Chant.* (Great Britain: Yale University Press, Biddles Ltd, Guildford and Kings Lynn, 2000)

Stolba, K. Marie. *The Development of Western Music.* (The McGraw-Hill Companies, 1998)

Hanning, Barbara Russano. *Concise History of Western Music Second Edition.* (W.W. Norton & Company, Inc., 1998, 2002)

Barbour, Murray J. *Tuning and Temperament—A Historical Servey.* Mineola, [New York: (Original: Michigan State-Press, 1951) Dover Publications, Inc., 2004]

Forte, Allen. *The Structure of Atonal Music.* (Yale University Press, 1973)

Michels, Urlich. *dtv-Atlas zur Musik.* [(Original version: KG, Munchen: Deutscher Taschenbuch Verlag GmbH & Co.; 1977, 1985) Translated version (Japanese) by Sumikura, Ichiro. Tokyo, Japan: Hakusuisha, Inc.; 1989, 2007]

Special Thanks to: Emily Eng, John Zorn, Zensho-ji, Corrina Collins and Shimpei Takeda.

CHAPTER
25

AARON NOVIK

SECRETS OF "SECRETS OF SECRETS"

The idea for *Secrets of Secrets* started with the name. I was reading a book years ago about the history of the Jewish people and came across a reference to a book written by a 13th century Rabbi, Eleazar of Worms called *Secrets of Secrets* and was immediately struck by the book's mysterious and evocative title. I ended up tracking down *Secrets of Secrets* online, but was dismayed to find that it was only available in Hebrew, which unfortunately I never learned growing up. So I ordered the book, got a beginning biblical Hebrew primer from a local library and a 20-pound Hebrew to English dictionary and naively attempted to translate the book on my own.

Secrets of Secrets is Rabbi Eleazar of Worms treatise on the hidden meanings in sacred Kabbalistic texts. The texts that Kabbalists consider most sacred are *Genesis*, *Song of Songs* and *The Book of Ezekiel*, all from the *Bible*, and the *Sepher Yetzirah*, which is considered to be the earliest Kabbalistic text in known existence. I began to gather information about the Rabbi and read every translation of his writing I could find, including excerpts from *Secrets of Secrets* piecing together what I could about the man and his ideas.

Eleazar of Worms was a 13th century Rabbi who spent years writing, mostly on subjects relating to ethics and the esoteric. During the Crusades, his wife and three kids were murdered by Christian soldiers right in front of him, but instead of giving up hope on humanity, Eleazar retained an optimistic view of life and believed that ethically, man was designed for good. His writings on the esoteric, specifically the Kabbalah, are what he is most known for, and the book *Secrets of Secrets* is his crowning achievement. He believed that there were secret codes in the *Bible* and that there existed rational systems that unlocked these hidden messages. That people truly believed there were hidden messages in the *Bible* and that there existed rational systems to decode these messages mathematically and scientifically, seems both insane in ambition and logical in its desire.

The Music

I decided to write a suite of music where each movement represented a different section of *Secrets of Secrets*. The book is split into five smaller parts each exploring a major Kabbalistic secret. *Secrets of Creation* tackles Genesis and the creation of the world, *Secrets of the Divine World* talks about the celestial plane, *Secrets of the Divine Chariot* deciphers the *Book of Ezekiel* and God's judgment upon mankind, *Secrets of the Holy Name* discusses the seventy-six different names used for God in the *Bible*, and *Secrets of Formation* illuminates the sacred texts of the *Sepher Yetzirah*, which includes how to build a Golem and bring it to life.

I wanted to reference Jewish music within these five movements and decided to do this a couple of ways. First, I based each piece on a traditional klezmer dance rhythm. To represent each of the five books, I used the khoisdl, bulgar, hora, doina and terkish rhythms. I then tried to relate each rhythm to both an acoustic classical setting, and an amplified rock or "metal band" instrumentation, writing the music to flow seamlessly between the two sound worlds.

With regards to scale I wanted to incorporate Jewish modes into the pieces similar to the approach used in an earlier composition of mine, *The Samuel Suite*. For that composition all seven modes of the harmonic minor scale were used equally, not just the modes based on the 1st, 4th or 5th of the scale, which are the three modes most commonly used. The more uncommonly used modes are awkward and had to be worked very carefully in order to sound right. This is because some of these scales don't have a perfect 5th, or might have both a major and minor 3rd. When used correctly they can still convey a sound associated with jewish music, but turned inside out. Using these modes strictly, without any accidentals, also created an older medieval sound to the music to my ears, as if it were written in a time where no one had thought to use accidentals or chromaticism. So here was something that sounded very old and very new, a perfect parallel to the orchestral and metal duality.

Kabbalah

Many Kabbalists when discussing sacred scripture talk about layers of meaning, where on the surface you have the literal meaning of the text, and beneath, lie hidden messages. To give an example of this type of study, here is the opening section of *Secrets of Creation*:

"Blessed are the secrets of the wise, who gave from 'his' (God's) wisdom to those that fear him. To give to us the law of truth. To announce his might to humankind and the glory of his presence. The power of his deeds, of *Secrets of Secrets* from on high (heaven) to down below (earth). The wealth and majesty god is hidden in his words, like honey and milk under one's tongue. Let there be you alone, and not some stranger."

The first word, "ברוך" or "blessed" is a common Hebrew word which begins most prayers. The letter ב (bet) starts this passage, which is the first passage in this book. It is also the very first letter of בראשית (In the beginning…), the very first phrase in the *Bible*, and is considered a powerful letter in Kabbalistic creation mythology. A popular myth related in the Zohar tells the tale of each letter of the alphabet standing before God, asking permission to help create the universe. Each letter argues their own worth, what powerful words they begin or end. The letter ב (Bet) is finally rewarded by God and is allowed to help him create the universe. This is the reason the *Bible* begins with this letter.

Another method Kabbalists used to discover hidden meaning is mathematically, through various numerology techniques. The most popular of these is called Gematria, a system where each word is given a numerical value creating new relationships between words with the same or similar values. With all of these techniques for finding new meanings and relationships within these writings, the possibilities when analyzing them are literally endless.

I bring all this up to illustrate the differing levels one can read these texts, and the mystery and contradictions they can create, every line eluding to something else, every word hiding potential meanings. Without the knowledge of these techniques and references one is lost on the surface.

The Codes

Inspired by these ancient cyphers, I created some of my own code systems to instill "layers of meaning" into the music as well. Entire sections of Eleazar's text were placed inside the composition, each by a separate code created explicitly with this task in mind. In the first track *Secrets of Creation* each letter of the Hebrew alphabet was translated into a 3 to 5 note descending pattern based in D harmonic minor. These rhythmic figures were strung together in the same order as they appeared in the very first passage of *Secrets of Creation.*

Figure 1 shows how the beginning of this pattern looked, with the Hebrew letters below the corresponding melodic phrase. This is the same passage discussed earlier, starting with "דורב."

For the second track *Secrets of the Divine World*, a different one measure terkish rhythm was created for each letter of the alphabet and strung together to spell out different sections from this book. Two beat pauses were placed between words, and four beat pauses between phrases. You can hear this code in the dumbek and strings section of the piece. Here is the beginning of this section, with the word "חכמת" or "wisdom" spelled out.

Another code system simply took the 22 letter Hebrew alphabet and allocated a different letter for each note ascending the scale. A three octave scale is exactly 22 notes, so this worked out quite well, and was used in all of the remaining tracks each in different ways. In Italy they built their synagogues with exactly 22 stairs between floors, to literally ascend the alphabet as they moved around the sacred space.

This code was used in *Secrets of the Divine Chariot* where Carla Kihlstedt and I double each other, the letters of the text creating awkward leaps in the melody which circles around the more deliberate linear sounding brass parts.

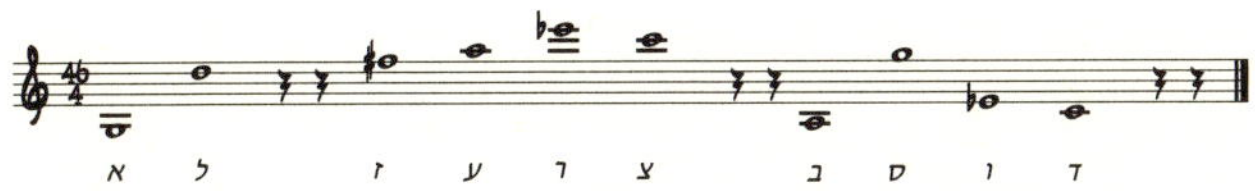

In *Secrets of the Holy Name*, the brass spells out the different hidden names of God that are explored in that text. According to Eleazar there are 76 different names for God used in the *Bible*, each one carrying with it a different Kabbalistic subtext. If Ein Sof is used instead of Yahweh, there is a specific reason why. For some names of God, this is obvious, but for others, again, a mystery.

In *Secrets of Formation* the brisk and relentless ascending pattern that dominates the majority of the piece is taken from this graph:

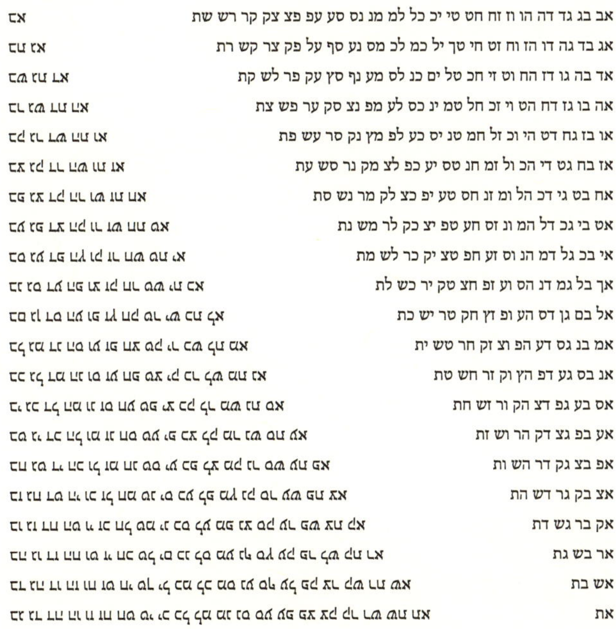

A big part of the Kabbalistic mythology concerns the alchemy involved in creating a Golem, or a clay guardian. Many know of the Golem through the famous silent film of the same name or the equally beautiful book by Gustav Meyrink on which the movie was loosely based. It was believed that if one were to incant every two letter combination in succession without a spare breath, this spell would bring the Golem life. There are many theories surrounding the correct order of syllabic invocation, the one shown above taken from the source, the Sepher Yetzirah. Eleazar had other theories as to what the correct order was, believing the enchantor could skip around and still say them all, but it is this chart from the Sepher Yetzirah that spoke to me visually and ultimately created what is the blue print for the closing track of this album.

When using the code created with the Hebrew alphabet ascending by three octaves, the pattern starts off by playing notes in 2nds (בא), then 3rds (גא), then 4ths (דא), until a final leap from א to ת finishes the cycle. This pattern starts with the first note of the alphabet, "א" goes through every single permutation with that letter first, then starts all over again doing the same syllabic combinations starting with the next letter in the alphabet. This cycle continues through all 22 letters of the alphabet, a grand total of 5082 different syllabic combinations!

Listening with this in mind, the pattern and the code come together and the structure of the piece becomes clear. Rabbi Eleazar among others felt this ritual would be a very physically demanding one to complete and could even take days to finish, with no room for errors or breaks. Playing God was thought to be no easy feat, and wasn't treated lightly. Below is one line from the same page viewed above with the Hebrew letters below each note to follow along.

The composition *Secrets of Formation* is 17 minutes, which is much longer than I would usually make a piece, especially something that serves so simple a function. The text was telling me that this piece needed to be a certain length for the message to be conveyed. Just as the ritual demanded a certain focus and discipline, so too does the music, as a performer, and as a listener. Each track was created by the text in this way. The music carries the words literally, but also spiritually as the tracks, through discipline, intensity and repetition hopefully create a meditative space for the listener to immerse themselves in.

CHAPTER
26

INTO THE ABYSS OF 1/∞

CHRIS OTTO

My violin octet, which you can hear at soundcloud.com/ottotelic/violin-octet, represents a significant part of my ongoing exploration of just intonation. I wrote the 111-minute piece in July 2012, and recorded all eight parts that fall in the Bushwick studio of my friend Christopher Botta, mixing it with him over the next 9 months. While I hope that the piece offers a meaningful experience to the listener on its own, I would like to give some context for it and explain some of the abstract principles behind it in order to illuminate what it means to me and add another dimension to the listener's experience of the work.

The pitch language of my violin octet is a form of just intonation (JI). While JI is only one of the ways that I deal with pitch as a performer, it has been the primary one for me as a composer for the last several years, and I have found it extremely rewarding and creatively stimulating in both capacities. For me its significance lies in the way it connects the abstract with the sensual, the universal with the particular, the eternal with the transient. As a tool, JI has served different functions for composers of widely divergent aesthetics, and my own understanding and use of JI has changed over time.

I first encountered JI when I was 15 or 16, through the work of Ben Johnston. Johnston had taught at the University of Illinois in Urbana-Champaign, where I grew up, and a former student of his introduced me to the central concept of just intonation, the idea that pitch can be organized rationally, that is, in terms of ratios of frequencies. He drew a diagram of the C major scale in an arrangement I had never seen before, a lattice:

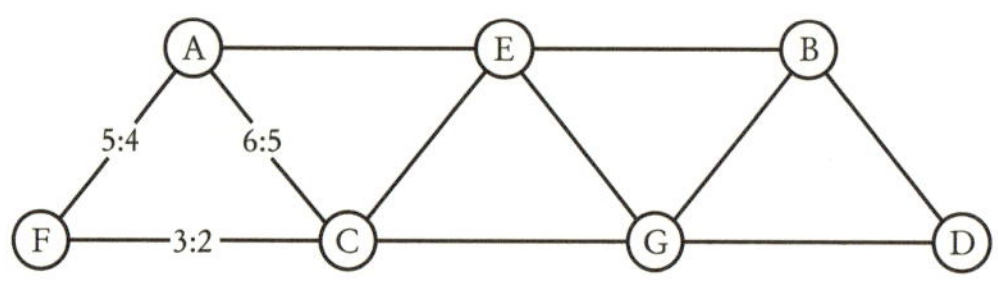

In this orientation, moving one unit to the right on the lattice means going up a perfect 5th, which, he explained, is equivalent to a 3:2 ratio of the frequencies. Going diagonally up and right one unit means ascending a pure major 3rd, 5:4, and moving down and right one unit means ascending a pure minor 3rd, 6:5. The F major, C major, and G major triads form three upward-pointing triangles, which represent frequencies in a 4:5:6 proportion, while the A minor and E minor triads form two downward-pointing triangles, representing the inverse 4:5:6 proportion.

The D minor triad, however, poses a challenge to this system. The existing D and A are not 3:2 apart, but 40:27, so a new pitch, called D- in Johnston's notation, would have to be introduced to the left of A to create another pure minor triad. The difference between this D- and D is a syntonic comma, a ratio of 80:81, or approximately 21.5 cents.

After seeing this lattice I realized that the syntonic comma was the same discrepancy I had heard several years earlier as a violinist playing Kreisler's Preludium and Allegro. I had noticed that if I tuned a B against my D string, it was lower than a B tuned with my E string, but I had no explanation for what I was hearing until I encountered this lattice.

I was beginning to realize that my theoretical conception of pitch and what I was actually hearing were somewhat divergent. JI helped explain the divergence, but it was some time before I realized the new conception of pitch it offered. At that point I had studied traditional music theory, and since starting on the piano at age 5 I had more or less thought that there were simply twelve equal semitones per octave. At the same time, as a violin student, I worked on intonation in part by holding double-stops without vibrato, and since any beating between the harmonics is very apparent in this case, I naturally adjusted the intervals to slow down the beating, which has the effect of pulling the intervals toward just intonation.

Most of the music I was playing at the time was with piano or in an orchestra, where tuning was generally based on equal temperament, and these discrepancies could often be swept under the rug in fast music or when playing with vibrato. However, as I started playing solo Bach and chamber music with other string players, particularly at Eastman, these tuning problems became more exposed in certain situations, and it was (and still is) helpful to know the mathematical logic behind them. I also explored temperaments, which are systems of adjusting pure intervals so that some of these discrepancies disappear.

As a composer, it took some time for me to incorporate just intonation into my music. I loved math and was interested in the mathematical side of music, but since the 12-tone universe was the paradigm I knew best, I initially explored serial music, particularly Babbitt and Schoenberg. I had a friend throughout high school whose father was a composer who had studied with Babbitt, and through him I was introduced the rich and varied connections between math and music within the 12-tone equal-tempered system. I also explored Xenakis's applications of math to composition, which exposed me to radically different possibilities of structuring sound.

From the end of high school to almost the end of my time at Eastman, I used mathematical structures regularly in my compositions. The structures became increasingly abstract in an attempt to create a deep network of meanings. What I lacked, however, was a connection between the abstract relationships I was imagining and how they sounded as music. I would spend many months devising compositional structures that I could understand intellectually, but I was often disappointed when I heard the finished pieces performed. My performing and composing sides diverged, as I was performing a lot of very exciting new and old music at Eastman, but relatively few of my own compositions.

I started bringing my ears into the compositional process in a more direct way with electronic music. I could hear the sonic result of a compositional structure much more quickly and use my perception of it to shape further iterations. I began to create slowly changing drones with sine tones that explored acoustic phenomena resulting from beating and attempted to bridge the timescales of pitch and rhythm.

At the same time, I began working on JI more seriously as a violinist. At UCSD I learned a lot from cellist Charles Curtis, whose mastery of the music of La Monte Young gave me a new appreciation for the amount of time and discipline it takes to develop and explore intonation. In particular, this was the first time I really considered the process of training myself to tune intervals by ear. I soon found that even the simplest task—tuning a single pitch in unison with a sine tone—was an enormously complex and rewarding experience.

The essence of tuning is slowing down beating. Any two frequencies will produce a third frequency equal to their difference, called a difference tone. The closer the pitches, the lower the difference tone, and when it is too low to be perceived as pitch, it becomes a rhythm, which is called beating. Beating can be described as a rhythmic fluctuation of a sound, but what parameter is fluctuating depends on the speed of the beating and the spatial position of the two tones. Faster beating and beating where the tones are not spatially separated produce rhythmic amplitude changes, while slower and more spatially separated beating produce perceptions of timbral fluctuations and rotations in space around the listener.

In the case of tuning a note on the violin to a sine tone, the task is very clear—out of all the sounds present, focusing on and slowing down the beating created between the fundamental of the violin tone and the sine tone. In attempting this task, I began to experience a kind of fusion of the mental and physical, listening with my mind and body. As I focused on slowing down the beating, I became aware of all the precisely coordinated physical adjustments I was making, for example adjusting the left hand finger position microscopically to counteract changes in bow pressure. The beating would slow down to the point where it became an irregular folding and unfolding of the sound, ebbing and flowing. At a certain point the mind—its perception of the sound and the physical sensations of playing—became indistinguishable from the sound itself.

I would also practice with a complex tone such as a sawtooth wave. For a unison, this meant slowing down the overall beating—since each harmonic of the violin note would be beating with the corresponding harmonic of the sawtooth, the task became more ambiguous and subjective. The harmonics of a violin note typically get sharper as they get higher. At a certain point, in order to slow down one beating, another would have to speed up, so I would focus my attention on the sound as a whole and slow down whatever beating was most prominent, a combination of its speed and loudness.

For intervals other than the unison, the beating to slow down would be the harmonics common to both series, the lowest of which I call the reinforced harmonic, which is the least common multiple (LCM) of the two pitches. For example, with a perfect 5th, a 2:3 ratio, the reinforced harmonic would be 6, as the third harmonic of the two beats against the second harmonic of the 3.

Practicing intervals as double stops adds the additional challenge of stabilizing two notes at once. I worked on a repertoire of double stops with one open string and one stopped note, starting with the simpler intervals and progressing to more complex ones (e.g., 2:3, 3:4, 3:5, 4:5, 5:6, 4:7, 5:7,

6:7, 5:8, 7:8, 4:9, 5:9, 7:9, 8:9, etc.)

Through this process I began to explore the distinctive character and quality of each interval. As the intervals become more complex, the reinforced harmonics become higher and higher, and the difference tones between the notes and their harmonics are particularly useful in defining the intervals aurally. The difference tones between the numerous pairs of harmonics of the notes tend to reinforce each other and grow louder as the interval's intonation stabilizes, and have the effect of filling out the dyad into an entire chord, pointing toward their common fundamental, which is the greatest common divisor (GCD) of the two frequencies.

For example, a 5:7 interval, the simplest just tuning of the tritone, creates this unique pattern of harmonics and difference tones:

5	7	difference
5		
	7	2
10		3
	14	4
15		1
20		5
	21	1
25		4
	28	3
30		2
35	35	5
40		5
	42	2
etc.	etc.	

While building up this repertoire of dyads, I started exploring the different ways these dyads could be combined. If the implied fundamentals of two dyads are the same, they have the effect of filling out and strengthening that fundamental. If they are different, but related by a just interval, then they imply an overall fundamental lower than at least one of the dyad's fundamentals. In general, the lower the implied fundamental, the more dissonant the chord, at least in my conception of consonance and dissonance.

I became particularly interested in sets of frequencies in which subsets would be in relatively consonant relationships, but taken together would reinforce a lower, more dissonant fundamental through difference tones or beating. For example, in a constellation of frequencies with proportions 24:25:35:36, the 24:36 reduces to 2:3, and the 25:35 reduces to 5:7, while the 24:25 and 35:36 create difference tones of 1, reinforcing the overall fundamental. These ratios with a numerator and denominator separated by 1 are called superparticular.

In my violin duo, written for and recorded by Erik Carlson, I experimented with ways of linking these types of tetrachords together to create a dynamic melodic/harmonic flow, and my violin octet expands these harmonies both vertically and horizontally to create a sound object that can be heard on many different levels, and to allow ample time for the ear to focus on different aspects of the sound.

* * *

In my violin octet, the open strings of violins 1, 2, 5, and 6 are tuned to the 4th, 6th, 9th, and 13th harmonics of a 42 Hz fundamental, while the open strings of violins 3, 4, 7, and 8 are tuned to the 5th, 7th, 11th, and 15th harmonics. Using the intervals I could tune by ear above and below each open string, I generated over a hundred pitches. Calculating the difference tones between each pair of these pitches, I picked the most frequently occurring ones, which form the basis of the first nine sections of the piece. Each of these sections has its own sectional fundamental, which is 42 Hz multiplied by the following ratios: 1, 1/2, 1/3, 1/4, 1/5, 1/6, 1/7, 2/15, and 1/10, yielding 42 Hz, 21 Hz, 14 Hz, 10.5 Hz, 8.4 Hz, 7 Hz, 6 Hz, 5.6 Hz, and 4.2 Hz.

For each section, I selected from the complete set of pitches those that are integer multiples (harmonics) of the sectional fundamental. From this list of harmonics, I constructed a chord with at most one dyad in each of the 8 violin parts that would maximize the number of superparticular ratios. These superparticular ratios reinforce the sectional fundamentals because they each create a difference tone of 1.

The chart below shows the collection of harmonics in each section relative to the sectional fundamental shown at the bottom. The absolute frequencies of the first section (which is the complete set of open strings) are shown at the left, and following each open string in a straight line to the right reveals how it functions as a progressively higher harmonic of the progressively lower fundamentals. The superparticular ratios are boxed, and we can notice how a ratio such as 24:25 in the second section recurs in later sections at lower pitch levels. For me each superparticular ratio has a unique flavor due to its unique set of prime factors, but as it is transposed lower it takes on different qualities due to the different beating speeds it creates. At the same time, within a section, the various superparticular ratios with their unique flavors are unified by their identical beating speeds.

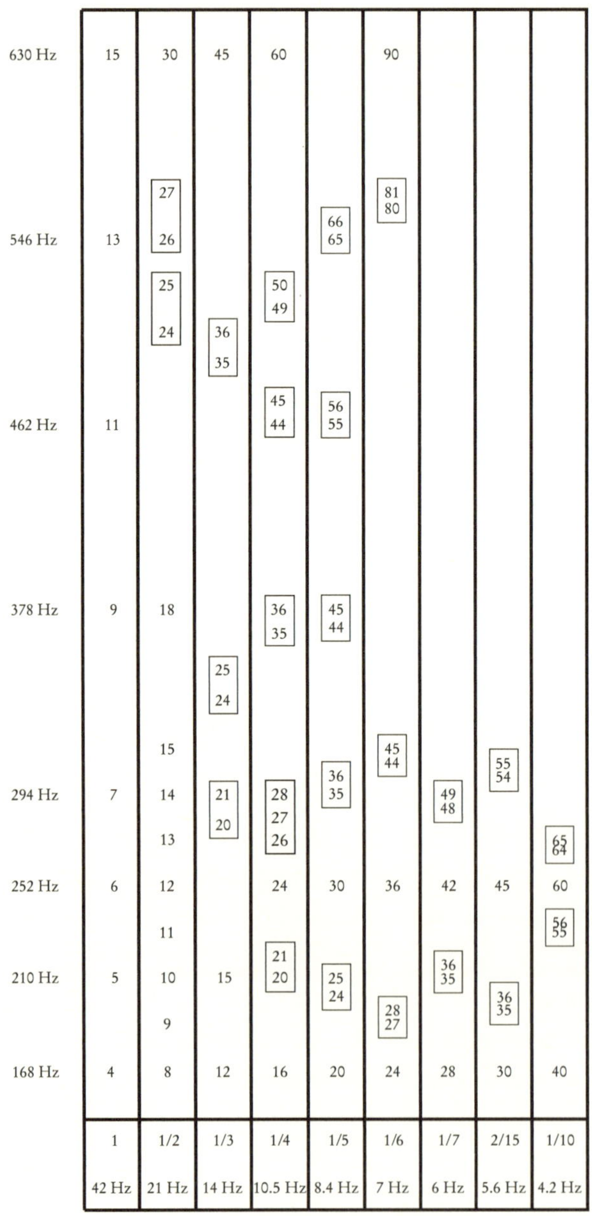

These verticalities are also shown in the Extended Helmholtz-Ellis JI notation, treating the 42 Hz fundamental as an E (A=448 Hz). (This notation indicates 5th-harmonic deviations with arrows attached to the accidental, 7th harmonic with a hook, 11th harmonic with a quarter-sharp symbol, and 13th harmonic with a backward flat with an extra vertical line. More information on this notation created by Marc Sabat and Wolfgang von Schweinitz can be found on their website, http://plainsound.org/ This notation and the work of Marc and Wolfgang has been enormously influential and helpful to me, and I recommend exploring their website to learn more about JI.)

Within the pitch collection for a section, the full chord is heard as well as various subsets which illuminate different internal relationships. Some subsets highlight the overall fundamental by emphasizing the superparticular ratios, while other subsets reveal higher fundamentals which are multiples of the sectional fundamental. For example, in section 2, which has the overall fundamental of 21 Hz, the harmonics 9, 12, 18, 24, 27, and 30 share a factor of 3, so when heard in isolation they become harmonics 3, 4, 6, 8, 9, 10 of a fundamental of 63 Hz.

As the piece progresses through the sections, the difference tones go from the realm of pitch to rhythm: from 42 Hz to 4.2 Hz in the first nine sections, and asymptotically approaching 0 in the final section. Just as each dyad has a characteristic sound and feeling, each of these difference tones has a unique quality. From the opening sonority, the perceived dissonance increases as the fundamentals get lower, but as the beating approaches 0 in the last section, we increasingly perceive the sound as a single entity, a subtly-fluctuating "unison" of harmonics whose fundamental is 252 Hz, the highest fundamental of the piece.

One of my goals in this piece was to create a unified sense of timescale, from the highest audible frequencies to the duration of the entire piece, as a continuum of frequencies/rhythms. The harmonics of the violins occupy the upper end of the frequency range—in particular, the reinforced harmonics of the dyads form a cohesive layer. The fundamentals of the violin notes occupy the mid-range, and the difference tones (and their reinforcement with sine tones at several moments) fill out the lower register and connect to the beating speeds, which occupy the faster rhythmic space (21 Hz to 4.2 Hz) and, in the last section, slow down and approach 0.

The slower rhythmic space is structured by the bow changes. For each dyad, the duration of the downbows and upbows is constant, in part because having a constant bow speed for each double stop helped me to stabilize the intonation and get in a groove. These bow durations (BDs) form a rhythmic counterpoint to the JI pitch relationships, forming polyrhythms and "cascades" which relate to the sectional fundamentals.

The overall tempo of the piece is quarter ("beat") = 63 bpm. I restricted the BDs available in a given section to those that comprise an integral number of cycles of the fundamental for that section. For example, in the first section a 4-beat BD contains 42 cycles/second × 60/63 seconds/beat × 4 beats = 160 cycles of the fundamental of 42 Hz. In theory, this means that the bow changes in all parts would align with the cycles of the fundamental, but as I have not yet been able to control the phase of the beatings so precisely, this is more of a conceptual connection.

Just as a dyad implies a reinforced harmonic and a fundamental, a polyrhythm (in particular one consisting of two constant durations) implies what I call a rhythmic quantum (RQ) and a cycle length. The RQ is the longest duration which subdivides both durations, and equals the

GCD of the durations. The cycle length is the minimum duration between alignments of the two rhythms, and equals their LCM.

For example, in the opening section, the four violin parts have BDs of 4 beats, 6 beats, 24/5 beats, and 5 beats. The GCD of these durations is 1/5 of a beat, so the RQ is a quintuplet-sixteenth duration. Since the LCM of these four durations is 120, the four parts align every 120 beats.

This creates a symmetrical structure corresponding to a major/minor triad, with an overall 20:24:25:30 proportion which contains a 4:5:6 (20:25:30) and an inverse 4:5:6 (20:24:30). Because of the symmetry, this 20:24:25:30 structure represents both the number of RQs in each BD and the number of bows in the overall cycle.

In addition to these polyrhythmic structures, there are sections in which multiple parts have the same BD, but are displaced successively at equal durations (the displacement duration, DD). The DD divides the BD evenly, so that the bow duration is subdivided into BD÷DD parts. BD÷DD is often larger than the number of parts present, in which case there is a gap of one or more subdivisions articulated. I think of these composite rhythms as cascades.

For example, immediately after the opening chord (but still within the first section), the 5-beat BD (containing 25 RQs) is adopted by all four parts, with each subsequent part displaced by one quarter note (DD=5 RQs) to create a constant five-beat (25/5=5) cascade of attacks (beat, beat, beat, beat, gap).

In the second section, this five-beat cascade in violins 1, 3, 5, and 7 is pitted against a second, slightly faster cascade in violins 2, 4, 6, and 8. The second cascade has a BD of 24 RQs (the 24/5 beats) and DD of 4 RQs, creating a subdivision into 6 durations: 4 beats plus a 2-beat gap.

Each of the pairs of violins 1 and 2, 3 and 4, 5 and 6, and 7 and 8 create a 24:25 polyrhythm, but start at different points within the overall cycle. Taken together, the two cascades produce a 4:5 polyrhythm (with gaps) at a smaller scale.

In this case, the division of the 8 violins into 2 cascades of 4 violins each mirrors the division of the chord into harmonics of the sectional fundamental that are divisible by 3 and those that are not. Over the course of the piece, the partitioning of the 8 violins into subsets varies, and I use different combinations of polyrhythms and cascades to delineate and connect the subsets.

These rhythmic relationships can be heard on multiple levels—one can listen to the overall composite rhythm, which has the fastest speed of articulation and also the longest cycle, as well as the shorter and slower rhythmic cycles created by various subsets.

* * *

For me, the process of recording and mixing the violin octet is as much a part of the piece as the composition on paper. I composed an earlier version of the piece in early 2012 while living in Bushwick, Brooklyn and recorded it over several all-night sessions in the nearby studio of my friend Christopher Botta soon after. A few months later, I realized I was missing an important conceptual link in the material, and recomposed the piece, recording the new version that fall in the same studio while living in Montclair, NJ.

These all-night recording sessions constituted a very intense training in attention. I listened to sine tone versions in headphones to help stabilize the interval. Tuning thus became a multifaceted endeavor—attempting to

> 1) slow down the beating of each fundamental to the corresponding sine tone,
>
> 2) slow down the beating of the reinforced harmonics within the interval,
>
> 3) maximize the difference tones, and
>
> 4) align my bow changes with the click track. The effect of bow pressure and speed on the intonation of an open string was extremely noticeable—I had to tune open strings at the correct tempo, because if tuning with an arbitrary bow speed I would notice a subtle difference in pitch at the actual tempo.

Attempting to slow down all these beatings while maintaining a steady bow speed engages the mind and body in a subtle and precise relationship. Manifesting the interval as clearly as possible given the physical nature of the instrument, the body, the air, the room, at that moment in time, I was imagining, perceiving, analyzing, hearing, and feeling in myriad ways the presence of a unified entity. For long stretches I felt this entity with my entire being, as different modes of perception became unified, while at the same time I could focus my attention on different aspects of the entity. In playing an interval continuously for many minutes, I could get into a zone where my attention was completely manifest in the sound.

Recording the full duration of each note in complete takes, sometimes lasting 10 minutes or more, was important in order to preserve this sense of a continuous evolution of the zone. In layering these zones on top of each other and mixing them with Chris Botta, I aimed to unify them into a still larger entity, encompassing and interrelating the journeys of each note.

CHAPTER 27

CULTURAL ROOTS

Connecting Time and Place in Musical Composition

HILDA PAREDES

"México no era una provincia aislada y virginal sino parte indudable de la raza humana y de su tradición cultural."

"...me acerqué al oro y al fango de México, el país imaginario, imaginado, finalmente real, pero sólo si lo veía desde una distancia que me asegurase, por el hecho mismo de la separación, que mi deseo de reunirme con él siempre sería apremiante y real sólo sí lo escribía."

—Carlos Fuentes

I have lived in Europe for more than half of my life and as time passes by, my roots pull me deeper into Mexico my native country. Time and distance have given me a perspective into a rich and complex country, with a diverse cultural heritage that keeps sprouting onto different layers of my music.

Living in London for several decades, I have become a target for invitations to attend what promoters in the UK believe to be a "Latin cultural expression." An example was a recent invitation to a *Serenata Latina* at the Queen Elizabeth Hall in London's South Bank, whose programme consisted of memorable tunes and rhythms that can easily be labeled as Latin without any further insight into the geography or the history of where this music came from, but is synonymous with repetitive syncopated rhythms and ostinato harmonic patterns. Strangely enough, several of these tunes were written by composers in the US and offer their view of what they believe Latin music should be about.

Often this is the kind of music that is expected from me and many of my fellow country colleagues and some, like me have refused to succumb to the expectations of a paternalistic industry of entertainment, because we cannot ignore and forget what the reality of our history and our cultural heritage means for us. As creative artists we also want to continue developing the wider musical resources we have at hand.

I have always believed that the power of music is such that does not need to be understood like a language and it does not require a passport to reach ears throughout the world. If you are open, music can reach the hearts through the ears. It doesn't matter where you come from in the world, it can still stir you soul and spirit.

Therefore, to limit music to one cultural realm and define it with some general features can be very restrictive if you are a creator and limiting if you are a listener.

I will try here to outline an overview of what Mexican culture means for me and how it leaves an imprint in several of my works, which I believe aim at the universality that music can achieve.

For more than 500 years, the history of Mexico is one of relentless cultural impositions on those who were natives in their country. The conquest of Mexico was the beginning of a history that has not ceased to look towards the first world for cultural stereotypes to try and shape an identity and its development. But another parallel reality has not been completely suppressed and this has stamped its distinctive seal in many artistic and cultural expressions, by integrating and assimilating foreign cultural models into their own. This phenomenon is what is known as syncretism, and it is embedded in every layer of Mexican life.

> Syncretism: the amalgamation or attempted amalgamation of different religions, cultures or schools of thought. From Greek sunkretismos: "unite against a third party", from sun: together + kres "Cretan"(originally with reference to ancient Cretan communities."[1]

1. *The New Oxford Dictionary*. Oxford University Press, 1998.

As well as the Spanish impositions since the 16th century, contemporary Mexican culture has been enriched by this assimilation and integration of multiple and diverse cultural influences.

Through the first half of the 20th century, the European immigrants fleeing the second world war where welcomed in Mexico, as were, later on those escaping from the impunities of dictatorships in Chile and Argentina. Since 1937 and up to 1942 many artists, scientists and intellectuals fleeing the Spain of Franco settled in Mexico and contribute to enrich and transform the cultural environment which also nourished there expressions. Amongst the many well known artists and writers who settled in Mexico were the philosopher José Gaos, musicologist Adolfo Salazar, poets like Pedro Garfias, the composer Rodolfo Halffter, the filmmaker Luis Buñuel who together with the surrealists painters Remedios Varo and the British born Leonora Carrington found in the new land a haven for their expression.

The works of Remedios Varo have been a constant source of inspiration for my music. I first wrote *Homenaje a Remedios Varo*, a sextet in 1995 as a homage to her work. This work is in five distinctive sections, each one of them making a reference to a painting of hers. More recently I wrote a piece for ensemble and electronics, which bears the title of one of her paintings: *Revelación*.

The idea of different concepts of time portrayed in the painting, is reflected in the score by different pulses beating against each other on the string section.

Example 1

To view image, please visit: http://img255.imageshack.us/img255/4482/revelacinoelrelojero195.jpg

Many aspects of both the contemporary and the ancient indigenous Mexican cultures have also left an imprint in my music. My Grandfather spoke Mayan, and this nourished my interest through my adult years.

As well as the language, the cosmology, the literature, both contemporary and ancient, the concept of time in the ancient Mayan culture has also given me food for thought for the make up of my music. *Tzolkin* is the name for their ritualistic calendar. It comprises of 260 days and has 13-day cycles with twenty different names. These are represented in glyphs, each with a unique combination of number and name that is repeated only after the 260-day cycle is completed. I had begun to explore the possibilities of applying this to music first in my solo percussion piece *Tzolkin* and later at the beginning of my concerto for ensemble *Ah paaxo'ob* (those who make the music) in which different instruments come to the foreground at different moments throughout the piece.

In the following example I also combine ideas, which I have developed from my contact with the music of India. Many of my decisions concerning ways of manipulating rhythm and structure have been influenced by those found in Indian Music. However, I do not attempt to quote any traditional music nor to recreate it. My interest in the music of India began when I was a student. Whilst the music and dance of Northern India was a source of inspiration to my musical thinking, I have since found that many Indian rhythmic procedures can be applied in Western music.

One of my favorite rhythmic cadential formulas in Indian music is what is called *tiha i*, which means third part and consists of a threefold repetition of a phrase. The main function of it is to bring to an end improvisations by setting a cadential rhythmic formula that repeats three times, often against the beat and concludes on the first beat of the next rhythmic cycle.

In the introduction of *Ah paax o'ob*, there are different layers of different beat lengths that repeat where two or three instruments conform each superimposed phrase. These weave around the melodic skeleton of thirteen pitches (one per quaver) that is shared by the vibraphone, glockenspiel, harp and violins and flute.

Example 2

This melodic cell is built of two melodic cells of six sounds that reflect each other intervalically and the seventh pitch is repeated at the octave to signal where the process is inverted.

This cell is played twice before is transposed down a semitone. The first two transpositions are repeated twice before descending into the next transposition.

Example 3

Transpositions:

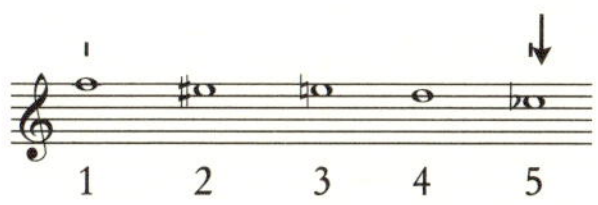

The descent is accelerated by means of not repeating the last two transpositions. When arriving to the 5th, which is a tritone away, the phrase of 13 quavers begins again on the first beat of the bar.

Another three phrases are superimposed on this material, each one of them made of different durations and gestures.

The clarinets share a phrase of 13 crotchets length, which opens the work.

Example 4

The phrases of both: violas and cellos respectively, are grouped in pairs.

The viola phrase, which begins in the second bar lasts 24 quavers and is repeated three times. These end exactly with the end of the fourth transposition of the phrase of harp and percussion.

Example 5

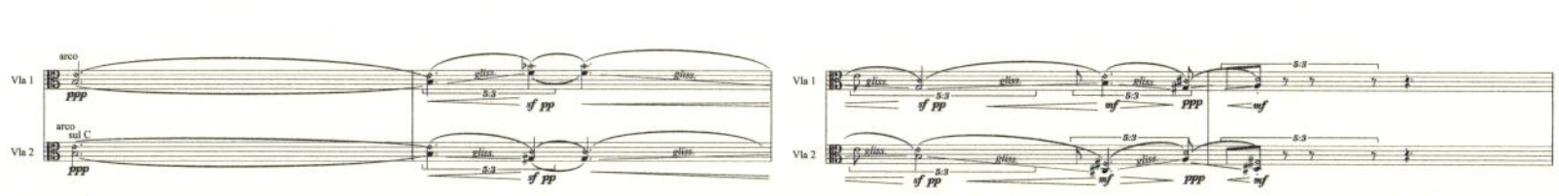

The cello phrase lasts 18 quavers and it repeats four times, also in different transpositions. The last phrase ends synchronously with the other instruments.

Example 6

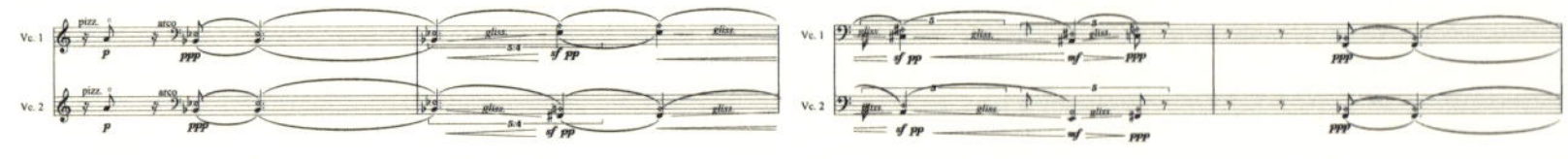

This counterpoint of phrases is also flanked by the celesta, which articulates every 20 crotchets and in this way the 13 and 20 beat cycle taken from the *Tzolkin* are represented in this introduction. The superimposition of phrases of different lengths is a transformation of the principles I found in Indian music in which phrases of different lengths combine and often work against the beat but coincide at the end of the structure of a section.

The Mexican Nobel prize-winner Octavio Paz once said that there is no modernism without tradition, it is this link towards our past culture that creates our present and gives an impulse to the future.

For several centuries, there has been a widening gap between the modern Mexico and the indigenous communities. In an attempt to achieve a homogenous Mexican society, many policies were practiced through the centuries to eradicate different indigenous languages and impose Spanish as the unique one. This practice damaged the development of these languages, which are often only spoken with fluency by the older generation. However, in the last two and a half decades, we have witnessed efforts to rescue this heritage. Their literature is now being published and several studies have been integrated in some of the University curriculums.

For some years, I have been attempting to integrate into my music the richness of our indigenous languages in an attempt to search into my heritage and pay tribute to my roots.

I have done several settings of texts taken from El Ritual de los Bacabe, a compilation of ancient spells from the Mayan healers. The language used in these texts belongs to the ancient Maya culture and particularly to that of the priests from the aristocracy of the time. This compilation contains medical, magical and religious concepts of the Mayas with almost no European influence. The use of a few European words makes us think that this compilation dates from the time of the arrival of the Spaniards. The imagery of this text keeps in touch with nature and uses this to explain the universe. I have written two works for voices and string quartet based on different spells found in this compilation. The first one *Can silim tun* (Precious stone of the great offerings), dates back to 1999 and *Kamex ch'ab* (Receive the creation) from 2010.

In *Kamex ch'ab* I kept the oral tradition of indigenous Mexican pagan rituals alive with ideas, which are repeated and gradually integrate new words as the ritual develops. The musical shape of the work flows following this principle.

The music also evolves by bringing to the foreground the emphasis of the sound of syllables and unique guttural qualities of the language, which enrich the music rhythmically as well as instrumentally. The semantics, rich in symbolism, triggered off my musical imagination.

Some ideas repeat constantly. Like the word *Tok*, (stone) that recurs semantically and musically. The instrumental treatment aids to enhance the onomatopoeic qualities of the word.

Example 7

There is a reference to religious sacrifices, which consisted in offering the heart of young victims that were taken prisoners from other ethnic groups. They would take their hearts out with a sharp stone in a ceremonial temple. The heart was offered to please the Gods.

Ch'ab tex	We have apprehended for you
Yutzil mehene	The best children
Utzi uile	For the subtle hunger
Caix u natab	And so it will be interpreted
Cuxanilon[2]	that we are still alive

2. *El Ritual de los Bacabe*. México: Instituto de Investigaciones Filológicas, Centro de Estudios Mayas, Universidad Nacional Autónoma de México, 1987.

To make a direct reference to the heart, I transcribed the sound of the pulse machines in a cardiology ward and turned them into thematic material.

Example 8

To underline the last line: *we are still alive*, I quote the only surviving pre-Hispanic melody known to us: *Konex konex*. This is the same one that the Mexican composer Silvestre Revueltas quotes in *La Noche de los Mayas*.

Example 9

When I wrote my opera *El Palacio Imaginado* in 2001–03, I too extracted some fragments from this compilation, which soon became an integral part of the drama and also provided me with a dual purpose: as a reference to the history from which the modern indigenous world comes from and as a commentary in the course of developing the drama.

In the foreground, I integrated carefully chosen contemporary indigenous poetry in Mazateco, Zapoteco and modern Maya. All read by their authors: Juan Gregorio Regino, Natalia Toledo and Briceida Cuevas and integrated on tape, which I was able to process electronically at the Experimental studio in Freiburg. While working there, I took good care to keep and enhance the musicality of these languages, as well as integrating their profound meaning to give the drama another dimension.

The libretto is based on a story by the Chilean writer Isabel Allende, entitled *El Palacio Imaginado* and was written in collaboration with the Mexican writer Adriana Diaz Enciso.

> *The story takes place in San Jerónimo, a village somewhere in Latin America where the natives had been living for several thousand years. These Indians were an ancient tribe, so poor that no one had bothered to extract taxes from them, and so meek that they had never been recruited for war. Gradually, the Indians who did not die in slavery or as a result of tortures, or as victims of unknown illnesses, scattered deep into the jungle. Always in hiding, they survived for centuries, speaking in whispers and mobilising by night. They came to be so skilful in the art of dissimulation that history did not record them. No one has seen them, but the peasants who live in the region where our story takes place, say they have heard them in the forest.*

This introduction, scored for electronics, and both instrumental and vocal forces creates this opening scenario. The vocal writing is made with a setting of fragments of *El Ritual de los Bacabe* and two poems read by their authors: the first one in Mazateco by Juan Gregorio Regino and the second by Briceida Cuevas Cob in Mayan, contribute to portray the essence of the setting.

3. *Ngata'ara stsee.* Juan Gregorio Regino. Escritores en Lenguas Indígenas, 1999.

Example 10

Poem by Juan Gregorio Regino in Mazateco[3]

Nijun uchan yibua nga kjín.	*Cuatrocientos zontles de distancia*	Four hundred measures of distance.
Nijun ucha legua k'ajmí,	*Cuatrocientas leguas al infinito*	Four hundred leagues towards infinity,
ndi'í, jnú, isien.	*Luz, obscuridad, imágenes*	Light, darkness, images.
Kiatjien fuchó nda chjinie,	*Hasta allí llega la voz del sabio*	The sage's voice reaches that far,
chjinie xi sié nga tsakí.	*El cantor sobador de dolores*	Singer healer of pain.
Nguijín isien k'a.	*Entre imágenes terrenales*	Amongst divine images.
Nguijín isien nguindié.	*Se escucha su voz suave,*	Amongst earthly images.
Nday'a anda anda ndaá,	*Su cantar divino,*	His soft voice is heard,
só tsjatsoó,	*Su plegaria piadosa.*	His divine chant,
Ndi nijmí ndasen.	*El cruza la senda de la vida,*	His compassionate plea.
Kuíxi fuatjún ndiyaá ngasandié,	*Llega hasta el lugar sagrado donde*	He crosses the path of life,
ndanga fuchó ndabua isien.	*existe la perfección.*	As far as the sacred place where perfection dwells.
Kía chjianijmí,	*Allá platica*	There he talks
kiá futí,	*Allá discute*	There he argues,
kia tsab'uxie'á	*Allá aboga*	There he pleads

nguijín Néná xi nchibutixamá ngasandié.	*Con los dioses que rigen el destino del mundo.*	With the gods that rule the world's fate.
Tjo ch'an b'itjijyá,	*La brisa lo arrulla,*	A breeze lulls him off to sleep,
chi'un kjifé ts'akunda,	*el rayo dormido lo acecha*	A dormant lightening stalks him,
bikjín nday'aní nda,	*retumba su voz piadosa*	His compassionate voice resounds
njuijín inima ngasandié	*en el centro del universo*	into the centre of the universe.

Poem by Briceida Cuevas

Yan maax tu júpchataj u xbajbi xánab k 'asanil	*Alguien se calzó las alpargatas de la maldad*	Someone has worn the sandals of evil
ka pechanaj ich k'u naj.	*Y dejó su huella en la iglesia.*	And left footprints in church.
¿Baan u bela u multal maak	*¿De que sirve una multitud*	What good is there in a crowd
ua ichil junjuntul maak tu xúxub ch'enaknakil—?	*si en cada gente silba la soledad?*	If loneliness whistles in every person?
Xkayeole tu chen dzíbtik u yich,	*La hipocresía se santigua,*	Hypocrisy blesses itself,
dzok u báaitik u tzem yétel u yich ikil u dzíbtikuba.	*Se ha enmarañado el rostro en su santiguar*	Face and chest entangled by crossing itself.
K'uxile tu payalchí,	*El rencor reza se mastica los labios.*	Remorse prays chewing its lips.
yétel u payalchíe tu cháachik u bóxil u chi.	*La mentira se postra Suavemente se da golpes de pecho.*	The Lie prostrates itself Softly beating its chest.
Tuse tu chen xolk'alánkal, tu chan lóloxik u tzen.	*La vanidad tiene en la mano tantas velas*	Vanity has so many candles in its hand,
Xmá bálile u machma p'enkech kib, u mek 'ma jun noj chaach lol.	*Tiene en los brazos un gran ramillete.*	Like a huge bunch of flowers in its arms.
¿Maax u yamaoob?	*¿A quien aman?*	Who do they love?
¿Maax ti ku payalchioob?	*¿A quien rezan?*	Whom do they pray to?
¿Ti maaz ku jach k'ubentikubaloob?	*¿A quien se encomiendan con vehemencia?*	Whom do they commend themselves to, vehemently?
¿Maax ti ku yok'oloob,	*¿A quien imploran*	Whom do they implore
ua mix maak tu k'ajotaj Yum K'u,	*si al mismo Dios nadie lo reconoció*	if even God himself remained unrecognized?
tumén u lak' pek'	*hecho a semejanza del perro*	Treated like a dog
tojoch'inta chen manak'tabi ti tu	*que fue echado apenas lo*	Who was cast out, as soon as they
jolnaji u yotoch?	*vislumbraron en la puerta de la iglesia?*	spotted him at the church door?

El Palacio Imaginado, provided me with a platform in which to explore critical political, gender and humanitarian issues, which have concerned me all my life. If setting a text to music always provides music with new semantic possibilities, opera adds a new dramatic layer to it and an opportunity to go deeper into complex issues, which can develop dramatically.

The "Imaginary Palace" is a metaphor of a historical reality in Latin America where foreign cultural models have relentlessly been imposed on a reality, which is ignored and oppressed. When referring to Mexico, the ethnologist Guillermo Bonfil Batalla refers to two different realities to explain this problem, profound Mexico and imaginary Mexico:

> "What has been proposed as a national culture in different moments of the history of Mexico can be understood as a permanent aspiration for destroying what we are. It has always been a cultural project that neglects the historic reality of the Mexican social structure and it therefore, does not accept the possibility of building a future on its reality. It is a project of substitution

in every case. The future is somewhere else, anywhere but here in this concrete reality. The task of building a national culture consists of an imposition of an alien model, a distant one, that would eliminate the cultural diversity and would achieve a unity from suppressing the existing."[4]

4. *México Profundo, Reclaiming A Civilization.* Guillermo Bonfil Batalla. University of Texas Press, Austin. 1996.

As in this opera, in *La tierra de la miel*, my most recent music theatre work, I was able to focus on these issues. This work is a collaborative opera project based on true events. It tells the story of women brought into the US and trapped in a cycle of prostitution and slavery in and around the US/Mexican border at San Diego and Tijuana.

The text of Jorge Volpi also gave me the possibility to address the imbedded idea in the minds of so many Mexicans who look for a better life across the border, given the lack of possibilities in their own country. This is why I chose to highlight one of Volpi's verses as the title for my piece: *La tierra de la miel* (*The land of honey*.) These are the words that Iris' father tells her to persuade her to go away with the men who will ultimately rape her and force her into prostitution once in the US.

As Violeta tells the story of her friend Iris, the musical dramaturgy addresses the overwhelming impact of abuse suffered by women by means of destroying the language as a way to reflect her destroyed inner world, which has become powerless and meaningless, after being raped and later murdered. To portray the victim's inability to speak, the text in the music is split amongst all performers, non of them articulating a whole word. In this manner the music destroys the language and at the same time expresses the inner pain suffered by the abuse.

Example 11

The works mentioned in this text are somehow representative of my attempt to render tribute to my cultural heritage and my humble contribution to the rich and complex cultural reality of my native country. Several of my works not mentioned in this text are also part of this continuing search to expand beyond the frontiers as only music can do. Hopefully this allows the music to be universal and break away from the local stereotypes that touch only the surface of a richer history and reality.

Music has led me to discover manifold meanings and mysteries of the human soul. More than an individual creation, I consider my work as one of discovery. Often I need to take risks to find a way to articulate the music and this often leads to more discoveries. A process that continuously gives meaning to music making and to life.

CHAPTER 28

THE SLOW ETUDE

JOSHUA RUBIN

I **needed the slow etude** when I encountered some music that relied on different standards of time and motion. Music without obvious fence posts for form (Figure 1), or with a form reduced to its simplest and most elegant state (Figure 2). Music that was on the outside edge of performance as I knew it, music that asked questions about what is possible to perceive as music (Figure 3). Music that was creating new relationships of sound and time (Figure 4), and music that made me constantly revisit what I knew about performance practice (Figure 5).

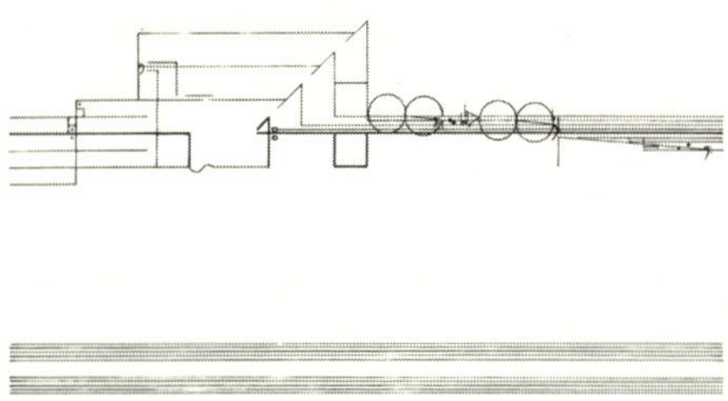

Figure 1. Cornelius Cardew, *Treatise*, 1963–1967, excerpt.

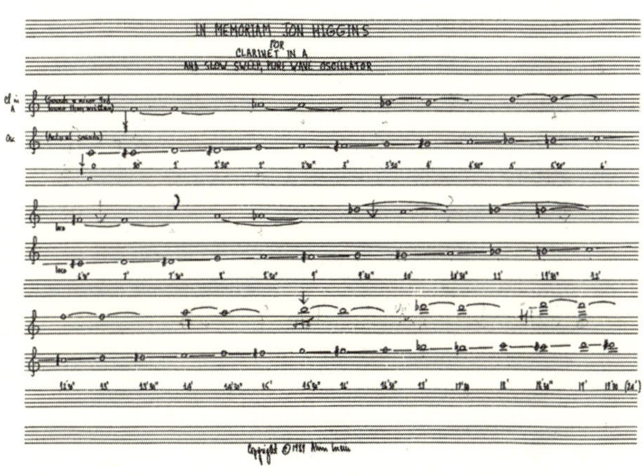

Figure 2. Alvin Lucier, *In Memoriam Jon Higgins*, 1985, excerpt.

Figure 3. Iannis Xenakis, *Échange*, 1989, excerpt.

Figure 4. Olly Wilson, *Echoes*, 1974, excerpt.

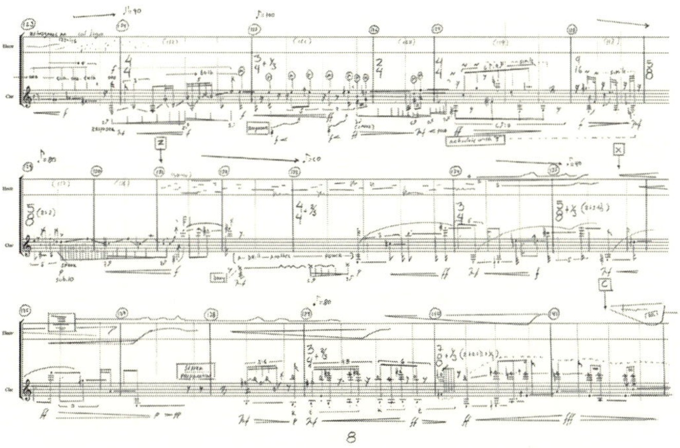

Figure 5. Ignacio Baca Lobera, *Salto Cuántico*, 2011, excerpt.

This is music that required a different point of entry, a different kind of connection to my instrument. It is also music that demands a deeper confidence of my own understanding and performance strategies in order to reach unfamiliar listeners that might have few reference points to the inner workings of this music.

My earliest hint of the need for the slow etude stems from watching some very young clarinetists struggle to achieve technical virtuosity through the endless practice of etudes and music of increasing quickness. Fast is impressive to others and is rewarding to work on; it is an important part of the development of young musicians. Fast has primal satisfaction that runs parallel to our desire to get to the finish line first. Slow is both muscular and cerebral, with few clear rewards deserving of sticky stars on notebooks. I identify with the satisfaction of quick music and I hold my pedagogy blameless for my impatience; speed is a crucial benchmark.

Some of the many considerations and expectations in forming musical phrases that are intuitive to experienced musicians:

—the idea that time is flexible and can be sculpted in the moment.

—the considerations, the obligations, and the intentionality of knowing as much as possible about the style and history of a piece of music. Once I inquired to a teacher about how to crack the nut of a piece that I found challenging; his irrefutable response was: "Have you listened to and studied every single piece by this composer?"

—just as important: when to ignore that knowledge. When to start from scratch in the moment and rewrite the performance practice, drawing on inspiration from a word, a book, a sound, a physical characteristic.

The complexity of these considerations are part of the roadblocks that steer students toward the fast rather than the slow. They will eventually find their way into these facets of music; perhaps the slow etude can help them. But the search for the slow etude is really about my own musical development.

What does the slow etude look like? I don't yet know its shape, how long it lasts, or the best technique for working with it. Will it be an exercise that changes and adapts while I'm playing it? Does working on it defy linear progress, in the same way that the some of the music that it addresses pushes far outside standard forms?

While the slow etude will require concentration, it's not a spiritual meditation. It is a corporeal practice: I simply want the instrument in my hands as much as possible. The slow etude gives me the chance to hold the instrument as much as possible, to understand it as a physical extension of my body.

* * *

Bar 1

Starting at the lowest note of the clarinet, E below the treble clef staff, I want to move infinitely slowly up the scale of the instrument. The clarinet is a mix of fingers covering holes, and mechanisms that cover additional holes. Uncovering the finger holes slowly is not a problem, it is limited by the muscle control in my hand, and concentration to keep the motion smooth and steady in my fingers. I become aware that if I'm tired or hungry my fingers will shake a little at their axes.

* * *

The typical process for learning challenging music is to incrementally increase the practice speed until a passage feels comfortable, until it sits right in the hands. Day after day of this kind of work leads to reproducibility which then presumably frees up the mind to start thinking about the meaning and intention of the music.

What if the core of music lies at the other end? This is what the slow etude is for me. It's not about slowing down fast music to work it to technical perfection; it's about slowing down music so much that it strips its capacity to hold meaning, becomes a pure physical action. Ideally, time stops all together and I'm forced to grapple with what this might imply for the music I'm trying to make. This is what I hope to achieve from the slow etude.

Music teachers and performers are always reminding themselves of the fundamentals—the building blocks that fit together to build the foundations of musicianship. The clarinet is a fairly easy instrument to learn to sound. Naturally, the heart of musicianship lies everywhere else but the mechanics of the instrument. But as with the process of learning fast music, the core of the slow etude might be about the mechanics alone.

Bar 2

There are a series of obstacles to manipulating the keys of the clarinet as true extensions of the body. Moving from the lowest E to F to F-sharp involves the closing of one pad over a hole, while two others lift up. These are controlled by springs and levers, manipulated by the tips of the little fingers. The points of connection between the flesh and the machine are where the smoothest motion translates into smooth playing.

In bar two of the slow etude, I transition from E to F. The pressure of my breath increases as the resistance of the instrument changes subtly. This is similar to how a singer increases the intensity of sound as she moves from low note to a high one. I move my right little finger slowly, assessing the weight of the spring, then guiding the button up carefully, and finally lifting the finger off of the key. The transition is complete; it takes 45 seconds, but my next goal is two minutes, then an hour, eventually a year.

* * *

Music is human control of the mechanics of the instrument, under the influence of layers of abstraction both in the effort of performing and in the reception of the listener; these layers are a hodgepodge of subjective, magical, temporal, perceptual.

Time begins in music when one note becomes two. For a monophonic instrument like the clarinet, connections between notes are the heart of expressivity. Smooth connections form the timeline of music.

I want to have the tools to span the lowest note to the highest, moving smoothly without any gaps, shifting from the loudest sounds to the softest that my instrument is capable of. I want to be able to drop every gradation of tone color along the way, emphasizing the darker parts of the spectrum on even the most shrill notes of the clarinet.

Bar 3

In bar three I'm considering where I came from and where I need to go: F-sharp. Each day the meaning of this might change, and I want to be aware of all of the expressive possibilities that are open to me at this moment. If I move aggressively into F-sharp, the F will retroactively have a sweet nostalgia. If I move even more slowly into F-sharp, I will have started the etude with a sense of playful motion, and now I'm moving into a more introspective mood.

* * *

The etude will give me the chance to imitate the silky interstitial connections of the cello, or the crystal clear movements of the piano.

The slow etude turns my attention to the details of the muscles of inhalation and exhalation, the most hairline movements of the violin bow, the chain of reflex and response to depress the piano key.

The etude will have to at least be slow enough to let me deconstruct the intuitive nature of these muscle movements.

Bar 4

Represent every type of attack and release throughout the scale. The softest attack and release: where the note starts with a gentle sweep of breath, ramping up from near-inaudibility (the clarinet's secret weapon) to a steady tone, and back to nothing. On the opposite extreme: The tongue is held in position on the reed by the force of air from the diaphragm. Release the tongue forcibly to create a harsh attack; quickly in a controlled fashion to create an inverse attack (as when recorded music is played back in reverse); smoothly but deliberately to create the perfect on/off attack.

Try to imagine attacks and releases outside of their context. Make a tranquil music built only with aggressive attacks.

* * *

The slow etude is fashioned around the idea that a greater awareness of what I'm doing will make me more aware of what others are doing. Chamber music is a miraculous real time game of evidence gathering, adaptation, and contribution. With a group, it's rare to have the opportunity to explore the type of listening that the slow etude allows. The slow etude is undoubtedly a solo enterprise.

Why spend so much time buried in the specificity of the slow etude?

Why not engineer a new instrument—one that facilitates only the smoothest musical connections between notes?

Computer tools make it easy to listen closely to music from many perspectives: We can visualize the entire waveform of the most complex piece as a simple chart. One slice of the auditory spectrum can be plucked for analysis. We can slow down the music to appreciate just one sound out of its temporal context, forever if need be.

The clarinet has a design history that predates by several hundred years the microscope detail that computers are capable of showing us. As my musical world broadens and I try to expand my capabilities within the open ocean of noise, I appreciate that the clarinet is a tool with some resistance, some constraints. It is a thrilling jumping-off point with historical reference to a dizzying body of great music already accumulated for the clarinet, and infinite opportunities to question what is now and next for the instrument.

Bar 5

Imagine an oscillator playing a single note in the room; slow disturbances would begin to rhythmically appear as my note diverges from the one sounding steady. As I move to bar four, I'm trying to do this in my head—conjuring that steady note and diverging from it. I'm picturing the physical sensation of emerging beats as they would materialize in the room. I'm trying to make the clarinet an agonist, activating the environment without the aid of other instruments or sound-producers. If my concentration falters or I need to take a breath, I lose those imaginary resultant frequencies. Start from the new note and begin the process again.

CHAPTER 29

MUSIC AS AN ART OF TOUCH

DAVID SCANLON

Saint Elias appeared before me in a dream
"They have begun marching to the sea, enormous in their approach"
The grey-eyed goddess followed
Explaining resonance and states of matter

Hearing is the detection and interpretation of sound waves by the ear and brain. A vibration is created and travels the distance between its origin and the receptive ear by exciting molecules in a long chain reaction. The vibration creates a wave. The sound wave travels into the outer ear where it is funneled toward the eardrum, causing it to vibrate. The vibration is then sent to the inner ear where it interacts with cells that translate the vibration into electrical impulses to be interpreted by the brain. Since sound is vibrating molecules, it is dependent on the presence of matter. Although we rarely think of hearing in this way, physical contact is needed to hear in the same way that contact is required when we touch something with our hands or taste something with our tongue.

The arts are delicately crafted gifts for our senses. Many art forms are dependent on this "touch." In the culinary arts the artist creates an art piece that is tasted by the consumer's tongue/brain and smelled with their nose/brain. The receiver is in physical contact with the art piece. Music is similar. The receiver is in physical contact with the art piece through the contact of vibrating molecules transmitting the sound wave. However, with music, and unlike the culinary arts, we are left asking where does the ambiguous art "object" live? Music is not the instrument or the record. Music is not the notes on the score. Music is carefully crafted sound waves vibrating and coming in contact with the listener's body. There is a tactile relationship between the art object and the listener/receiver. Music is an art of touch. The tactile nature of sound emphasizes the intimate relationship between the composer and the listener. The music vibrates the body. In some ways, the body also sings.

Many art forms are dependent on sight and almost all art forms have an element of visual presentation. Sight has both similarities and differences with hearing. When we see something our eyes are sensing and interpreting light. Light is reflected off an object and is received by retinal photoreceptors in our inner eye. Sight is dependent on the perception and interpretation of light. What differentiates this from sound is that light requires no matter. Unlike sound, light can travel through and exist in a vacuum. A good example of this phenomenon is that we are able to see light from stars incredibly far from earth: between those stars and earth is vast empty space, area where there is no matter. The physicality of sight is different because there is no matter with which the body is in physical contact. Think of a painting: the painting may be 10 feet in front of you. You receive light reflected off the painting in your eye and perceive it in your brain. It differs from sound because there is no matter that you are in physical contact with, despite the painting 10 feet in front of you.

Now imagine that there is a sculpture 10 feet in front of you and due to the materials and the angle of the sculpture light is refracting as it passes through. It looks as if the object is bent, however, if you were to touch the sculpture, examine it, or measure it, the object is in fact straight. This is an art piece that is being taken in visually, however the "finished" form and effect exists in our eyes and brain, and is different from what lives 10 feet in front of us. This relates to music because of the external/internal relationship: the art object exists internally, but it is informed by something external. Music exists internally in the brain where the sensation of the sound wave that touches the body is perceived and interpreted. Music is informed by an external sound wave.

As composers we must work with the physicality of sound. The volume a piece of music is performed at should be critically examined during the compositional process. By volume I am referring to actual decibels not the dynamics. Musical dynamics are based on relative relationships. Two ensembles may play at extremely different volumes but the difference between fortissimo and pianissimo may be the same for both (that is, the fortissimo of a rock band will be much louder than that of a string quartet but the sonic "distance" between each ensemble's fortissimo and pianissimo might nevertheless be the same). If a piece of music is meant to be extremely loud that is all well and good, but why? Sound has the ability to do permanent physical damage to the body. That is a powerful thing to either leverage or avoid, however, whichever path is taken should be taken with intent. Silence, an absence of sound, means there is an absence of touch. Few things can project aloneness and solitude the way that silence can, and it should be used purposefully. I believe that volume can effect the content of a piece. If the same music is played at two different volumes I do not feel that it communicates the same thing, or one volume may communicate the content more effectively.

Words like "Big" or "Huge" or "Heavy" are very common when discussing loud music. These terms imply physicality. They imply size and weight. However, a larger size may not be what is compositionally appropriate for certain musical content. Listeners describe quiet music as "soft." If we use the word soft we are describing something that exerts a very small amount of force on another object. This is a physical relationship. Think of how we use the word "space" in terms of our relationships with other people. Space implies a distance. If you ask someone for space you are asking them to move a bit further away, and you do not want to be touched. The word "space" is often used when discussing very quiet music. I find the words soft and space very telling of the way we hear quiet music. These words describe quiet music's absence of touch. (Space rock is different, and as much as I would like to talk about phasers, flangers, and chorus pedals it would really distract us).

When you communicate in your relationships with other people throughout the day you make decisions with regards to volume constantly and intuitively. You raise your voice in celebration and in anger. You lower your voice to console or in sadness. Even if a listener does not understand the language in which the words are derived the listener does know the difference between what is expressed when something is harshly yelled and when something is gently whispered. Parents also use abstract vocal communication to communicate with their babies before they have developed verbal language skills. A quiet soothing voice is used to comfort and relax a child, and a child understands that when a louder scold is used she or he has done something wrong. The difference between vocal communication and tactile communication is ambiguous due to sound's tactile nature, and their intersection is crucial to the way we communicate. Pure tactile communication, such as gently rubbing someone's back or simply putting your hand on someone's shoulder, expresses both concrete and abstract ideas. A gentle caress may at times express an abstract positive feeling of comfort, or if a child is reaching for something they should not have their parent may quickly push the child's hand away communicating a very direct idea that says, "No, you cannot have that right now." This same communication is very common among other species as well. Elephants walk very close to their offspring so that they can feel their presence. This communicates safety and loyalty to both elephants. Also, it is a combination of tactile and vocal communication that we use in our interspecies relationships. Music communicates along these same audio-tactile pathways. Music is a form of tactile communication. Music's touch communicates both abstract and direct ideas. We understand what aggression feels and sounds like in both our physical relationships and in music. Audio-tactile communication often lives outside of this realm of clear/direct/concrete ideas, or ideas that can be shaped into words. Language is a code used to ease the exchange of information. Many words are connected to objects and images. What is communicated when you touch someone or something with your hands is not always understood in a way that can be shaped into words or connected to objects, but information is still exchanged. The same principles apply to music. For example, when music is at its best, the information that is exchanged when you hear a solo piano piece is not just the idea, "I hear a piano", but the sound of the piano touches your body, vibrates your eardrum, is perceived by your brain, and graciously gives ideas that are felt and somehow understood.

The wood floor's changing brown hue is infinite in the grandmother of a house
Boards cut by men's hands and laid parallel
As I do nightly in joining my body to geometry
Your inconsistency is your beauty
And equally beautiful you were in previous forms

I stand in a lake, water midway up my thighs
Childish net in hand
Singing to myself
"Bring me your gold and I will sleep soundly."

CHAPTER 30

TOUR DIARY FOR MY EUROPEAN "PIANO SUTRAS" SOLO PIANO TOUR

MATT SHIPP

1.

Playing solo piano can be exhilarating, dizzying, dangerous, fulfilling, perplexing, all of the above, none of the above. It is such a naked and pure way to bare one's soul. It is a dialogue between one's mind and soul—an alphabet of ivories and ebonies sequenced in a unitary whole before you. Doing a solo piano tour can be an exhausting endeavor, and like any tour it can be a micro/macrocosms of the many issues one has to deal with in music. I will try to elucidate a few things that came up on this 2013 solo tour.

2.

Sometimes after gigs, music students came backstage to talk with me, and it was interesting to see where they were coming from and what was on their minds. What I found most interesting was the students' perception of the different aesthetics that are out there and what they were trying to take from each. One kid I spoke with was trying to synthesize aspects of what he had gotten from my aesthetic with things he had learned from Tim Berne's work and from John Zorn's music. This same student—though not from a so-called "straight-ahead" jazz environment—was studying composer/theorist George Russell's book *Lydian Chromatic Concept of Tonal Organization.*

Another student was trying to balance the various aspects of the New York Vision Festival School and the Chicago post-Ken Vandermark scene.

A pianist I spoke with, who seemed to be from a "quasi-straight-ahead" background, wanted to branch out in a more "modernist" way as far as generating a series of compositions to be used as a vehicle for improvisation—sort of the Monk model. This pianist claimed that the way I phrase—

especially my pianissimo passages—was something he had been searching for his whole life. We talked about how to listen to the silence and how to let the silence generate the phrasing, all the while allowing one's touch on the instrument (articulation) to make a musical statement at various dynamics.

Several students had questions about musical personalities I've been involved with. One was interested about my time in the David S. Ware Quartet and another about my work with the great Mal Waldron (he somehow knew I had opened for him a couple of times.) We both shared a great appreciation for Mal Waldron, one of my favorites. This opened up a conversation about the huge worth of Mal's under-appreciated legacy: how Mal's work touched on everything and how he was completely himself but at the same time a weird synthesis of certain aspects of Monk and Bud Powell.

Every once in a while, a student would know I had been close with the late great composer and reed player Joe Maneri, and I would get questions about what was he like.

And sometimes I would get a real surprise—like the student who asked about my CDs with altoist Rob Brown. This particular student said he considered Rob to be one of the most important voices on the instrument since Eric Dolphy.

I got a lot of questions about what students might need to know (or not need to know) in order to be out here and make a musical statement. In general I encouraged them to study and explore everything that's out here; to listen to their own conscience; to keep pushing until they get a vision. And once they are confident enough about that vision, and a course opens up before them, listen to nobody and plow ahead.

Of course I always got a few questions about gossip from the New York scene like who hates who.

3.

Every solo gig is a process of self discovery. Who am I? I don't know. There is not one person on earth who can tell you what the mind is anymore than they know what improvisation is. All we know is that the mind is, and that we use it. Therefore, no improviser can really tell you who they are. All I know for sure is that some type of process is happening. I do know that I feel very confident that I can always make something happen. I do know that there are some black and white keys in front of me that form a sort of alphabet, and that my job is to push them down in some kind of configuration. Hopefully I feel some freedom and exhilaration while doing this, and I am able to transmit this feeling to the audience. I have no idea if I play jazz, some offshoot of jazz, free jazz or some new emerging genre that is improvisation-based rather than genre-based. Nor do I care. Classification and exact definitions are for morons of the highest order.

When one is in the middle of inspiration—that religious-ecstatic feeling that playing can bring you to—what type of pathetic moron would care what it is called? At that point it just is—in the "is"ness of what it is.

Obviously, I realize that I come from a tradition (or maybe a few traditions)—but so what. A child is always a different person from his or her parents. I subscribe to the Bruce Lee philosophy (articulated in Jeet Kune Do) that all styles are limitations. I simply try to use what seems right in the moment to express myself.

Expression is all that has meaning at the second of inspiration if one is really in the moment. At the second of inspiration, the only thing of consequence is the flow of language from the universal mind through the improviser/composer within that unitary framework. At the second of inspiration, the flow of language is all there is, and those names in the jazz firmament—whether Coltrane, Parker, Armstrong, etc.—are incidental, for you are dealing with the impersonal aspect of the flow of language, not with personalities. And those names—at that moment only—serve as fucking worm meat in fucking graveyards.

It is all about the flow of language.

CHAPTER
31

WE ALL BREAK

A Crossroads of Haitian Vodou Drumming and Creative Music

CHES SMITH

For the last 10 years or so I have spent a lot of my time studying and performing Haitian Vodou drumming, working with many different teachers and performing on the New York scene for dance classes and Vodou ceremonies. For quite some time I already had a full schedule playing the drumset and writing music for groups on different music scenes ("jazz," "indie," and "creative music"), so I always thought of my interest in Haitian music as a kind of hobby, something I did for no other reason than loving the music and hanging with the musicians, dancers, and participants of the Vodou religion. I didn't really notice that maybe in the last 5 years, the time I spent on this "hobby" had increased to the point where I was devoting as much time to it as I do the music I make a living playing.

Recently, I was invited to present some new music at Bimhuis in Amsterdam, so I thought, why not up the ante in my pursuit of Haitian music and attempt to connect it to creative jazz music? So I began working on two sets' worth of music for pianist Matt Mitchell (an incredible improviser and interpreter on the "jazz" and creative music scene), two Haitian Vodou percussionists (both teachers of mine, Daniel Brevil and Markus Schwartz), and myself on drumset and Haitian drums. Embarking on this, I soon hesitated. What if Daniel and Markus couldn't connect with the music I was writing? Although it utilized traditional Haitian drum rhythms and structural devices, the harmonic world I was operating within was decidedly polytonal, and the overall sound was far from any Haitian music I had heard. What if, culturally speaking, it didn't make any sense to do this? After all, there is no "avant-garde jazz scene" that I know of in Haiti's capitol city, Port-au-Prince, let alone in the Haitian countryside (a recent trip to Haiti confirmed this). On the other hand, the drumming of Vodou shares a lot with jazz and creative music of the last 50+ years, especially with the music I play presently. I kept my focus on these elements and went ahead, hoping to create a composition and context for improvising that would highlight these commonalities.

In this essay I would like to share my ideas on these connections. But first, some background information for the reader with no experience with the music of Haitian Vodou. Here I beg you to *please* check out the sources cited at the end of this essay as they offer much more in-depth information on the religion and music of Vodou than you will find here. My approach to this paper is not that of a scholar who has dedicated his/her life to studying Vodou in the interest of thorough documentation, but merely as a musician and outsider with a very particular slant who is excited to share what he has learned so far (albeit between rehearsals, touring, composing, gigs, recording, etc.)

The Port-au-Prince Tradition

Vodou drumming is an expansive tradition with innumerable rhythms, variations of which you can find from region to region, city to city, even neighborhood to neighborhood. The drummers I have studied with mostly come from—or are versed in the music of—Haiti's capitol city, Port-au-Prince. The Vodou drumming of Port-au-Prince represents a syncretizing of traditions and influences to establish a repertoire of iconic rhythms that any drummer steeped in this tradition will know at least some version of. Most Port-au-Prince Vodou rhythms fall into two main categories, *Rada* (which has a dominant influence from the former West African kingdom of Dahomey, presently the Republic of Benin) and *Petro* (aka Petwo, which has a religious and rhythmic influence from the African Congo). Each category breaks down into subcategories, and so on, producing a vast number of rhythms in each division. There also are important and frequently played rhythms that fall outside of Rada and Petro, but for my purposes it will suffice to focus on the rhythms of these two categories.

There are two different sets of drums utilized in Rada and Petro. Rada drums have tuning pegs that affix cow skin heads to the drum, and are played either with two sticks, or one stick and one hand. Petro drums have goat skin heads wound to the drum with rope, and are played exclusively with hands. In the USA drummers often use conga drums in place of the Rada or Petro drums, as it can be difficult to import the traditional drums from Haiti. Lately in New York and Haiti the African djembe is sometimes being used as well.

In either set, the largest drum, the *manman*, is also referred to as the "lead drum" or "master drum," as the drummer with the most experience typically plays it. He or she is responsible for knowing exactly what rhythm and variation to play for each song, dance, and ritual activity. The drummer on the smaller and higher-pitched *segon* must play the correct compliment to the myriad things the manman drummer calls, choosing among dozens of melodic variations and "conversations" within each main rhythm. The percussive and highest-pitched drum, the *boula* (called the *kata* in Petro), typically has only one pattern for each main rhythm, and need not change its part for each variation of the manman and segon. The boula's main job is to provide a relentless, driving feel that creates buoyancy for the rest of the ensemble to float on.

In addition to the set of three drums, a traditional ensemble might also include a piece of iron called the *ogan* (a hoe blade or a cowbell could also be used) which plays the fundamental rhythm of each main division, and one or two low-pitched frame drums called *bas* (or bass). As of late the bas has taken a much greater role in the sound of a Haitian Vodou ensemble, with one drummer playing complex bass lines on 3, 4 or 5 conga drums.

Tension

The rhythms of Vodou have polyrhythmic tension built in to them. The basic 6/8 bell pattern of the staple Rada rhythm *Yanvalou* features a 3:2 polyrhythm, spelling out 3 beats in the first bar, then in the same amount of real-time space, it slows to two beats in the second bar. The priest's *ason* (a maraca-shaped shaker made of gourd and beads) marks these downbeats on the two side, landing on the "1." Together, the bell and the ason look like this:

This polarity of a strong 3 side/weak 2 side creates an imbalance that pushes the music forward. The songs that accompany Rada rhythms often highlight this dynamic by embellishing the second bar with a 4:3 polyrhythm:

The fundamental Petro rhythm called *Petro Franc* has a melody played on Segon using an array of hand techniques. The rhythm can also be played outright on the kata drum with sticks. It can be phrased in cut time like this:

However, some ensembles (or at least the lead drummer) pull it toward 5. There is a Petro piece on the Smithsonian Folkways release *Drums of Haiti* recorded by ethnomusicologist Harold Courlander that feels pretty much like this:

Other ensembles play it decidedly in the middle of 4 and 5. Although perhaps a bit unwieldy to sight read, a way to notate this was devised by one of my teachers in New York, John Amira. He applies 32nd note rests to the second and fourth notes of the rhythm to produce this:

In this example, notes 1, 3, and 5 of each bar still fit into a 4/4 grid, but notes 2 and 4 are displaced toward, but not all the way to, the comparable notes in 5:4. True, you might be hard pressed to find a Haitian who describes the feel in this way, but after years in pursuit of the feel between 4 and 5, I find this to be pretty accurate notational representation of how many drummers phrase Petro.

Whether the Petro is phrased in 4, 5, or anywhere in between, the singers will fit the songs over it, and the dancers can dance the various Petro steps to it. Amira told me a story of being lost listening to the Courlander Petro recording until his wife (the great Haitian dancer Mona Estime Amira) began dancing to it, whereupon suddenly he could hear where the time was. The singers and dancers of Vodou routinely transpose melody and choreography on the spot to make it fit with the drummers' interpretation of the time feel.

Challenging the Time: The Kase

An effective Vodou drummer must display a mastery of the complex, nuanced feels above, all the while pushing and pulling against the time feel with a running rhythmic commentary. This is what piqued my interest in the music in the first place: I tend to listen to drummers who engage in a counter line, one that creates a lot of tension, as it can push an ensemble to new places. There are many devices available to do this: polyrhythm, cross rhythms, beat displacement, flexible phrasing in relation to the beat, multi-directional ("free") playing, or, even, *bad drumming* (Trey Spruance and I have spent many hours listening to recorded examples of rushing, dragging, and enthusiastic overplaying in search of time-keeping ideas for the drum parts of Secret Chiefs 3).

The *kase* (pronounced cah-sey, meaning "break") in Vodou drumming is to me one of the most exciting events in all of music. It is an event of indeterminate length in which the manman drummer dramatically increases the intensity and plays in an unpredictable, rhythmically complex manner, challenging the time and causing severe tension. At the lead drummer's cue, the manman and segon drums break from their main rhythms to play new parts that emphasize a polyrhythmic relation to the basic pattern. In the Petro kase, the manman drummer riffs on a slow 5 phrase in the space of 8 beats:

The Yanvalou kase emphasizes the half note, so although still on the same 8th note grid as the main rhythm, a 3:4 polyrhythm is created over two bars:

Granted, 3:4 and 5:4 in and of themselves should not be too hard for a musician to follow. What disorients is the way in which a master drummer embellishes the shifted pattern. An introductory phrase in the Petro kase utilizes rests to create a further shifting cycles within the 5:4 polyrhythm:

This repeated grouping of 3 on the 5 side of the 5:4 polyrhythm is orchestrated using hand techniques such as slaps, basses, open tones, and presses to create further subgroups of the 3 cycles within the 5:4 context. To introduce a Petro rhythm the lead drummer might omit more notes, creating a slow 5 over 16 beats. This phrase is typically used to call the other drummers in at the beginning of a song:

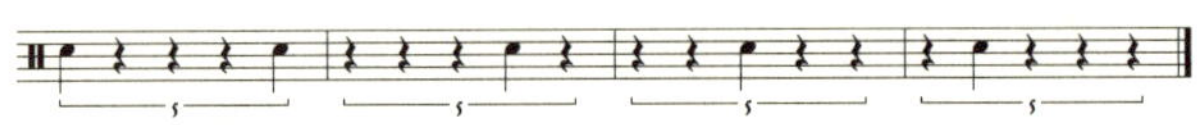

This Yanvalou kase phrase adds accents to the slow 3:4 polyrhythm to create a longer cross rhythm, then moves to offbeat accents to finish the combination:

Great Vodou drummers also have command over where they place their notes in relation to the beat. Often in the kase, the lead drummer will lean so far back on the beat that it feels like he or she is about to take the whole rhythm section down. A solid, driving boula and segon are crucial in these moments. The situation has an analogue in jazz: when the late, great Haitian drummer Frisner Augustin concludes a frenetic polyrhythmic sequence by pounding the downbeat, finishing it off with a heavy, laid back thud on the fifth 8th note of the bar (the "kase note" in 6/8), it is like Elvin

Jones ramping up a triplet figure on the turnaround of a tune, hammering it down on beat 1, and finishing it off with a way-laid back, thunderous crash on beat 4 while the bass player charges ahead with the time. I heard once that Elvin used to listen incessantly to a tape of Tiroro, known then as "Haiti's Greatest Drummer." I totally believe it.

The Kase's Function

When I first learned some kases, I was excited about the rhythmic challenges for their own sake. The polyrhythms, cross rhythms, and beat placement sounded like a lot of things played on drumset in post-bop jazz music, and I was happy to find them in another musical context. Later I found out this kind of playing in the kase actually served important functions in the religion. As a "secular musician" this idea was new to me. The kase reinforces song structure: the manman drummer calls a break at the beginning of any song cycle for a spirit, and each time a new song is introduced within a cycle. It also reinforces ritual activities: breaks are called each time the *houngan* or *manbo* (male or female priest) approaches the alter to perform a choreographed *vire* (spin). By far the most important function of the kase, however, is to facilitate possession: The kase's violent interruption of the of the trance-like, predictable dance of the main rhythm causes an imbalance in the devotees, moving them further from regular consciousness, creating a psychic space for the spirit to enter.

Possession by *loa* (spirits) is an immanent feature of Vodou, a condition necessary to allow spiritual work to be done. Karen McCarthy Brown explains: "These possession-performances, which blend pro forma actions and attitudes with those responsive to the immediate situation, are the heart of a Vodou ceremony. The spirits talk with the faithful. They hug them, hold them, feed them, chastise them. Group and individual problems are aired through interaction with the spirits. Strife is healed and misunderstanding rectified. At these ceremonies, crucial community bonds are reinforced through the process of giving gifts of food and entertainment to the Vodou spirits."

The master drummer's job is to help facilitate possession through a combination of several means, including the polyrhythmic displacement described above. Another key ingredient is timbral variation, using cracking sounds produced by slapping the drum (with sticks or hands) as well as drawing out the bass frequencies by striking the center of the drum head with a cupped hand. I have seen John Amira go so far as to slam his conga drum on the ground to shake the floor with low end in order to bring on a possession.

Dynamics are also important, and by this I include the ability to play *really loud*. Although it is true that loud volume doesn't *necessarily* equate with power, it is also true that loud volume *can* and *often does* equate with power. I spent a long time trying increase my top volume on the drumset, along the way discovering that it helps to use the biggest drumsticks you can find. When I met Frisner Augustin, I was really happy to see he used the same huge marching drum sticks I use when he played the manman drum of the Rada set—I knew I had met the right mentor! Sometimes I'd be playing the lead drum in his group class, and he'd come over and demonstrate how he wanted the part to be played. He would take the stick and play it literally twice as loud as I had been playing it, barely straining to do so. He was one of the most powerful drummers I have ever heard. However, he also stressed the importance of playing dynamically—in order to play for the spirits (and to make it all the way through a ceremony from 9PM to 6AM), you must know how much energy to give, when to lay back and when to when to give it all.

Perhaps the most important feature of all in a kase is the element of *surprise*. A master drummer uses all of the rhythmic, timbral, and dynamic considerations at his or her disposal to invent new meanings in the moment, "shocking" the congregation with combinations of phrases that suddenly take the listener far from the rhythmic and melodic construct of the dance's main pattern. When I listen to a great drummer kase, I get the same sense of wonder and surprise as I do listening to improvisations by Charlie Parker or Sonny Rollins.

Frisner was a master of surprise. Literally every time you would try to anticipate where one of his kase phrases was headed he would change direction and improvise another path. Then, instead of using the standard reentrances to the main rhythm of many drum companies, he would create those anew each time. Yet, somehow you knew where you were supposed to be. Daniel Brevil also improvises particularly unpredictable kases, but infused with virtuosic technique and rhythmic command, and the ultramodern vocabulary favored by the "new generation" of Haitian drummers. I was surprised, amused, and humbled to find that after years of playing solid time backing up some great lead players, I still could be thrown by a kase delivered courtesy of Daniel Brevil.

Some time ago I was in a conversation with a poet about my experiences playing for Vodou ceremonies. At that stage in my development I only played segon and boula, as I knew the correct rhythm to play in each instance, even though I couldn't yet follow much of the ritual activity, and I only knew a limited number of songs. But, it had taken me 7+ years of hard study to get to that point where I was a reliable member of the lead drummer's team—a fact appreciated by the lead drummer and those present at the ceremony. I explained "I can do my part in the ceremony as long as I know all the support drum parts that go with the rhythms the lead drummer may call..." she interjected interrogatively—"um... as opposed to knowing any *content*?" I agreed with her that I did need to push further ahead in my study of the religion's rituals and songs. But now it is clear to me that she harbored an assumption that information related to the drumming or music in general couldn't possibly be content. But, insofar as the drum team works together to provide the master drummer a solid bed to kase and bring about possession, it seems safe to say the drumming is a huge part of the content.

We All Break

I wanted the group with Daniel, Markus and Matt to work with the improvisation at the core of both Port-au-Prince Vodou and the creative music tradition. The kase is where the lead drummer of the Vodou drum ensemble, through creative improvisation, takes the listener far from the trance-like flow of the dance to a peak energy level, allowing for the transformation of the consciousness of the devotees. There is an analogous space in collective improvisation: there are moments where everything comes together pointedly in a noticeable shift from a previous flow of energy, transforming the musicians and audience. Perhaps a music could be constructed using the kase—the break—as an improvisational crossroads which connect both musics. In order to keep this idea in the front of my imagination, I named the band We All Break.

I felt composition was needed to create a common ground to facilitate improvisation. As I saw it, the writing wouldn't reference the harmonic tradition of Haitian music including Kompa, Misik Rasin, Haitian Jazz, or even the classical music tradition (such as the guitar music of Frantz Casseus, although his efforts were definitely an inspiration), but instead meditate on the relationships present in a ceremonial context. The work wouldn't be a *blend* of Haitian music and American improvised music, but a study and extrapolation of Vodou elements, put back together in an art music context, albeit one that happened to work with traditional Haitian drums. In doing this I hoped to create a sound world like I have experienced while taking in the entirety of a ceremony—the composite tonalities, rhythms, dance, personalities, smells, room temperature, vibe, etc. As such, my artistic motivation was probably more in line with a kind of self-conscious European "abstract impressionist" art tradition, rather than an attempt to create a genuinely Haitian music. I hoped the band intuited this (and was cool with it) as I started sending them demos. At some point I stopped worrying: what the hell?—it was a paying gig...

"Drum-centric" Harmonic World

In western concert music, care is taken so that percussion doesn't interfere with the orchestra's ability to express tonality clearly. The instruments must speak quickly and get out of the way, such as the snare drum, or they must be able to be tuned, like timpani, concert toms, mallet instruments, orchestral bells etc. Jazz drumming employs a different concept, particularly among players whose toms are woven into their comping patterns, such as Ed Blackwell, Elvin Jones, Jack DeJohnette, and Steve Ellington. Perhaps because jazz is such a highly chromatic music, drummers rarely tune to specific pitches (Max Roach, in this connection, pointed out that the drumset "has the privilege of being of an indeterminate pitch"). The paramount concern with tuning seems to be that the drums resonate—"sing," and sound good together in a set. As such, drum solos in jazz appear as a momentary break from the harmonic fabric of the tune. You hear the harmony in the soloing of many drummers including Roach, "Philly" Joe Jones, Roy Haynes, Paul Motian and others, but the harmony is expressed through the filter of the drumset with its own internal tuning logic. Vodou extends this concept further: as there is no chordal or harmonic instrument, the manman, segon, boula and bas are left alone to interact with a chorus of singers. This allows the drums a greater harmonic role.

In the last 20 to 30 years, the increased presence of the bas in Vodou drumming has brought a perceptible polytonality to the overall sound. The repetitive, low-pitched, melodic patterns made up of clear intervals imply a key center often in remote relation to the interval created by the manman and segon. When the Vodou songs are sung over this, in simple modes that clearly spell out major or minor tonalities, an understated polytonal texture results.

I have transcribed and analyzed many of these relationships on recordings, and noted what I've heard at ceremonies and dance classes. Although I do know a few Haitian drummers who feel the bas must tune to the key of each song (especially when recording), I have found that the bas, manman and segon, and the songs more often than not stand in polytonal relation to each other. Part of the reason for this could be pragmatic: a vast number of songs, each with a distinct tonality, must be started in the heat of the moment in rapid succession, apace with what spirits need to be honored in the houngan or manbo's estimation. There is no time to transpose the songs to be in harmony with the drums; whoever starts the song barely has time to select a key comfortable for them and the chorus. Perhaps the harmonic world comes from the pressing needs of the moment. I have seen that a lot of care goes into tuning of a Vodou ensemble, generally speaking: each lead drummer I play with is very particular about what pitch relationships they accept among the drums, and each song must be correct down to the most minute vocal nuance. So perhaps this is simply *how the music is*: the music sounds "right" so long as the sonic integrity of the bas and three traditional drums remains intact, the song is sung correctly, and most importantly, sufficient energy is generated to elevate these constituent parts to something greater than their sum.

I envisioned Matt Mitchell's piano parts having a "drum-centric" sound. Using the examples of bas/song relationships that I had transcribed as a starting point, I ultimately devised my own relationships, in order to construct a coherent harmonic journey that would traverse two sets. I further harmonized most melodies by juxtaposing at least two key centers. Lest it sound as though drums were the sole influence on the harmony of the piece, I should mention other influences. Rapper Kool Keith puts together tracks in which the bass lines outline one key center, a sample states another, and the chorus—often sung in falsetto—are in a third key. I find the way he puts it all together to be quite hypnotic. Other things I have spent an inordinate amount of time with include Messiaen's Turangalila symphony, Ornette Coleman's harmolodic improvisation, and, even more so, Marc Ribot's and Tony Malaby's improvised line playing which freely traverses keys (although probably these latter two are influenced by Ornette). Ribot often chooses the most straightforward constituent elements to create his polytonality, layering triadic constructions in remote keys—it was actually his music I thought of first when I started analyzing the Vodou bas-song relationships (recently Marc, Shahzad Ismaily, and I went to Haiti together and jammed with a Rara band—another extremely poly- and microtonal Haitian music. Marc spent the most of the session with his head buried in his acoustic guitar, which no one else could hear due to the loud drums and horns. He eventually emerged, grinning, and called out the two distant triads superimposed on each other in the melody and bass of the plastic horns and bamboo *vaccines*. He had been dealing with that bitonal relationship the whole time he was playing).

"Drum-centric" Structure

Through many years playing with Matt Mitchell in Tim Berne's band, and more recently in his own projects, I knew well his highly developed rhythmic sense and ability to respond to aural cues. Thus, rather than confine the piano to a melodic/harmonic function, it made sense for Matt to handle duties normally reserved for the drums. His left hand was usually in the role of the bas, and had to answer to Daniel's lead drum calls as Markus and I did. Matt's parts changed with variations of each basic rhythm, working around the composite melody of the manman and segon. In a ceremony, or even a dance class, the sequence of rhythms and how long to stay on each one is never planned. One must hear the new pattern and immediately change to the appropriate bass line.

During kases the bas drops out to highlight the contrast to the trance-like flow of the main rhythm, laying bare the polyrhythmic and timbral challenges of the lead drummer. Similarly, when Daniel called a kase Matt would cease playing the left hand part while continuing the written or improvised material indicated for the right hand. Thus, the listener would follow the thread of a line into a radically changed, and often combative, rhythmic environment. In some cases I wrote accompaniment to the kase highlighting the polyrhythmic element that most opposed the dance's regular pattern. Matt would shift into this with a free hand when the kase was called, continuing his lines while simultaneously highlighting the element most antagonistic to the flow of the main rhythm.

I also wrote piano accompaniment for various "conversations" in the Vodou repertory. These are figures of a finite length in which the manman instigates a hocketed interplay with the segon before returning to the main rhythm. Matt had to respond to Daniel's call with a harmonized, composite version of both drum parts. Between the calls for conversations, kase, variations, not to mention the beginnings and endings of tunes—all called by the lead drummer, Matt had a lot to keep track of.

In addition to this "drums-up" writing, there were also piano parts that worked with the classic rhythmic and melodic phrases of the songs and drum rhythms of Vodou. I often followed the traditional song arrangement, where a verse sung by the leader is then repeated by the chorus—anywhere from a few to dozens of people. This is a mix comprising different registers, characters of voices, vibratos and inflections. Matt would play an unadorned version of a melody, repeated in a harmonized version, typically close-voiced to evoke the indeterminate blend you might find in a chorus.

Finally, on a few pieces I referenced extra-musical elements of a ceremony. One such piece features fortissimo clusters in the bass register of the piano which become progressively figurated as the piece goes on, moving through sections in which clarity and light in tonality and texture emerge. This is meant to simulate an appearance by the Nago spirit Ogun at a ceremony. An Ogun possession evolves from its violent beginning, giving way to a calming of the spirit's demeanor to engage with those assembled—depending on which Ogun shows up, he might light a cigar while moving in the traditional choreography, dance skillfully with a machete, or shake hands with those assembled as a powerful politician might. Perhaps there will even be candid, one-on-one consultations where important information is gleaned.

Relations of Syncretism

The Bimhuis gig, and a subsequent trip to Haiti culminated a year of intense involvement with Haitian music for me: I played many ceremonies, played drumset alongside traditional drums for the first time, studied a lot more with Daniel Brevil, and found a few more great drummers to study with—Gaston "Bonga" Jean Baptiste just an hour away from my house, and Eddy Jean, just outside of Port-au-Prince, Haiti—and I finally started applying the Haitian Creole I have been working on basically in a vacuum for the last couple of years. Getting the music together for the gig made me reflect on relationships: between harmonic worlds, between performer and audience, between English and Haitian Creole, between insiders and outsiders of a culture, between Vodou musicians and creative musicians, between affluent countries and the impoverished, between oppressor and oppressed, between Haitian culture and that of the USA. On one hand I now feel even more connected to, and invested in, the music of Haitian Vodou. On the other hand, this experience cemented the idea that I will never transform into a Haitian, no matter how well I know the music, study the language, the culture and the history. That might sound like a dumb thing to say, but it was a striking realization to me as I worked on this project. I still plan to spend a lot of time in pursuit of Vodou music, and I'm still positive the drumming is the greatest in the world. But now I see that it would be disingenuous to turn away from my whole musical picture, and should maintain the proper respect and appreciation for the creative, improvised, punk, noise, new music, jazz, etc., etc., etc. scenes that have shaped me thus far. Perhaps you could say that the tradition of Vodou drumming—itself a syncretism—mirrors the melding of elements that make up a person. I invite this tradition, to whatever extent it wants, to be a contributing factor in its own right to what I will become.

Thanks

Teachers Daniel Brevil, Morgan Zwerlein, John Amira, Mona Estime Amira, Markus Schwartz, Eddy Jean, Bonga Jean-Baptiste, and Steve Deats. This is dedicated to the memory of Frisner Augustin. Skooter Fein, Michelle Martin and Johnny Scovel for turning me on to the music.

Works Cited

Markus Schwartz. *Rhythms Without End: Haitian Vodou Drum Music.* http://www.windowsonhaiti.com/windowsonhaiti/rhythms.shtml

Lois Wilcken. *The Vodou Kase: The Drum Break in New York Temples and Dance Classes.* http://www.nyfolklore.org/pubs/voic36-1-2/vodou.html

Lois Wilcken. *The Drums of Voodoo.* (White Cliffs Media)

Karen McCarthy Brown. *Mama Lola: A Vodou Priestess in Brooklyn.* (University of California Press)

Arthur Taylor. *Notes and Tones: Musician-to-Musician Interviews.* (Da Capo Press)

Recordings Cited

Various Artists: *Music of Haiti: Vol. 2, Drums of Haiti.* (Smithsonian Folkways) http://www.folkways.si.edu/music-of-haiti-vol-2-drums-of-haiti/caribbean-world/album/smithsonian

This is the Courlander recording referred to in the straight 5:4 Petro example. Scroll down to "Petro Dance." You can also buy the whole record here, which I highly recommend.

Haitian Folk Artists and Maya Deren. *Voices of Haiti—Mid Century Haitian Recordings.* (Global Village Music)

This is on iTunes—type in these exact words and it will appear. For an example of the Petro feel in between 4 and 5 (the example of the John Amira notation), check out the track *Miro Miba* (congo), which is a Petro Franc played in the old style with 2 only two drums, plus *ogan* and *cha cha* (Petro's *ason*). At 2:48 you can hear the Petro *kase* entrance, with a slow 5 directly into a 5:4 broken into groups of three.

Societe Absolument Guinen. *Voodoo Drums.* (Soul Jazz Records)

http://www.souljazzrecords.co.uk/releases/?id=157

This is a great example of "new generation" Vodou drumming, complete with three drum *bas* parts.

Societe Absolument Guinen. *Sprits of Life: Haitian Vodou.* (Soul Jazz Records)

http://www.souljazzrecords.co.uk/releases/?id=220

Same crew as *Voodoo Drums* but with the addition of songs for the loa. This is polytonal Vodou music.

Kool Keith. *Matthew.* (Funky Ass Records)

One of my favorite records ever. Polytonal and phraseologically insane.

Kool Keith. *Spankmaster.* (Gothom/Overcore)

Check out track two.

Ches Smith and These Arches. *Hammered.* (Clean Feed)

Sorry to cite one of my own records, but it has some great Tony Malaby bitonal improvising on it.

CHAPTER
32

GEORGE STEEL IN CONVERSATION WITH JOHN ZORN

GEORGE STEEL

January 27, 2014 New York City.

Zorn: So—life after the opera. You mentioned you wanted to talk a little bit about the programming that you did there, your successes there...and I think we should touch upon your programming at Miller also because the 11 years you spent at Miller really changed the face of new music in New York.

Steel: Ah, thank you.

Zorn: It really made a strong impact and continues to make a strong impact. And the sign of a really successful project is one that carries on even after you're not involved. So do you want to talk a little bit about programming ideas, what attracts you to pieces, how you put programs together, the team that you have with you?

Steel: Yeah. Well, sure. I'm working on programming now, so I'm reminded again just what my process is. Part of it is just making sure to really listen to everything, because the ideas come from the pieces, and usually not the other way around. Not to say you can't have a framing idea for a program, say, "I want to do all pieces that are about this idea," but the pieces have to exist. You don't create them *ex post facto* to support the programming conceit.

The framing ideas for concerts or events come from having listened to lots of music, or having looked at lots of work. The old fashioned model for putting together a concert had to do primarily with variety and with demonstrating the learnedness and virtuosity of the performer, but I think that's a less and less interesting model. Unless it's a player you have a love affair with, somebody who's incredibly intriguing. But really programming should be about the work itself.

I find that there are two fundamental modes: programming things together because they're similar, and programming things together because they are contrasting. And this connects to something, a sort of a paradox, that I'm always struck by: the moment someone starts telling you why two things are similar, they've already admitted that they think the two are fundamentally dissimilar—or else why would they be telling you, right?

Zorn: Absolutely.

Steel: And the same is true the opposite way: if somebody's telling you why two things are different, then they're probably fundamentally very, very similar. And so this idea of programming music because it contrasts, suggests to people that there's something underlying and they're just the same.

Zorn: It's connected.

Steel: Correct. And if you play two pieces that are very obviously similar, two sets of pieces called, "Theme and Variations," you're immediately looking for the ways that they are different. It is, of course, the way the brain is wired—to compare two things. And at some point your brain makes a decision and says, "Well, if I have two identical coffee mugs, to make a list of the ways that they are similar to each other is an infinite and trivial task." So your mind immediately goes to how they are distinct from each other. And I think playing with that idea, asking people to hear, see, feel things that are similar between two works, or to try to find distinctions, opens up what a composer was doing. Why is this piece different from that other piece? And all of the assumptions that you made about the implacable surface of the piece start to fall away, and you realize that everything is a choice. And you realize that it's not inevitable that a piece sounds a certain way, even a piece of Mozart that seems as if it comes out of some unending stream—it's always the same, it always has this elegant composure, you don't feel the sweat behind the music. But when you compare a piece to another piece that's very similar, suddenly you see the number of choices the composer's making.

Zorn: Your programming has focused on composers, which has been very successful and very unusual in a certain way, because audiences seem to find it easier to relate to the visceral experience of seeing a performer on stage. In a way the composer has been in the back, invisible—but the composer-performer model is changing all that.

Steel: You know, the classical music industry (which is changing a lot) in the glory days of the '40s, '50s, '60s, '70s, you know, they were about stars. And to a degree that's still the case. It was really about, "I want to see a star performer do their thing. I want to see Luciano Pavarotti. What's he in? I don't know, but he's great." You know. "I want to see Glenn Gould," who is one of the greatest of all time. You don't even need to know what he's playing. You just go to see the artist. (Though Gould is a special case, because he was so composer-centered.) But in reality, absent a sort of movie star performer, that kind of approach falls apart quickly. The industry was trying to make everybody else, the other 99% into stars too, because it's a much more efficient way to sell tickets if you say "Luciano Pavarotti is singing at Carnegie Hall," full stop—you've finished advertising. You don't have to tell what he's playing. Doesn't matter.

But I think for people to develop a real connection to the work, they need to understand that the composer is at the absolute center. And the moment you acknowledge the composer's centrality to the whole question, it changes the way you program. You're not programming as you plan a meal, with a soup, entrée, salad, *etc.*—this fixed progression: something intellectual and then little encore pieces at the end—you're programming something that's about a learning, hearing experience.

And I think also, my approach to programming is not presuming that people already know the work. There was a kind of fiction in the post-war period, you know, a quixotic project to get all Americans to know the classical music they were supposed to know. Get them to listen to their Time Life records so they all recognize Schubert's *Unfinished Symphony.* Now there's so much wonderful music from so many categories, it's impossible to know it all, even for you or me, people who spend our lives in music. So it's totally liberating. Instead of announcing to the world, "There's this common body of work and we should all know it," it's the opposite: "Put something interesting in front of me and give me a way in to the piece." That's the challenge: not, "Show me another way to do this Chopin mazurka," but, "Blow my mind."

Zorn: Contextualization is something that's become very important in the late 20th century and now into the 21st—*where and how* you contextualize your work.

Steel: Yes.

Zorn: Where you put a certain piece on the program; what else is on the program.

Steel: And there's still a super-intuitive quality to putting a program together. In the end, it just has to *work*. So one of the beauties of our digital age is that I can put all these programs together and listen to them, which would have been really hard to do even 30 years ago. I used to do it, painfully, on cassettes ... but now I can do it like this [snaps fingers]. I can listen to how a piece transitions, I can listen to the tonal relationship, which is really fundamental (even with pieces that are not in any key, the general tonal palette changes from one piece to another), and I can listen to the show a hundred times in a hundred different versions. So you can really pore over a show and make it into an object rather than just a bunch of music.

Zorn: It's a way of composing.

Steel: In a sense. It's like a lot of things. It's like making a movie. I think of it sometimes as liturgy. You know I grew up as a choirboy, and there's all this extraordinary music that has its special place in the service and it has tremendous emotional power. It's a theatrical, liturgical progression of music and affect. And when you're making a concert your doing that. You're taking people on a journey.

Zorn: Another thing that you do—and I thought of this when you mentioned that you were a choirboy, because you continue to have a passion with the voice and with liturgical vocal music—is that you program things you love. You program things because you're passionate about them. You're not just looking at how many asses you can get in the seats or how many tickets are going to get sold or how much money you're going to make—you follow through on a project because you believe in it, and that is sadly rare these days.

Steel: Well we did your opera with Feldman and Schoenberg and we got great crowds. The key is doing something strong. When you temper a great idea, or hedge your bet, you just knee-cap the idea.

I used to say that the Composer Portraits program that we had a Miller Theatre was very, very simple. And it was really an empirical discovery. I didn't say, "This is what it has to be." I just observed: when we did a one-composer show the house was packed. If we did a two-composer show the house was empty. Didn't matter. I don't care who the composer is. Berio and Stockhausen: half house. Stockhausen alone: full house. Because, somehow, there's a message. When you do an all-Stockhausen program it says, "This show matters." And when you do Stockhausen and composer X it says, "I'm not sure that one composer is enough to fill the house, so I've got two! See?" Suddenly no one wants to go. It's an invisible but nonetheless powerful disincentive.

In a world where there's so much new to learn, people need an opportunity to learn the music. The best situation in which to learn about John Zorn's music is in a program of John Zorn's music. That's the strongest possible context for John Zorn's music.

Zorn: I agree completely—it makes total organic sense to present music in that way. It's interesting to you, to me and to many others, but it's still quite unusual for a large institution to have a program dedicated to a single contemporary composer. Is this changing?

Steel: Yes. Well, there's a big challenge for big institutions with fixed ensembles, like most of the ones at Lincoln Center—and of course it was true for the New York City Opera. A presenter, like Carnegie Hall, doesn't have a company of dancers or an orchestra.

Now, that's a fundamental problem, because we need these big institutions. There is something very special about the continuity of an ensemble of amazing musicians. And those ensembles are at the center of musical life for the city and for performers. Yet it's very, very tough for the programming model for that kind of institution to evolve. I think it needs to get much more flexible. You know, Alan Gilbert's having a lot of success at the Philharmonic: they break up into smaller groups. They do new music. They do chamber music.

The problem is that these kinds of fixed-ensemble institutions are by nature *retrospective*—"let's make an ensemble appropriate to perform the important works of the last 100 years." They are in some senses automatically cut off from the future. It's very tough for it to move forward. A traditional orchestra, for example, isn't really designed to deal with a work like *Pierrot Lunaire*—they just don't play that piece. And that seems a little crazy.

It's like the story I used to tell, about when I needed a glass harmonica for the Mozart glass harmonica quintet, and my guy copped out. I remembered that I'd seen in the musician's union book a listing for a glass harmonica player—amazing! It reminded me of the old joke about the definition of an optimist as "an accordion player with a pager." So I called her up, "It's your lucky day, are you free on such and such a date. She said, "Yeah, yeah, yeah, yeah. By the way, what's the gig?" I said, "What else, it's the Mozart glass harmonica quintet," and she said, "Oh, I don't play that."

Zorn: [laughs] What *does* she play? A Beatles medley? [laughs]

Steel: But the story illustrates the point that if you run a big ensemble that's too retrospective and too tied up in being the ensemble, some of the great masterpieces of all time will pass you by, because they're not for you. So those organizations have a tougher time being advocates for the work that they love. So they have to commission more, but they really have to strive.

The bottom line is this: audiences don't consume music based on the size or makeup of the performing ensemble. But standing ensembles are compelled to sell it that way. And that is a serious and inherent problem.

Zorn: Flexibility is really an important word in today's world. Not just for composers, performers or ensembles, but for people who do programming. You have to really do your homework and know a wide range of music to put together an exciting program. Also the venues themselves need to be flexible. The idea of one 1,500 seat hall where everything happens doesn't really work anymore. A lot of modern architects are addressing that issue and creating modular spaces that can accommodate different size audiences—150 people—open it up and it accommodates 500 people—open it up again and it accommodates 1,000 people. It functions well for a new world that has more variety in it than ever before.

Steel: Well, it's fascinating. Changeable spaces make me nervous because they tend to get very expensive to operate. But that's another problem. But they also tend not to be *amazing* for any one kind of music. Think of it this way: the architecture and the ensembles of performing arts centers fix in stone the Nation's artistic priorities of 50 years ago.

If you look at Lincoln Center as a complex (and, you know, it's complicated for me to talk about Lincoln Center because of all of the Opera's drama there) but there are many kinds of work that have no suitable home at Lincoln Center. *Many* kinds. Where would you do Thomas Tallis's *Lamentations*, some of the most important, most beautiful music—ever written? There is no venue there that is actually good for that piece of music. Where would you do a Bach cantata? There's not really any venue that's really good for a Bach cantata. The greatest composer who ever lived, 80% of his output is cantatas, and yet there is no home for the work. And if we add his organ music, we are at something like 95% of his output that is "homeless" in a traditional performing arts center. So to me, you need a palette of venues. And the work has to drive it. "What piece are you doing?—Great! Where does it want to be?" Not, "I've got this hall and I got these ten guys. What can we do together?" That's the least interesting way to pose the question. And you know, museums are better places for flexibility because they build walls and they change spaces and they can say "what work are we hanging, and why, and what's the best way to show that work?" And it's going to involve, most of the time, walls and spaces. Sometimes MoMA has to build a pavilion next door, sometimes it's got to go out to PS1.

Zorn: You once said to me that popular opinion is manipulated opinion.

Steel: Yes, I suppose that's true.

Zorn: That's stayed with me for a long, long time. Large corporations like Sony/Columbia, Universal or Warner's are in financial straits now, crumbling under the weight of their own pomposity and with all the bean counters in charge there's little hope of having them spend huge sums recording an experimental musician like they did in the '60s with Partch, Varèse or Stockhausen. What might we see in the future as far as building New Music "stars"?

Steel: I think they're out there and I think we'll get more of them. And interestingly, about the death of recordings, it's more visible in pop music: It used to be that you toured to promote the album—this is an old saw—and now you make your album to promote the tour, that's where you make your money. So you've got to go on the road to make money. Which, for all the horror it creates, is in some ways good, because it puts people in seats watching live musicians. It puts that experience as a priority.

It's bad for a host of reasons. I mean, I was around for the glorious era when *everything* was reissued on CD. Suddenly there was a huge amount of money in the system to record stuff that had never been recorded—you went over to Tower Records on Broadway and everything was coming in from every corner of the globe—all the crazy stuff from the '40s, '50s, and '60s, the Harry Partch stuff, would be reissued, and unknown music (new and old) was recorded—there was just a tremendous amount of music available. Now that pool is constricting and the money's falling out of it, and it's tough. The early days when Columbia was saying, "OK we'll do every note of Stravinsky conducted by Stravinsky." Those kinds of projects were funded by the classical music stars.

And I think that in the United States it was a patriotic project, an express project, after the Second World War, to build American culture to something of international importance. And there was terrific philanthropic energy and generosity on every side of that equation: to build the organizations, to educate audiences, to fund school programs, and to get classical music on radio and public television. You know when I was a kid you turned on the TV and there was George Crumb's *Ancient Voices of Children.* That was crazy, weird music on TV within a few years of its being written. That's not happening. Tell me the last time you saw a major world premiere on public television. It just doesn't happen.

Zorn: It happens in Europe.

Steel: It happens in Europe. But that project of getting stuff on TV, of educating audiences and of building the institutions—in the last 20 years the energy behind that has waned terribly.

Zorn: It's interesting that you take World War II as a kind of a landmark that perhaps caused America to become more serious and sophisticated about its place and role in world culture. Let me take another landmark and ask you what's happened since 9/11.

Steel: Well, that's a tougher question. And to tell the truth, I really look at it as a New Yorker, and not from the global vantage. I know since that day audience behavior for live events has changed. I saw it at Miller Theatre: I saw different behavior. And looking back, when I arrived at the opera, looking back at the old numbers, you could see it was a huge fall-off. And it's very, very strange. I can't tell you who the people were who stopped coming, or why they stopped coming, because we saw after September 11, we saw people wanting to be together, and coming together expressly *to be together.* But there was also a kind of emotionally hermetic quality: people dealt with things on their own. And I think people became more jealous of their own time, and the idea of subscribing—"Here's $200 of my money. You tell me what I'm going to see 8 months from now."—that was too passive a response to one's own destiny. And I think people really got into "What do I want to see right this minute?" That is a more vital response to the world—it just makes it tougher to run a performing arts organization.

Zorn: Wow. That's an interesting way to analyze it, in terms of existing in the *now*.

Steel: I think that's what it's about. Which means that if you can create the energy—and this goes to programming—of a thing, of an event, people will go. It's sort of a classic New York, "Well, what's the longest line? Well, that's the event. I got to go get in that line." If you can create something that matters in the culture at that moment, or persuade people that it matters, they'll come. They'll come out.

Zorn: Let's talk about some of the things that you have planned for this next year, because now you're free and clear as an artist, as a conductor, as a producer. You can call your own shots and do what you want. What are your plans?

Steel: Yes. Well in the very near term, I mean in the next few months, I want to conduct as much as possible. Every kind of music.

I want to do some of the music that means the most to me, 19th and

20th century orchestra music, 16th century music—Eton Choirbook music, lamentations—and do crazy modern music, and then, in about a year, I'm working on a semi-secret project that is really very close to my heart that will involve theater and dance and visual art and fiction and poetry and music, all tied together. And every event will be treated as an installation; every artwork will be treated as an object in a gallery. And I don't mean coldly or dispassionately, I mean placed in a context where it can be observed from a lot of different angles, and I try to strip away as much of the social ritual around whatever the art form is as possible. Put it in an appropriate room, but imagine an orchestra concert where you really can move around and look and shoot video and post it on the Internet and interact with this thing. Or a dance performance where you have a similar relationship. And to show the connections among art forms, because I think that has disappeared a lot. I think music has lost its tight connection with even dance. You know, the greatest choreographers are often not picking the greatest music. It's a problem. And I think I could be helpful in connecting those things up again.

And it's true of visual art. Visual artists have lost a little bit of connection to ... I think nowadays if you asked a sculptor from Brooklyn, "What is your favorite music?" they would name a pop music artist. And that's fine in some ways, but they have fellow artists and fellow New Yorkers who are making *art music*, and they need to be connected to that music. And I feel as if that's fallen away a little bit.

Zorn: Yeah. There's a malaise going on in the film world, in the dance world, where music is being used as a backdrop. And it's all too easy to put your favorite Rolling Stones song on in the back of a Mafia kill scene...

Steel: Right.

Zorn: It's happening in dance as well, where choreographers are excerpting music from divergent sources—we used to call it "dropping the needle"—to construct a dance score with a little bit of Bach, a little bit of Rock and Roll, a few minutes of the Taraf de Haidouks, some Meredith Monk... they stick it all together and they've got a whole new piece that functions for their needs but has little or no musical integrity—or worth!

Steel: It's really the idea of music as background music or mood music, or soundtrack—as you were saying about film.

Zorn: It's not the way Balanchine dealt with Stravinsky.

Steel: Precisely right. And I think film has done a lot of violence to music, oddly, because very often it's pushing it to the background: "I want to feel sad here. Stop doing so much, Composer." You know? "Don't do anything but make me sad." That's an extremely problematic thing for an art form to do. It's about the priorities: so, the filmmaker says, "The film is what my actors are saying and what my shots look like. And the music matters less."

Zorn: It becomes purely illustrative, one dimensional—rather than engaging in an artistic dialogue. And that's a shame, it restricts creativity.

What venues are you looking at for the future, because venues matter.

Steel: Matter a lot.

Zorn: You went into Miller and took a hall that didn't sound very good, was way uptown, was not so comfortable to sit in, and you turned it into one of the most vibrant, exciting cultural institutions in the City. Now, you're not with any one particular house. You can choose your venues. What kind of venues are you looking for?

Steel: My sense is I'm looking at the work first and trying to find the space, a space that matches it. But I'm also looking at work in a new way, where I'm trying to reinvent the experience of consuming art. It has become too much like going down Madison Avenue and saying, "I'll take two of the green ones. I don't really go for the blue ones."

No. I don't want that. I want people to interact, to experience work as much as possible. So there's a series of pieces we're doing that will be installations, really. A single work—whether it's 2 minutes long or an hour long, I don't care—but a single work set in a totally perfect, apt situation. Sometimes it involves reinterpretation of the piece or some kind of spatialization of the piece, or theatricalization, but focusing on a single work and presenting it to people so that it rocks their world. In a way that's about the piece—it's not like I'm going to show movies of fireworks while we play

Souza marches—something that is about the piece. Let the piece determine the experience. And we'll launch the whole series with invitation-only events. So it's not, take out an ad in the paper and say, "Oh, hey, look over here! We have a new project." No. It's, put on something that will blow people's minds and invite them to it.

Zorn: One of the things that really excited me this past 60th birthday year (2013) were the shows at museums where I was able to actually perform in a room with art that had inspired the music, near beautiful work. Tickets weren't sold, concerts were free with museum admission. The ritual of looking in the paper or online, buying a ticket, standing in line, sitting in a prescribed seat, the players enter, play, leave, you go home—was kind of turned on its head.

Steel: Yes.

Zorn:: I was very excited by that. That's a context that I want to concentrate on in the next few years. Performing in museums, in front of art, and really putting art *with* art. It's more intimate, more special and is very much like what you were talking about. Maybe this is something that's in the air.

Steel: Well I agree with you in a lot of ways. And my first invitation-only concert experiences were *your* pieces: the Theatre of Musical Optics at your apartment, and your invitational premieres which are set in private context. It's an amazingly strong way to see work.

I think my role is to get more people into the tent. You know? "Come on, come see this." Rather than the whole ritual where you subscribe and it's this and it's that. That's for people who are already a part of it. People who are already in the classical music universe, we can change their world, and we can make their life more interesting, but I'm really interested in getting everybody in. Let's pack it out. The discussion is too small, and it's among too few people. It doesn't mean the work has to be less interesting. In fact the work should become *more* interesting to draw people to it. And I think that's the response. People think, "Well, if we water it down—it's a little too strong right now—let's water it down then more people will like it." No. That's not true. Do the most exciting, most vibrant, most vivid, most dangerous, most edgy, most extreme work—and draw more people in. And people can say, "That's too extreme! That's too edgy!" or "Wow, you blew my mind!" OK. Great. Now we're having a conversation.

So I think my job is to bring people into the conversation and to get artists looking at each others' work. And just to open up the sense of vitality and the presence of art, and the idea that it's happening now, and that you have to respond.

Zorn: How do you find your venues? I find my venues mostly by going to people I know. It's more about the people than the space. Do you go to friends? Or do you go to a space that works for the piece and try to convince them...

Steel: That is what I do. And there are a million ideas to consider. One is, what's the social context of the space? And in what way is that interesting for the work to be in it. For instance I want to do a piece of Twyla's choreography. I think it would be much more interesting to do it in an art museum than in a dance theater, where it's an object and it happens ten times a day. And there's wall text describing it and you come in and you're like, "Oh!" It changes your relationship to what a dance is. Suddenly it's something different and you have to look at it in a fresh way. So that's the social context—right?—the intellectual frame of the venue.

Then there are the very boring but extremely important practical things: it's got to have a sprung floor, it's got to have a miked floor, the dancers need a place to change, they're going to sweat, they have to have a shower, all of that, which, you know, you learn from years of being in the business, all the kinds of stuff they need and don't need. It's a lot, lot, lot of those things. And you have to work through all of that very, very carefully or else the whole thing will fall apart. No matter how cool it would be, you can't fill a gallery at MoMA with water and have somebody swim in it, you know, it's just not going to happen. So, there's that side of things.

And then you have to think about more practical acoustical considerations. What does the music sound like? What does the dancing sound like in there? What does it look like? What are the sight lines? How many people can get in? Capacity is a huge question, because, with capacity it is not just one question. It's not, "this piece would attract 2,000 people." It's, "well what if an audience of one person heard the Elliott Carter *Orchestra Variations*?" What would that be like? Crazy! And wonderful! What would it be like if a million people heard them? You know there's a lot of different ways to contextualize the same piece, and to change the quality of the experience for the listener or the viewer. And you have to be conscious about what you're doing.

You know, one of the things that I want to do in this is to offer very special experiences where you are maybe the only person. Maybe you have an hour with a painting in a private collection that you would never see, ever. That's never been shown publicly. One person, 1 hour. That's the whole project. It's amazing. Something special. And it touches people who don't even get the experience. And changes. And people say, "What do you mean, he got an hour with that Rothko painting? Nobody's ever seen it!" And it changes your feeling about what you're entitled to and what kind of relationship you ought to have with a painting next time you see one. You can alter all of those expectations about the depth of the experience, about the intensity of it, about the commonality of it or the individuality of it, about the way a work sounds, you know. You can play Mahler's Resurrection in the Park Avenue Armory. It sounds great. It's a big, churchy acoustic. Or you can play it at Carnegie Hall. Totally different experience. Same piece, different sound. The piece is durable and can go in both spaces. Of course, there are other pieces that wouldn't work in both spaces, plenty of them.

So there are all of those issues. And then for me—because my project is about New York and about a love affair with New York City—yeah, I want to be in Queens, and I want to be in the Bronx, and I want to be in Staten Island, if there's any way to do it. Yes, around Manhattan.

I need to know: how much time do I need to be in the space? Who runs it? What are they about? So I have some collaborators who are very specific, where there's one choice. There's a project I'm doing where there's one outfit in New York that's got the technology and the smarts and the passion to back up my vision for this project, so it's about them. Their availability drives the timing. But a concert of string quartets, there's 200 places I could do it. It's about availability and context and social meaning and acoustics and support services and capacity.

Zorn: What you're talking about is bringing value back to music. That it's been devalued—in a way by it's proliferation on the net.

Steel: I think it has been.

Zorn: Anyone can download anything off of YouTube—it's there all the time, streaming away. And by giving one person a chance to be with a Rothko painting for an hour in a room, it's all about that idea of *treasure*.

Steel: Yes. Yes. The good news is that more people will be broadly familiar with more music. But the denatured quality of music in crummy fidelity over the Web lacks so much that is central to the art.

Zorn: Specialness. Art really needs to return to the world of the special. People need to value art more.

Steel: Valuing present time. And as a programmer, the things you can do are these: curate, make interesting choices about the performer and the work; juxtapose works (which is super important); or isolate them, contextualize, as you say. I want to make totally beautiful, finished performance objects and give people a very considered experience with those works. It's like when you walk into a dinner and the table is immaculately set. Something's going to happen. There's an expectation.

Zorn: It's all about bringing the sacred back into the music world, and, man, it's *time*.

Steel: Yes. The liturgy.

Zorn: And I think people are ready for that.

Steel: Without question.

Zorn: I think they're sick of having been spoon-fed crap for decades. They want that religious experience. They want that sacred experience. They want that transcendent experience.

Steel: Absolutely.

Zorn: And the bottom line is that it's the responsibility of the presenter, of someone who has resources and power to help make those things happen—I wish more people took that responsibility. But it's very rare—large institutions are so mired in finances and fashion. It's something that artists can do down here on the grass roots level—something we have always been doing on our own.

Steel: I think it's coming back. Vision and leadership—*cultural* leadership—people see their value again. Slowly, slowly.

Zorn: Yes we're on a wave. It's coming around again.

Steel: Yes.

Zorn: It may be 20 years, it may be 50, it may be a hundred years for the big picture to swing back into focus—where consciousness comes back to valuing integrity, but we are on the swing.

Steel: Yes.

Zorn: And it is coming back.

Steel: Absolutely right.

Zorn: And there we go.

Steel: Thank you, JZ!

CHAPTER
33

ON A LIFE IN MUSIC

Ivory Tower Not, or Right Place Right Time Right Luck

KENT TRITLE

All my life I've felt extremely lucky. Lucky to have been placed in an amazing family, lucky to have wonderful friends, lucky for having the best colleagues in the world, and lucky for the countless good things that have come to me in music. And yet countless people have reminded me that I had something to do with bringing that luck about.

You've got to be ready when the moment comes, and you've got to be able to take a risk and jump when you see the ring on the merry go round.

This article is for my students at Juilliard and the Manhattan School of Music—and for young people who are thinking of a career in music. You see, I'm now in mid-life. It's a great place to be, because now I can see the LONG VIEW—something I could never have seen in my 20s and 30s. And what I see is that perseverance, preparedness and courage are really keystones to a career in music—as important as the talent. And sometimes those flashes-in-the-pan who shoot out of the cannon in their early 20s don't end up with a career anywhere as interesting or rewarding as those who work hard, work diligently and consistently, and, by the way, also figure out how to relate to those around them.

I'd like to share some real life examples of how this all works, or at least how it all worked for me. When I say I've been lucky, I really mean I've been blessed. I've had a modicum of success here in New York City; some would say an overnight success that took 30 years to achieve.

I'm the organist of the New York Philharmonic. I love my orchestra. Never did I dream that I would be the organist for this incredible ensemble. In school I always expressed my interest in being a part of something larger than myself, and jumped at every opportunity to play the organ part in orchestral works. My teacher invited me to sub with the Phil, which I did twice. He was their regular guy back then. After I graduated, we fell out, and then he died. And someone else had that job. I never considered that I might one day play again with the NY Phil, but I did keep my resume going in their direction. One day I got the call—the former organist had left, and they needed a sub. That was about 20 years ago. Anyway, I jumped at it—and turned my schedule upside down to make that opportunity work. After that came 6 more years of getting calls, sometimes at the last minute (this is the way the business works) and every time I turned my life upside down to make it work. And I went the extra mile—always getting ahold of not only the organ part, but whenever possible the full score so that I would know the larger context in which I would play. After those 6 years I was appointed by Kurt Masur to the roster of the orchestra, and it has been one of the great joys of my life to be a part of that music making. I've learned more about conducting from sitting on that organ bench and observing than I ever learned in a conducting class! For me, playing in the New York Philharmonic is a privilege I can never let up on and never take for granted.

Now I'm the Music Director at the Cathedral of St. John the Divine. It's a great place to be—a place that captures the imagination of New Yorkers and really lives up to its charter to be a House of Prayer for All Peoples. We're building a program here which I hope will recapture the glorious musical tradition of this place, but also blaze new trails in fulfilling the potential of this, the world's largest [neo] Gothic cathedral. But I didn't get here the normal way. The normal way in Cathedral society is to progress through other Cathedral music programs, or at least through the same denomination until you reach this kind of appointment. Nope. I came quite differently, and I wouldn't change a bit of that. I also applaud St. John the Divine for taking a risk on me because of that. You see, I am a Metho-Presbo-Catholic now Episcopal musician. I'm a born Methodist from a small town in Iowa, served a Lutheran congregation on my way to NYC, and, once here, served Presbyterian-Catholic-Presbyterian-Catholic, and finally Episcopal denominations, in that order. Before coming to the Cathedral, I was at the Roman Catholic Church of St. Ignatius Loyola on the East Side of Manhattan for 22 years. I loved my work there—it was the ride of a lifetime! I had for the most of my time there the greatest boss ever, the Jesuit Fr. Walter Modrys. He brought me on, church mutt that I was, to broaden the scope of the music program. We started with a small almost non-program, and built it into one of the leading church music programs in the US. (Which means in the world, because churches in the US are in general FAR more alive and well than their European counterparts....)

It took a long, long time to build that program, and once it achieved a certain level, people took to it as though it were a huge overnight success. My boss was expert at walk, don't run, and be sure you crawl before you walk! We started slowly to build the music series, which we called "Sacred Music in a Sacred Space"—and when I left, I had conducted over 150 choral concerts with our professional choir, overseen the installation of one of the most important tracker action pipe organs on the East Coast, and witnessed the growth of the music staff from one (me) in 1989 to five full timers by 2010. In the end, I hit a kind of glass ceiling, and knew it was time to go build again. Which is why I'm here at the Cathedral of St. John the Divine.

I'm the Music Director for the Oratorio Society of New York. It's an awesome chorus, founded in 1873. I knew about this chorus from the moment I came to New York City, but it was when their director became ill that I received an SOS call to help them out interim. Lyndon Woodside died quite suddenly, and the work of nurturing the chorus through a period of mourning began. But when it came time for the chorus's annual performance of Handel's *Messiah*, we together found their zest again. We had a blast—so much so, that the chorus offered me the music director job.

It is particularly in the music-making with these 200 volunteer (some say avocational) singers that all my work of the last 20 years—studying the great masterworks of Bach, Brahms and Mozart—pays off! During my St. Ignatius years I would spend the better part of an entire season taking apart Bach's *Mass in B Minor*, or Brahms's *Ein Deutsches Requiem*—so that I knew EVERY NOTE, and everything that I could possibly know about the piece. So as I balance my work now—in addition to the Cathedral and New York Philharmonic I've had a radio show at WQXR and am Director of Choral Activities at the Manhattan School of Music...and I'm Music Director of Musica Sacra, a professional chorus—I rely on all that hard, hard work to give me the depth I need. On my desk for performance this spring, for example, are the Beethoven *Missa Solemnis*, Bach's *Mass in B Minor*, Bach's *St. John Passion* and Bach's *St. Matthew Passion*. I know all these works intimately.

Which brings me to the human relationship side of all this. I have the greatest life partner ever. He's my muse, and my companion. And he's been incredibly patient on those many long and late nights when I would be practicing the organ at the church until midnight, or studying these masterworks until the wee hours. He is Arthur Fiacco, cellist. We met rehearsing John

Rutter's *Requiem* in Danbury, Connecticut. I persisted in getting his number—it wasn't until 3 months later that a chamber music friend of ours, Donna Elaine, connected us. He's been a part of everything since then—we built the series at St. Ignatius together and every part of our life reflects our commitment to the power of music, our love of nature, and our friends.

My mentor in choral conducting was the late Richard Westenburg. The first *Mass in B Minor* I ever heard in live performance was one of his, at Avery Fisher Hall in about 1983, with Samuel Ramey as the bass soloist! I was an undergraduate organ major at that time, but got to know Dick and when I determined to stay at Juilliard for graduate study, was able to get permission from the Deans of the school to embark on a double major in organ and choral conducting. Little did I know that I would one day lead Dick's beloved Musica Sacra, New York's longest-running professional chorus.

It was at the funeral for Lyndon Woodside, the late director of the Oratorio Society, that Dick Westenburg conducted a church full of singers—I mean hundreds of people—in choruses from Handel's *Messiah*. He called me up before that event to ask if we could have coffee after. We did—and he brought up what had been on his mind. Dick told me that he had been thinking of Music Sacra and its legacy, and that when he died he hoped it would continue. He said that of all his students, he most hoped I would be the one to lead the group forward. And he proposed a plan—I would become Associate Director, then Co-Director, and finally I would become the Music Director and he would become Director Emeritus. So we embarked on that journey, which ended abruptly when he died of colon cancer, relatively suddenly. And so I became the Music Director. And to this day marvel that I happened to connect with Dick in those early days, never once imagining that it would lead to this.

To my young readers who are thinking of going into this career track, I have this to say: work hard, hold your standards high, but don't be snooty. And never bite the hand that feeds you. Be ready to fall out of bed and perform major repertoire—for organists, it's something like the Widor *Toccata*. You've got to be fabulous at the get-go with no notice. The only way you'll get to that level is to build your technique and your repertoire one slow block at a time. When you are 26 you can be impatient. Don't worry. One day you'll hit 50 and look back to see that every bit was worth it!

1/13/14

CHAPTER 34

RANDOM COMPOSITION

KENNY WERNER

I've never been a fan of styles. When someone has said to me, "Please come hear my band. We play Ska." I would say, "Oh, you play Ska? Now that I know that I don't have to come hear your band!"

I find the raw elements of music to be much more fascinating. Those are rhythm, harmony, and melody. Judging music by style is like judging a person by the clothes they wear. There is something beneath the surface of style and it is what all music is made of; rhythm, harmony and melody. Its applications can be emotional, intellectual, even sexual. But the manipulation of those three elements produces shapes and forms and themes that delight with their lack of predictability. Allowing the notes to form themselves through random edits leads to new and exciting music.

For example, if one sets out to write a samba then the bad news is, he's written a samba. That means he's tended towards the chords, notes and rhythms typically used in a samba. Does the world really need another generic samba? Especially since all the great ones have been written already.

I can often anticipate what someone is writing early on in their piece. Once that happens my mind wanders. "Did I leave my keys in the door?" "Where did I park?" I am not being held by the music.

Classical music is often a repository for conventional wisdom. Phrases often have to be played twice. (Hall-le-lu-ja, Hall-le-lu-jah!) There is a motif, then exposition, and a return to the motif. Of course these are the structures used by the greatest composers in history but, like the samba, all the greatest pieces may have been written by now.

There are infinite variations of the elements which can be put into the context of a samba at the last minute, and then you have a new samba. As a student, writing a samba that sounds like a samba is good practice. One of the essential elements of studying music is imitation. But like the various stages of a rocket or the training wheels of a bicycle, eventually you can shed the skin of stylistic reference and graduate to the point of manipulating the music to your own essence or delight.

Deciding the kind of piece you are composing at the onset may lead to conventional choices while failing to consider all others. 12/8? Likely minor dorian, voicing in 4ths, etc.... (if it's a bass player's group the tune is in E minor with an unaccompanied free bass solo before the piece) Ballad? Typically the prettiest chord changes the composer is capable of.

Harmony, by the way, is usually the least developed of most young jazz composer's skills. While jazz and improvisation has progressed to near miraculous levels in other areas, the development of harmony has regressed, neanderthal compared to a tune written by Bill Evans in 1960.

But whatever limited capabilities the composer has harmonically are usually on display in his ballads. Up tempo? Less chords, less movement of the chords. Jazz waltz? The use of certain types of post diminished chords and, oh, don't forget, at least one "4 over 3 phrase." So how about taking the chords that were envisioned for the ballad and apply them to the 12/8 piece? Try taking the elements of the minor Dorian 12/8 and make it a ballad. Those suggestions are random. That's an example of what I'm talking about. Simple ideas like that produce something we might call original music, music with a surprise, with a distinct difference from other music in it's so-called category. Whatever standard characteristics there are for whatever type of music, haven't we heard enough of that?

As I said, writing sambas is good practice, and imitation is essential at the start of one's musical journey. After that music becomes a private journey. One needs to be able to edit the elements with an open mind and then allow it to trend towards one's own passion. If the composer plays with the different elements, the rhythm, harmony and melody with detachment, playing with notes the way one doodles on paper or note pad, perhaps he may arrive at certain points, like a tempo for example, and then at the last minute say, "Wow, it would be kind-a kinky if this was a samba!" Notice I used the word detachment as key to this process. We'll discuss that concept more later in the article.

The idea of random composition is to take some selection of notes, which can also be random or based on a system, or a child's song, anything, and subject it to random edits, that is to say doing anything to the notes without regard to the results. Just doing it and seeing what happens. One edits over and over again, watching the music morph into other ideas or into longer versions of the original idea. The edits are done so indiscriminately that they should not sound good but so often, they do! It's the sort of modern day "chance music" idea that John Cage was playing with, only instead of doing it with "chance sounds" e.g. coughing or car horns beeping, it's done with notes, rhythms, harmonies and melodies. The way they stack up or spread out is done randomly and they work out the way they do by "chance." When one trusts this idea they find out that most music "works."

Save As

I enjoy playing with notes. I look more than listen. I watch the screen. Computers were heaven sent for me. I am left-handed. Just the act of writing is difficult. Righties "pull" the pen. Lefties "push" the pen. When a composer is left-handed the side of his hand will actually slide over the part he just penned, smudging the written notes that came before. I was taught to tape two nickels on each end of a six inch ruler, like a mini scaffold and then rest my hand on it. Add to that the fact that I was a very bad student who hated writing anything. Those characteristics were severe inhibitors to writing music. When the computer came along I gained two very important allies. One, I could use an actual piano keyboard to enter the notes and the other was "save as."

With "save as" I could write carelessly, enter notes, move them around, make the melody the bass line, add or subtract notes, stack notes, harmonize a melody, erase the melody, write another melody to that harmony, erase that harmony, put the two or more documents together, and on and on. And it can all be done without losing the original document. The way these arbitrary moves interact creates a sort of "chance" or "random composition."

This is the way I have developed my larger works. I use "save as" to write and rewrite ideas until they morph into other ideas. Rather than writing "forward" I write "downward," taking the progressive rewrites and laying them side by side. Then I "smooth out the creases" between documents. I edit the creases between versions to "glue" them together. This creates a progression of ideas that naturally evolve rather than trying to think of how to "extend the piece."[1]

Buried in the progression of ideas are certain elements that were in the original idea.

1. Examples of this concept of extended composition are in evidence in several of my published CDs: *No Beginning, No End*—35-piece wind ensemble composition featuring Joe Lovano and Judi Silvano; *Institute of Higher Learning*—a Jazz Orchestra CD played by the Brussels Jazz Orchestra. *Naked In The Cosmos*—another one with the Brussels Jazz Orchestra. *Paintings*—a 1990 CD for octet featuring pieces written for several 20th century painters. For the latter two CDs you have to be a private detective to find them!

It happens automatically, you don't have to "plan" the recurring ideas. It has to happen because all your ideas are coming from an embryo which was at the start of the journey. Echoes of that original statement will always be heard or felt. The idea of motif development is still active, but in much more subtle ways. Little random elements recur, sort of buried among the leaves.

Leaves...As I watch a tree's leaves blowing in the wind I see endless variations of movement. At least they are so diverse that they seem endless to me. There are returns to rest periods, or cadences, but you can't predict when they will occur because you can't predict when the wind is going to stop blowing. When I observe nature I see patterns that are much more diverse and much harder to read. Do you know what happens when you can't "read" what the action is? You have to "follow" and that is what makes a piece of music riveting. When I compose randomly and even when I rearrange the order of the snippets randomly I usually get surprising and enchanting results. If one can't predict the bar counts, cadences and alike, one has to just follow the piece. That keeps one's (my) attention.

After all that "stuff" is created the editing continues. I can inject more order into the chaos. The repeating of a phrase here and there, repeating a rhythm rather than having it be endlessly variant, taking the randomness and giving it threads of uniformity, this begins to give an intentionality that it didn't have at the start, but it feels like it had that intention all along. Again, it is so much more stimulating to decide the tune is a samba at the last minute than at the beginning.

I like taking random stacks of notes, otherwise known as "harmony" whose randomness creates dissonance and walk it back to consonance and vice versa. That's as simple as moving the notes up or down by a half step. I could walk it all the way back to drone, a "sa," and give it raga-like clarity. But one could still feel the chaos behind the consonance. Conversely, I can take the prettiest melody and warp it by exchanging the sweet intervals with more disturbing ones.

None of it follows the standard path because there is no standard path. Most of the time a composer starts with order and tries to guide the piece towards some kind of controlled chaos. He wants us to believe the chaos is real but usually you can hear the composer's thoughts, like a movie that's trying to be a certain style but you're too aware of it while watching. I see what the composer is trying to do but the chaos is not nearly dangerous enough. Writing this other way, it is so easy for the piece to get free because it starts from chaos, from random elements. One can return to the original randomness or chaos at any time. One can release oneself from order as soon as it bores.

The first musical ideas aren't necessarily the beginning of the piece. Sometimes you come upon something fresh and compelling way into the piece and decide, "This is now the beginning of the piece."

I released a CD titled *Institute of Higher Learning*. It was my jazz orchestra (really a big band) music played by the Brussels Jazz Orchestra. One day I was playing drums, or I should say, playing at the drums. Anyway, I was doing a bass drum pattern that I liked. Then I had the idea of composing off of that bass drum pattern. I wrote all kinds of crazy things against it. Many of them became consecutive events, as if they were written concurrently. They didn't sound unrelated because they were all in response to the same stimulus, the bass drum pattern. Somewhere way into the process I had an urge to quote the old pop tune, *The House of the Rising Sun*. This also starts to happen as you randomly play with notes. Actual music ideas are induced along the way. The random musings irrigate the imagination, so to speak. I thought it would sound kind of wild in the middle of all this other crazy stuff. I wrote the song in one way, then another and then it suddenly hit me. "I think I am writing an arrangement of *The House of the Rising Sun*!" I didn't even decide that until sixty percent into the composition. You don't even hear the tune until over 2 minutes into the piece. With random composition anything can become anything at any time.

The concept of "save as" is not new, just the technology. What is different about this kind of re-writing is that the moves are random. Just do this, do that, etc. Editing with detachment can produce surprising results. That means one is willing to shape and reshape the rhythm, harmony and melody like raw clay and not be hampered by a preconception of what the piece should be. The idea of "save as" is not unlike how classical composers work.

In the mid-'90s I taught several years at Gunther Schuller's music camp in Sandpoint, Idaho. That was where my feeling for composition, writing for orchestra in fact was rekindled. A big part of that was hanging out with Donald Erb, a great American composer and an under appreciated one at that. As I listened with him to his music he would stare at me with a fire in his eyes as if to say, "This is the truth. do you get it?"

Don played me a recording of one of his works for orchestra

recorded by the Cleveland Symphony. It was an amazing piece. He gave me a great lesson about composing when he said, "To create that 45 minutes of music I had to throw out a whole room full of paper." He was saying that for every perfected phrase there were countless edits. Every edit meant a fresh piece of paper. Erasing wasn't an option because then you would lose the original idea, which one might want to return to.

The best way to edit is ruthlessly. Even your favorite moments, edit them. Why not? You can always go back to the original idea. What do you have to lose? Unless one is too attached to do so.

Bob Brookmeyer taught a similar thing. His teaching was a real epiphany for me. It changed my way of arranging overnight. He said that many jazz composers write a tune and act as if the tune is their baby. They shouldn't do anything to upset the baby. But he pointed the way to freedom by telling us to dissect the baby. Poke out the eyes and put them between the baby's toes. Cut off the baby's arms and see what they look like sticking out of the baby's head. Those and other indelicate suggestions. Thinking that way liberated the very next composition I wrote, even while still using paper. Then I took it quite a bit further than that and this became my process until the present day.

I made menus of everything you could do to and with notes. Playing with the elements, rhythms, harmonies and melodies, various musical episodes would evolve. I avoided trying to imagine the context for these episodes because if I decide that too early then all my subsequent choices would be stock choices for that kind of piece. It also slowed me down.

If you're not a hostage of styles you can watch the notes shape and re-shape. As they morph into different things you might even make several pieces out of it, like material you can sew with. You might make an apron, but you might also make a bridal gown or any other garment. By delaying the choice of context until much later I create a lot of "stuff," interesting combinations of R, H and M. I can then sculpture that raw material into a tune, a multi-movement piece, a string quartet or whatever. But they all have the similarity of moving organically rather than <u>self-consciously</u> because <u>they</u> were "arrived at" through progressive edits.

The music forms itself in all sorts of unexpected ways. And I think that is the point. "Unexpected" is key for me. I am hyper-active with a short attention span and have had turrets all my life. The element of surprise is the only way to keep my focus in the moment. (People like me were made for the psychedelic periods of the '60s and '70s. Reality moves much more predictably I'm afraid.) I was always ashamed of my short attention span. Now I regard it as a most useful ally.

As stated before, the concept of "save as" is equivalent to the classic way composers have always written. Their pieces evolving through editing, again and again, the composition. Editing with detachment produces even more interesting results. This is a free-flowing way to compose, that feeling you are being led towards something you haven't defined yet.

But doing that with paper is far too ambitious for me and I think many contemporary jazz composers. Most jazz composers don't have that kind of patience or even that kind of time. Many are attached to the original phrase. That is a weakness.

Those of us who would have never edited that much can do it many times and do it fast because of "save as." One caveat though, when you enter notes digitally you also have the ability to playback. Careful with this. Don't get too caught up in playback after every edit. It's another way of limiting the possibilities by what you are hearing. The greater freedom with this is to pay attention to what you're *seeing*. Watch the notes forming and reforming. It becomes more like a video game. There is more detachment in visually moving the data around than listening and contextualizing.

Few composers are known as being spontaneous composers, those whose compositions are in tact virtually as the piece was originally set down. Mozart was said to be like that. Thad Jones too as I was told. Mel Lewis told me some of Thad's pieces where the different sections are interacting in intricate ways were done without a score!

Then there are some of the world's greatest composers, such as Beethoven, who could write any silly idea but through editing that idea became the profound music we are so in awe of today. Don told me that he had traveled to Bonn, Germany, home of the Beethoven museum and had seen some original drafts of his compositions. He said some were corny, silly statements that wouldn't have been highly regarded at all.

In the movie, *Immortal Beloved*, the biography of Beethoven, there is a very hip reference to this. At one point late in the movie Beethoven is deaf and seemingly to most, quite out of his mind. There is a scene where his nephew Karl, whom he tormented to the point of attempted suicide, is sitting with Beethoven's life long supporter and associate Anton Schindler in a cafe and Karl is complaining that living with his uncle is intolerable. He says, "He doesn't work. All he does is [sic] incomprehensible phrases. Then he bellows this stupid, childish tune at the top of his lungs. 'Da da da da da da da da da da da da da da Da....'" It eventually turns out to be his *Ninth Symphony*!

I like to start from the chaos of random composition and remove things until the illusion of order has been reached. For me that is much closer to the truth. In my view chaos is the overall reality, or at least an order beyond anything we can comprehend. We cling to threads of societal order so as not to be aware of how little control we have, how random the events in our lives can be. This does not mean we have to act chaotically. We do have the option of allowing ourselves to be a channel for an energy that is beyond our understanding. Through various consciousness-raising techniques we can surrender to it and act in alignment with it. We can't control it, but we can be part of it. Thinking that the logic of the universe is linear and behaves in a rational way is usually the construct of religion.

What we are really talking about here is detachment. To enjoy life, go through pain, experience all of life's fruits, the sweet and the sour with equanimity, it is necessary to achieve a detached state of mind. This is the objective of Eastern-oriented spiritual practices.

Even in the *Bible* it says or is translated as, "If thine eye be single, thy whole body shall be full of light." Thine eye being single refers to the equanimity between good and evil. In terms of Indian philosophy it means seeing God in everyone and everything. This is one of the most difficult and frightening concepts for human beings to grasp. To regard all events as happening for the best may be divinely correct, but extremely hard to endure. But at least we can joyously write a bad piece and celebrate it as if it were great. After all, *it's only music!*

I learned a lot from Donald Erb but this idea messed him up a bit. I had played him some of my music, particularly a piece I wrote back in 1990 for an album titled *Paintings*. I wrote pieces for different 20th century painters and one of them, titled *Kandinsky* was the most far reaching of them all. Don and Gunther liked it a lot and as a result Don asked me to talk to his composition class. I basically said, "Want freedom? Write a bad piece of music." I said that this might also result, through reverse psychology, in a great piece of music. Ironically when one composes with the idea, "Let me write something terrible," one usually gets excited about those first few notes. The electricity of the moment is amped down, so to speak, by that very excitement. One may have come to the process with a detached state of mind, but upon hearing something possibly great, they immediately re-attach.

The next year at Gunther's camp Don asked me again to address his composition students. Again I said, "Want liberation? Write a bad piece." This time Don was ready for me. He said, "You know Kenny, I tried that. I wrote some bad music and it didn't feel very particularly liberating." I said, "Ah, but did you *try* to write a bad piece?" He laughed out loud. No, he hadn't really tried to write a bad piece, he just held his nose and did it. Real liberation can be found by celebrating the good and the bad with equanimity. That takes away all the drama of "trying" to compose.

Possibly Benefits:

If you're really ready to write a bad piece of music then the notes should come out with relative ease and speed. After all, why get stuck on the next note?

What fills a writer with anxiety more than a blank piece of paper? Staring at blank music paper is just like an author with writer's block. The paper is only blank because one is stumped trying to write something good. So get over it. Write something bad. It is always easier to edit something already written then to initiate the first notes. Just get some notes on the page. Whether the music is good or bad, now you have something to edit. Just like Beethoven, it can be the most inane statement, that musical idea you've tried desperately not to write because it is so completely un-special and un-clever. (Most composers would rather be dead than not clever!) But then by submitting the music to random edits one may come up with astounding music never heard before.

In the history of jazz there was a period where many musicians played in a "style" that was called "free music." Free music, hmm… The biggest joke is watching a musician trying to play free music "correctly." There is only one kind of free music, music that is free from self judgement. The actual music can be anything. It is the state of mind that makes it "free music." And so it is with composition. Editing randomly liberates the mind.

What delights you often defines you. One has their own style because one is constantly drawn towards the similar harmonies, as in Bill Evans, or rhythms as in Steve Coleman, or melodies as in Ornette Coleman. What style is Ornette playing in? Or Monk? One of my favorite and most often quoted licks is "If Thelonious Monk were alive today, he could never win the Thelonious Monk Competition." (The audacity...quoting myself!)

The same thing can happen while interpreting other's music. When pianists play Bill Evan's music they try to be as pretty as possible. When they play Thelonius Monk's music they try to sound ugly. The context in their minds makes their interpretations predictable. Try doing it the other way around. Stomp clumsily through a Bill Evan's tune like *Very Early* and play a Monk tune like *Trinkle Tinkle* as you would a lullaby. It's so easy to be different if one wants to be different. Just look at what everyone does and do the opposite. Is you're next CD an "organ project?" (don't know if that refers to a music event or medical research.) It is most likely neo-blues that recalls Jimmy Smith, Jack McDuff and alike. Cats like Larry Young and Lonnie Smith make an indelible impression because of their unique voices. Wanna do something different? Play organ and make it be the most avant-garde CD. We weren't expecting that. Glen Gould's interpretation of Bach is as counter to conventional wisdom as has ever been performed. Who is as well known for Bach as Glen Gould? What if the latest hip hop tune talked lovingly about the police? Not that I care, but that'd be some new shit, wouldn't it? Play the sweetest Christmas Carols in clusters with the elbows only but don't fall in the trap of thinking that it is now dissonant and angry. Although playing with elbows, play it as you would with the most religiously reverent approach. You'll hear some original music alright, guaranteed! (Note to self, "this has to be my Christmas CD. I've meant to do it for years!) These suggestions are....random!

You don't have to live and die by random choices. At any point you can steer those choices towards your inner desires. One of my strongest influences is not music but movies. That is what delights me. Once I embraced that my music became a lot stronger. In your final edits it's good to ask this question. "Does anybody need to hear this?" That means as hip as all the random stuff sounds, does it add up to anything that can stimulate not just musicians but *human beings*? I compare the power of the music to the power of a good movie. I can sit in a movie theatre for some hours with a good movie, not even a great one, and lose myself completely in the story until the lights come up. That doesn't happen too often for me when attending concerts. Even generally acknowledged "great concerts" can often fail to capture me in that way. Music, even brilliantly played music, can so often be two dimensional where as movies tend to be three dimensional, the third dimension being story, drama, humor, characters, etc. Call me a populist, but my tastes run very similar to audiences who care more for entertainment than art. But what really turns me on is when a great work of art is also great entertainment. These days when one of my pieces works fully for me I say, "That's a movie!"

Other things I like: I like to toggle between the sweet and sour, the reverent and the profane, the heart and the genitals. The thrill of the change is what keeps me stimulated. That's just me. To find music that humans need to hear you have to find what stimulates or inspires you as a human, then use the music to describe that. Those are the final edits, the ones that outline as honestly as possible your deepest desires, your deepest aspirations. Random composition liberates one from the tyranny of art. Random edits allows one to expand the music in any way and finally, to steer it directly towards one's passion.

CHAPTER
35

INVISIBLE SCULPTURE

THERESA WONG

Diagram 1: Performance setup for *The Crass Menagerie and The Chorus of Fear*

The illustrations included are selections from *The Crass Menagerie and the Chorus of Fear,* a piece I created and performed as a graduate student at Mills College in 2004. The performer stands with a white box placed over her head and each drawing is projected onto the box from a slide projector. The audience, which stands in a circle around the performer, is instructed to let out a raucous scream after each fear is announced.

* * *

How can I see the cello and free it from the cultural and historical connotations connected to it? How can I rediscover the core of this instrument, as wood and string and hair—or even simply as a tree?

Projection 1: "*The fear that someone has already done it.*"

* * *

Nightwatching is a song I wrote for voice and detuned cello, inspired by the roughly 7 years I spent off and on working as a deckhand on the tall ship *Californian*. I was bit by the bug in high school, and the summer after graduation drove across country with my brother Glenn to work the summer on the schooner *Edna*, based in Boston Harbor. Inspired by Tania Aebi's book *Maiden Voyage*, I contemplated whether going to college or sailing around the world was the better path to take. I realized though that I had too little courage for the latter and so went on to my studies. But "the flung spray and the blown spume, and the sea-gulls crying"[1] have remained strongly imprinted in my bones.

1. From *Sea Fever*, by John Masefield.

In this song for cello and voice, the tuning is I:G, II:D, III:G, IV: *flabby*. The C-string is slackened to the point where it makes a growling sound when bowed but tensioned enough so that changing overtones can be perceived when the bow pressure is varied. A tiny piece of tin-foil is placed folded over the A-string to simulate a kind of high-hat sizzle.

No danger under a savage sky
Meteorites falling, a dozen an hour
I count them and then I stop counting them
While below nocturnal swimmers grace the bow
Rocking to oblivion in a narrow cocoon
Liquid mother vessel sounding planks by my ear
Could there be a better lullaby?

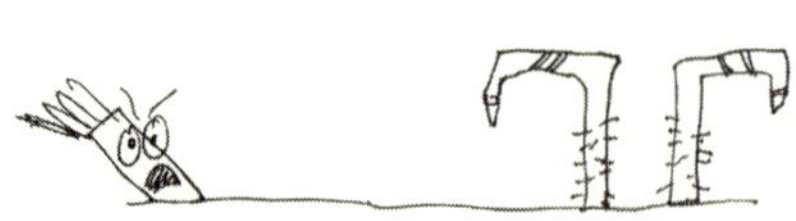

Projection 2: "*The fear that I'll never make it.*"

* * *

From a journal entry, Nov. 21, 2013 after performing in duo with Fred Frith at Duende in Oakland, California:

> *Last night's gig with Fred was spot on. What does that mean/how does it feel? During the day ... and days leading up to it, I really wanted to see this as a chance to transform. Not just "another gig"—but going back to the awareness (that I have when I perform often, esp. improvised music) that the concert could be totally transformative. During the day yesterday, I took my usual walk at the Aquatic Park and set an intention that I be able to connect with the spirit—to let that flow happen. At home before the show, I was also nervous as I was getting my electronics set up and ready... the nervousness seemed like a good sign.*
>
> *We got to Duende and had a calm time to set up—I arrived, then Fred. I found myself feeling my own insecurities—the usual shyness sound checking and being forthright with my sound—but I was also aware of this feeling and told myself it wasn't necessary. It was easier to listen—be silent and not make small talk when I didn't want to.*
>
> *Fred set up in a jiffy—we just played a few minutes. I trusted in my setup and left it, even though that insecurity lingered.*
>
> *We had a really nice dinner—H, F, E, and their friend M. Everyone was in good spirits and we were very relaxed—hardly like we were about to play...*
>
> *There were only about a dozen people at the start of the set—a disappointment, but I just willfully ignored that feeling, a part of me very determined that I wanted this to be a special concert for those who were there.*
>
> *Fred began, and I closed my eyes to just listen—just wait for the music to come—or be moved by it—and I had a very particular feeling when I closed my eyes. I felt "wohl"[2]—for lack of a better word, deeply and right there without doubt or settling—but like the soul was alive that instant.*
>
> *The second I began joining with my voice, the sound was good—meaning the tone, the levels, everything felt like it flowed—*

2. *sich wohlfühlen; German,* to feel well, comfortable, at ease.

as if music were a stream going by, and I could effortlessly drop petals or stones into it... I felt that instant that the spirit was there.

I love the sound world we share—it can be tonal, noisy, loud, delicate, songlike, totally abstract and wild—but always with musicality and sensitivity. The entire set (about 1 hour) unfolded, and I felt great trust in Fred and great freedom with myself. I had my eyes closed for most of it—and at first when I opened them, I felt a slight disjunct of going back to "waking consciousness"—but then I was able to go back and forth between the modes with much ease, adjusting my amp if needed, moving the vocal mic when necessary, looking at pedals, etc.... I felt a fluidity of being "lost" in this flow and conscious of my surroundings, which was somewhat of a new experience.

As often happens when the music is flowing—it unfolds and continues and I have the feeling that the possibilities are endless—this is a very profound thing! How does one tap into this more regularly?

Projection 3: *"The fear that I will hurt my body and not be able to play."*

Throughout the years, I have found many commonalities in the situations and performances when improvisation seems to work:

1) Setting an Intention for a Larger Purpose

Giving! Setting an intention that the music is for the benefit of a specific person, the entire audience, people not even present at the concert or any and all of the above.

2) Trusting and Connecting with Other Players

This seems to be necessary both in the context of the musical setting as well as outside of it. For example, having a meal and connecting with each other before the show, or in the days leading up to the show and sharing good conversation are merely extensions of the music that is played. This is all the more apparent with friendships and collaborations that have continued and deepened through the years. The exception to this has been playing with people for the very first time and having the synergy equally present. This likely comes about because 1) the players are strong and confident in their own sound 2) the individuals and I share a good sonic chemistry and 3) there is a heightened sense of listening precisely because we are playing for the first time together.

3) A "Sound" Set-Up

If the acoustics and or amplification are working well, there is a feeling that the music makes itself. This connects to the notion of entering into a picture that is larger than the self. I recently read about acoustic research being conducted in the Hagia Sophia in Istanbul, which has a near 11 second delay. A singer in this space can create a sound that *effortlessly continues beyond themselves*, which affords them a feeling of connecting with the "divine." This is also reflected in José Maceda's writing about how gongs reverberate for a long time after being struck. The human action of creating the sound is brief compared to the duration of the sound as it continues in the flow of a larger metaphysical vibration. A bowed instrument, on the other hand, has a very close durational correlation of action-to-sound. This has been a major challenge for me in playing the cello, especially in the context of solo performance (as many other monophonic instrumentalists may agree). A satisfactory sound, from the instrument to the amplification to the room acoustics, can enhance the feeling that the performer is merely "igniting" vibrations that are ready to speak for themselves.

4) Creating a Bubble For Myself

The bubble can simply happen just minutes before actually playing, but to have this space to go into my own concentration alone as well as with my fellow performers seems very valuable. Sometimes this means that I remain relatively quiet (not talking), or warm up (stretching or warming up my voice), stay in an isolated space (when possible if the venue has a green room), or when the situation is too chaotic—to simply remain focused on my internal awareness. Other times the bubble may just be a 5 second powwow with my band mates all doing some nonsensical ritual gesture.

5) Absorbing the Surroundings

I recall reading somewhere that before a gig, Milford Graves would stand in the back of the room and simply take in the feeling of the crowd, the space, the situation. I try to remember that in focusing on what I'm about to do as a performer, the other half lies with the receiving end of where all the music is going. I feel it's important to consciously take in the audience's energy, whatever it may seem—warm, hostile, weary, enthusiastic, disinterested—and simply acknowledge this state.

6) Listen!

Deeply, constantly, viscerally.

7) Entering the Flow of Sound

This experience of *flow* or *channeling spirit* is somewhat mysterious, but nonetheless something commonly described in many creative processes. For me, this entails letting go during performance into a certain state of mind which includes emptiness, non-judgment, letting go of fear, joy and playfulness. When this flow is happening, I often have the perception that I'm just behind the sound, which is happening a micro-second ahead of me. I am following the sound. When it's *not* happening, I'm at the front of the sound trying to lead and control it, but the sound isn't unfolding easily. I experience this state of positive flow as *channeling spirit* because there is a great sense of wonder and euphoria, as if another force were moving through me. It seems like something beyond my own capabilities and that the musical ideas are infinite. No sound is "off" or "wrong", and the materials at hand suddenly open up with a multitude of variations and possibilities.

(Thanks to those who have shared these expansive moments with me, including: Luciano Chessa, Gianni Gebbia, Fred Frith, Ellen Fullman, Kiku Day, Annie Lewandowski, Søren Kjærgaard, Maria Friis, Vinny Golia, Carmina Escobar, Dohee Lee, Kjell Nordeson, Joëlle Léandre, Frantz Loriot

and many others to come...)

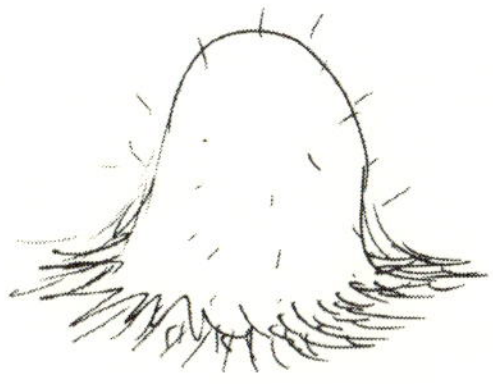

Projection 4: *"The fear of not realizing my potential."*

* * *

When my partner Ellen's mother passed away, we went to Memphis for her funeral and were invited to go to church later that week with Mary, one of her mother's most devoted caregivers. Mary was thrilled that we were coming, and when we arrived into the tiny one-roomed congregation in South Memphis, she welcomed us with a fully rapturous introduction to a gathering of twenty-some people (most of whom were related). After we each stood up to say a few words about ourselves (there was no sitting back and just observing here!), a gorgeous and rousing gospel service proceeded. Towards the end of the service, Mary went up to receive a blessing from the pastor and began speaking in tongues. A strongly built African American woman with a beaming smile, Mary broke out into a spirited splattering of vocal utterances, pointing her arms and jerky her body abruptly: "d-d-d-d-d-d-d-d-d, m-m-m-m-m-m-m-m-m!! Eh! e! eh eh eh eh eh eh! woa woa woh wo!! Ah Ba-ba-ba-ba-ba-ba-ba!!" As the pastor and dean (holding a plastic yellow mustard bottle filled with holy oil) looked on in joy with their palms extended out, Ellen and I sat in the pews moved to tears. I was struck by the commonality all of this had with my own work and extended vocal techniques, sound poetry and channeling spirit.

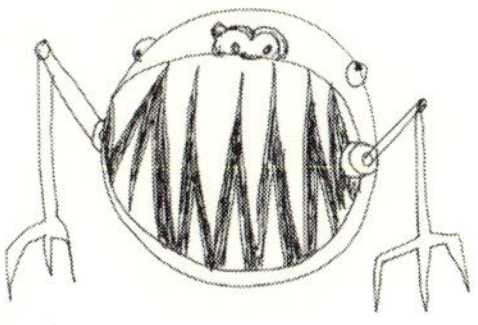

Projection 5: *"The fear of being chewed up by the machine of society."*

* * *

The need for wholistic thinking—to integrate and value connections rather than compartments. To place value on intuition and empathy and not just knowledge and intellect. To develop and cultivate spiritual technology that empowers us rather than makes us more dependent. *Cross-disciplinary-inter-departmental-trans-media-multi-cultural-biodiverse-pan-gendered.*

Projection 6: "The fear that my work will be cheesy and lame."

* * *

Sculpting Air—Vocal Adventures in the Body

I have been exploring the use of my voice now for many years without specific training. I was initially exposed to the work of Koichi Makigami and Phil Minton while working as a designer in Italy, and took part in a workshop with Makigami which allowed me to peek into the delights of what he aptly calls "paradise from vocalbox." Experimenting with my own voice in improvisations, compositions and live performances, I also began giving workshops exploring the voice through connecting with the body and movement. Below are some insights that have arisen during the course of this practice.

Back to the Basics: Breathing

Time and again, I come across the inescapable truth that the voice begins with *the breath*. The unfortunate side to this very simple idea is that many of us (myself included) forget *how to breathe*. Through years of socialization and learning "proper" behavior in society, managing the stresses of everyday life, building up emotional and psychological inhibitions, we both intentionally and inadvertently suppress our body's natural breathing mechanism. To reconnect with one's voice, one must go back to this inherent knowledge. If you observe someone sleeping, you will see their abdomen rise and fall in a very natural way as their breath returns to a less fettered cycle. Upon waking, the mind's restrictions on the body will usually kick back in, resulting in a compromised process of breathing. The beauty of this dilemma is that we already have the skill to breathe naturally and can access this easily. Often I begin by having workshop participants simply lie down on the floor and with eyes closed, place their attention on their breath. If you, dear reader, do exactly that (which I have just done between writing my last sentence and this one,) an inkling of insights and awareness about the state of your body and mind may begin to bubble to the surface. The more attention one puts on the breath, the more one can observe the fluctuations in quality of breath throughout the day; as we rise, as we are working, as we are in the company of certain people, as we are driving, as we are alone, etc. To use the voice, we are merely giving sound to the breath, so we must begin with the source of the instrument.

Invisible Sculpture

Although I enjoy working with people of all ages and experience, I am particularly fond of those who come without the belief that they can sing or have a good voice. I don't like to emphasize "having a good voice" or even defining what that is for others, because the voice is such an incredibly versatile and powerful instrument that the quality can only really be determined in the experience and meaning that it creates for the singer or for a listener. Sure, there are formal attributes to singing such as "being in tune" or "holding down a harmony" in a musical context, but what interests me is the joining of this more traditional idea of a "musical" realm (harmonies, rhythms, melodies, etc.) with the primal, "wild" or noise-based soundworld that the voice can produce. Thanks to spending time in Anna Halprin's dance classes (at the encouragement of filmmaker Daria Martin), where Anna asked me to vocalize as a part of the movement exercises, I have come to experience singing largely as a physical act of "sculpting air." Moving my body and quite literally shaping the air around me, I perceive vocalizing as an act of creating forms in the air, the vibrations making invisible sculptures all around me. Playing with others is a collective act of making these invisible sculptures in a real-time setting.

Allowing the Voice to Take Flight

The voice has infinite expressive capabilities—not just the ability to articulate a beautiful melody or language, but the potential of accessing a palette of sounds as wide as human experience itself in all its vastness. In workshops, people have been in tears of laughter as well as sorrow because of sounds they were able to create. In my vocal research, I came across the work of Dr. Gottfried Schlaug of the Beth Israel Deaconess Medical Center and Harvard Medical School, which deals with using singing to help stroke patients regain their capacity of speech when struck with aphasia, the loss of ability to understand or express speech. Because melody and pitch are largely processed by the right side of the brain and language by the left, patients who are unable to speak have shown remarkable progress in their speech recovery when retrained to use words in a melodically intoned way. Workshop participants often experience a shift in their attention and experience when focused on language based processes versus abstracted sound based production. If we incorporated more noises, wordless sounds and bodily gestures into our form of communication (well, props to *la lingua Italiana* for this), I'd be curious to see the repercussions in everyday life. Imagine an argument with your friend in which you both had to sing to heighten your points of view, or a doctor's visit in which you had to give voice to your ailment with noises, squeaks, whizzes, pops and melodies?

Community and Singing Together

Conspire: *Con* (the state of being connected; union), *spirare* (to breathe) could mean a truly subversive thing; to sing together. There is something of great value in coming together with others in the act of singing, breathing and vocalizing, which perhaps has been diminished in our modern times. In one session, I led the group in my "empathy" score—an exercise where each person creates a sound and a physical gesture, which the whole group joins in mimicking in their own way. When the group has settled into that one sound (in all its variety), we continue with the next person's sound. One participant had intuitively begun to cradle her arms and create a lamenting cry, and the whole group joined in a collective non-verbal expression of sorrow. This workshop was held right after the mass shootings of Sandy Hook elementary school in 2012, and we were all moved and overcome with the release of this collective weight which was difficult to express otherwise. For many of us, the process of mourning has somehow detached itself from the body. We sing to our children when they are distressed, but why don't we sing to each other when we grow older?

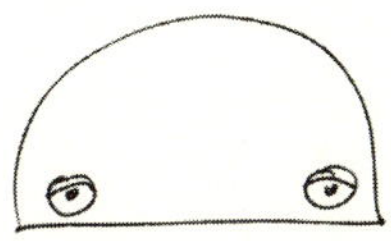

Projection 7: *"The fear of being mediocre"*

* * *

Projection 8: *"The fear of fear"*

CHAPTER 36

LET'S FACE IT, I SHOULD NEVER HAVE BEEN A CELLIST

JEFFREY ZEIGLER

Fear I: Oxymoron

I've been playing string quartets professionally for roughly 15 years. My first group was the Corigliano Quartet and, most recently, I was the cellist of the Kronos Quartet. I am very fortunate to have performed close to a thousand concerts all over the world in most of the world's most prestigious venues. I have premiered several hundred new works and collaborated with many of the most innovative artists across several different genres. So it might sound a bit odd to read that I have never had a very strong desire to be on stage.

This has nothing to do with stage fright (although I have had to overcome my fair share of that). Some people know from an early age that they love performing or that they want to become famous. But not me.

I love playing the cello and I love making music. I enjoy playing with others and it is my passion to be a part of the creation of new works. But honestly, I could be happy if I never set foot on stage ever again.

So why then do I continue to do it?

Fate I

I grew up in the '70s in Fremont, California. I always thought of my family as being very small because my parents, my brother and I didn't have anybody else. We barely knew my father's family and my mother's family in Japan had disowned her. They never approved of her running off with an African American GI.

I did not come from a musical family. In fact, looking back, I completely stumbled upon the cello. I was 8 years old and had signed up for a workshop to explore music. We got to play the recorder, violin and sing. As fate would have it, the violin teacher was actually a cello teacher. On the last day of the workshop, she asked me if I would like to play the cello. My response was, "Sure. What's a cello?" I wasn't going to let not having a clue what a cello was from stopping me from trying out something new.

Practice

I never practiced. In fact, during the first 4 years of my cello career, my focus was primarily on becoming a professional soccer player. But for some inexplicable reason, I progressed to the point that my parents thought I should join the San Jose Youth Orchestra.

The first concert we played included Beethoven's *First Symphony*. It was love at first sight. I practiced every day from then on.

I played in San Jose for about 3 years and 2 years with the Oakland Youth Orchestra sitting principal in both. When I was a freshman in high school I decided to audition for the San Francisco Youth Orchestra.

Somehow I got in by the skin of my teeth! The cello section rotated around, but I pretty much just rotated around the last stand. But that was OK. I was in!

Playing in SFYO was one of my happiest memories as a kid. We rehearsed every Saturday afternoon in Davies Symphony Hall and we worked very closely with members of the parent orchestra.

Looking back, one of my fondest memories was sneaking into Symphony concerts. I would stick around after rehearsal and practice in one of the practice rooms. About 5 minutes before concert time, I would head up the back stairwell and boom, you were in the hall!

It was this way that I was exposed to some of the greatest symphonic literature from Mozart to Mahler and from Beethoven to John Adams. Hearing those concerts opened up my ears and my imagination in a way that was absolutely priceless.

Gamble

When it came time to choose colleges, I pushed my parents to allow me to go to music school. My logic was that if it didn't work out I could always switch majors. This all sounded good, but really I had absolutely no clue what the world of music was going to be like.

Just to give an idea of my level of musical knowledge, before enrolling at Eastman, my cello teacher sat me down and showed me what a tonic and a dominant chord were. Thus I began my college career at one of the country's best music schools with only two chords under my belt.

Fear II: Test

After completing my Master's degree at Rice University, I decide to enter Indiana University in the Fall of 1998 both to join the Corigliano Quartet and to study with the great cellist, Janos Starker. When I arrived, I still had not been given a teacher assignment. So I went to Mr. Starker's studio and knocked on the door. He answered. When I asked him if he had any room in his class he told me, "Monday, 12:30. You will come here and play something."

When I showed up on Monday, there were about a dozen cellists standing outside of his studio. I realized right away that this was their class meeting.

When 12:30 came Mr. Starker welcomed us all in. For those of you who have not been to Room 155, it was a very small room with a platform in the middle. All of Starker's lessons were open so there were chairs lined up around the sides.

As I sat there listening, I learned about all of the studio logistics from how lessons would be run to master classes, etc. After about an hour, Mr. Starker looked over at me and said, "Now you will play something."

About a dozen horrified eyes looked my way. I quickly opened up my case and grabbed my cello. As soon as I took my place on the platform, Starker said, "Play a concerto." So I played some Elgar. Then he said, "Now play some Bach." I played the *Prelude* of the *3rd Suite*. Finally he said, "If there are no objections, I am happy to accept you into my class."

Fate II: Never Say Never

In the late Fall of 2004 I decided to move on from the Corigliano Quartet and to give a stab at New York freelancing. Whatever the future held, I knew that I was never going to play in a string quartet ever again. That lasted about 6 months.

In May 2005, I received a phone call from David Harrington, Kronos' first violinist, discussing the possibility of my coming out to San Francisco and subbing with the quartet for the summer. Three days later I was on an airplane bound for SFO. I thought I had the coolest summer job ever! It was a summer job that ended up lasting 8 years.

Fear III: Indeterminacy

That first season with Kronos I must have learned well over a hundred quartets. One of the most interesting projects was a concert in France where we were going to play John Cage's *Thirty Pieces for String Quartet* with the Merce Cunningham Dance Company.

With everything else that we needed to prepare, we ran out of time to run the piece with me before the tour. But that was OK. We figured that we would just find some time while we were on the road. Unfortunately, we never found the time.

The night before the Cage concert, we played a show at the Barbican Center in London. The following morning, we were picked up at the crack of dawn by a splitter van that drove us down to cross the Chunnel.

Not 1 hour after we crossed over into France, our van broke down.

After spending the morning and early afternoon trying to find a way to fix the van (it was a Sunday), we ended up renting cars and driving at light speed to the hall. We managed to arrive in one piece right when sound check was finishing up. We had just enough time to plug everything in and to make sure that everything worked. There was no time to rehearse.

This was the only instance during my entire tenure with Kronos that we ever performed a piece without playing it together. Honestly, I was pretty scared at the time. But it all worked out in the end. In retrospect, I think that John Cage himself would have enjoyed our degree of indeterminacy due to our lack of rehearsal.

Karma

I don't believe in Karma. However, something happened to me many years ago that tests my beliefs. It was the day that Paola Prestini and I got married. Many of our friends came down to Tucson to suffer the heat and to play in our ceremony. Not to brag, but this group was filled with some really world-class musicians. Nico Muhly wrote our processional music.

All went well with the ceremony until the processional. Nico's piece began and within 10 seconds everything fell apart. After struggling through it a bit more, the musicians decided to stop and give it another shot. The same thing happened again, but this time they plowed on through and somehow made it to the end of the piece. Paola shook her head. Nico was horrified. But I just smiled. I knew that it was all my fault that this had happened.

You see, I used to play a lot of gigs when I was in college. You name it, I played weddings, Bar Mitzvahs, parties and everything in between. But one wedding in particular sticks out in my mind.

This wedding called for the usual repertoire: Pachelbel's Canon, some Bach and some Mozart. But for some reason, we bombed our way through the processional. When we finished, I remember looking up at the bride. She wasn't happy. What I didn't realize at the time was that at that moment she had planted a curse on me: a curse that would finally be fulfilled during the processional on my own wedding day.

Epilogue I: Give Back More Than You Take

I have just completed my first year teaching at Mannes College the New School for Music in New York City. I feel very fortunate to be able to work with so many talented young musicians. Especially after spending so many years performing nontraditional repertoire, I have found teaching in a conservatory to be an enriching experience. I often think of a quote by Robert Mann, the founding first violinist of the Juilliard Quartet, "You should play new music like it's old music, and you should play old music like it's new music."

Epilogue II: Ownership and Risk

So let's go back a bit and discuss why I kick myself onto the stage as much as I do.

Performing is very hard work. You have to practice a lot in order to master your instrument and the music you are playing. You have to execute the most difficult passages under a great deal of pressure and, if you are on tour, often while being half asleep. Concert stages are often either too hot or too cold and you get blinded from the bright lights that are focused on your head. Why would anyone in their right mind do this if they didn't have to?

For me, it is because I believe that music is not something that one can own. I believe that each one of us owns a share in the world of music. So when I perform, I am not interested in selfishly placing the spotlight on me. I am sharing the world of music with everyone who is listening.

I still remember the day that I chose to play the cello. I am grateful for the fact that I was not afraid to try something new. Remember, I didn't even know what a cello was. I was never going to let that stop me.

ABOUT THE CONTRIBUTORS

Irvine Arditti was born at a very early age. After graduating from his cot and the early wireless-set experiences, he then went on to play in most major concert halls in the world and above a few of them.

Chuck Bettis was raised in the fertile harDCore soil, nourished within Baltimore's enigmatic avant-garde gatherings, and currently blossoming in New York's Downtown musical tribe. His unique blend of electronics and throat has lead him into various collaborations. He has performed live with John Zorn, Fred Frith, Jamie Saft and Afrirampo to name a few. Some of the musicians Bettis has recorded and played live with are as follows: Ikue Mori, Nautical Almanac, Audrey Chen, Yellow Swans, Toshio Kajiwara, Mick Barr, etc., plus a long history of punk bands he was in (most notably the experimental punk band Meta-matics as well as the enigmatic All Scars). Currently he is working on many of his experimental projects such as Mossenek with Mick Barr, Brown Wing Overdrive with Mikey IQ Jones & Derek Morton, Mudang Rouge with Jerry Lim & Evan Rapport, Period with Mike Pride & Charlie Looker, Hell Hoarse with Brendan Murray, Pretty Clicks with Berangere Maximin, and Chatterblip with Dafna Naphtali, in addition to improvising, recording, or composing with an array of musicians from around the world.

Irvine Arditti

Chuck Bettis

Shanir E. Blumenkranz

Shanir Ezra Blumenkranz acoustic bass, electric bass, oud, gimbri—was born 1975 in Brooklyn, NY to Egyptian and Polish parents. He was given his first instruments, pots and pans from the kitchen and a three-string guitar at the age of two. Since 1999, Shanir has been featured on over thirty-five releases on John Zorn's Tzadik label, producing and arranging many of the bands he works with, including Rashanim's *The Gathering*, Edom's *Hope And Destruction*, Pitom's *Blasphemy And Other Serious Crimes* and the *Kef* self-titled debut. In 2011, Shanir produced and arranged the CD *Caym*, featuring Cyro Baptista's Banquet of the Spirits comprised of compositions by John Zorn as part of the Masada *Book of Angels* series on Tzadik. Other CDs by Cyro Baptista include the self-titled debut of *Banquet of the Spirits* and *Infinito* with compositions and arrangements by Shanir. Tzadik releases featuring Shanir include *Abraxas*, *Psychomagia*, *The Treatment*, *Workingman's Death*, *Notes on Marie Menken/Ray Bandar*, *Belle de Nature/The New Rijksmuseum*, *FilmWorks*

Anthology 1986–2005, *In Search of the Miraculous* and *Protocols of Zion* (with Shanir on oud) all composed by John Zorn. Other releases on Tzadik include Pharaoh's Daughter and Satlah. Shanir has performed in concert halls and festival stages all over the world with John Zorn, Abraxas, Banquet of the Spirits, Yemen Blues, Edom, Pitom, Rashanim, Satlah, Kef, Pharaoh's Daughter and recently joining Yo-Yo Ma playing oud, bass, gimbri and arranging music for the Silk Road Project.

Born and raised in New York, Rob Burger is a Portland based multi-instrumentalist, film composer, arranger and music director. Burger began playing piano at age 4 as it was discovered he had the unique gift of perfect pitch, and went on to study formally with world-renowned pianist Jeffrey Marcus throughout high school, while playing in local and school bands. He received his formal education in classical piano performance, as well as improvisation and African American Studies at the University of Massachusetts under the direction of Yusef Lateef, while expanding his eclectic interests in various folk and experimental musical forms. It was at this time that he picked up an accordion as a natural extension of his keyboard studies, and his unique approach to the instrument was made apparent by a recruitment to a 1990s rendition of the Bill Frisell Band. Burger moved to the Bay Area, becoming an integral part of the scene in the mid-'90s. It was there that he founded the chamber collective Tin Hat Trio, and with them he composed and co-produced four critically acclaimed recordings for various major labels. Burger moved back to New York in 2001, where he established a close artistic relationship with composer John Zorn, releasing two full-length solo recordings for his Tzadik label, entitled *Lost Photograph* and *City of Strangers*, while contributing to many of Zorn's brilliant scores. Burger has utilized his multi-instrumental skills, gracing the stage and studio as a producer, music director and/or arranger for artists including Elvis Costello, Marianne Faithfull, Rufus Wainwright, Iron & Wine, and Laurie Anderson, among others. He has been a featured soloist with the Chicago Symphony Orchestra, and has scored and contributed to a number of acclaimed films including *Everything is Illuminated*, *The Disappearance of McKinley Nolan*, *Nebraska*, *Diminished Capacity*, *The Good Girl*, *Bully* and *360*, among others.

Armed with a diverse spectrum of repertoire and eclectic musical interests, cellist Jay Campbell has worked with some of today's most important musicians, including John Zorn, Pierre Boulez, Matthias Pintscher, and countless others from his own generation. Still in his early twenties, Jay made his debut with the New York Philharmonic last season and has appeared as a soloist in major venues around the globe including Alice Tully Hall, Carnegie Hall's Stern Auditorium, and Kongresszentrum Luzern to critical acclaim. Equally committed to chamber music, Jay has performed at the Marlboro, Moab, Heidelberger-Fruhling and Lincoln Center festivals.

Rob Burger

Jay Campbell

Eugene Chadbourne

Eugene Chadbourne was born January 4, 1954 in Mount Vernon, New York and grew up in Boulder, Colorado where he began playing guitar in teenage garage and psychedelic rock combos at the age of 15. His father, Dr. Richard Chadbourne, taught at the University of Colorado until relocating the family to Calgary, Alberta, Canada in 1971, saving Eugene from the possibility of being included in the upcoming year's Vietnam draft. Rather than finish high school, Eugene chose to go to work at the *Calgary Herald* as initially a copy-runner and then the youngest reporter and editor in the newspaper's history. Eugene also taught guitar, hosted programs on pirate radio in Calgary and in 1976 began recording solo guitar pieces highly influenced by avant-garde jazz. Pardoned by President Jimmy Carter, Eugene relocated to New York City by 1977 and was part of a thriving community of creative musicians there until moving his own family to Greensboro, North Carolina in the early '80s. By then his groundbreaking LP *There'll Be No Tears Tonight* had been released, setting the stage for decades of international touring with a unique combination of songs and improvising, primarily as a soloist but also a leader of and collaborator within many ensembles. He has a wife Emily and three daughters Jenny, Molly and Lizzie. The ultimate satisfaction in his career continues to be getting to play so much music with so many musicians of so many ages from so many styles.

GLORIA COATES'manuscripts look very simple, wrote Kyle Gann, but on closer scrutiny, reveal hidden, inner complexities such as canons, palindromes, polyrhythms, dissonances, glissandi, microtones, overtones, even tonal melodies and are distinguished by a wide expressive and emotional range. Born in Wausau,Wisconsin, Gloria Coates began composing at an early age, winning a National Federation of Music Clubs composition contest at age 14. Although she has resided in Europe (England and Germany) since 1969, she maintains a base in her homeland. Her musical education has been in the United States; Louisiana and Columbia, earning not only a Masters of Music, but a BA degree in theater and art. Gloria Coates has lectured on her music at Harvard, Brown, Princeton, New Delhi Conservatory, Calcutta and Bombay Max Mueller Bavahns, and Oxford University. From 1971 to 1984 she produced a German American concert series in Munich subsidized by the Ministry of Culture, Ditson Grants from Columbia University and the Munich America House. She has written and produced radio programs on American music for the Cologne Radio (WDR) and has written articles for *Die Musik Forschung* and *Musica*. She has been the recipient of numerous prizes and awards. In 1972 Gloria Coates demonstrated her work with vocal multiphonics in Darmstadt. Her music has been performed on festivals such as Warsaw Autumn, New Music America NYC, Dresden Festival, Berlin Festival, March Music, Other Minds, Musica Viva Munich: with orchestral performances by the Milwaukee Symphony, St. Paul Chamber Orchestra, Brooklyn Philharmonic, Munich Radio Symphony Orchestra, Stuttgart Philharmonic, and the Radio Symphony Orchestra Vienna; recordings by ORF Austria, BBC London, Radio Poland, Berlin Radio, and others. Her oeuvre covers sixteen symphonies, ten string quartets, chamber music, solo, instrumental music, vocal music, electronic, multimedia and opera.

Gloria Coates

Jacques Demierre

JACQUES DEMIERRE is a pianist, composer and improviser based in Geneva. Whether acoustic or electro-acoustic, respectful of traditional music writing or embracing free improvisation, his experimentations feed into music as well as sound poetry and sound intervention in situ. They are all driven by the same constant search for consciousness of sound. Author of numerous pieces for ensemble or voice, he also explores the power of everyday noises. Extending the sound possibilities of the piano instrument, Jacques Demierre also interrogates the ways in which it can approach the sphere of language. He develops a very cross and interdisciplinary critical conception of music which gives him the opportunity to work with artists from very different backgrounds. Regular performances in the field of language art in duo with Vincent Barras and collaboration with Chris Mann, Caroline Bergvall, L'Encyclopédie de la parole, Christian Kesten. Interdisciplinary projects, with choreographer Cindy van Acker, Noemi Lapzeson. He has performed with improvising and experimental musicians, including Barre Phillips, Urs Leimgruber, Thomas Lehn, Martial Solal, Joëlle Léandre, Radu Malfatti, Axel Dörner, Fritz Hauser, Sainkho Namtchylak, Lou Mallozzi, Urs Blöchlinger, Isabelle Duthoit, Brandon Labelle, Hans Koch, Jason Kahn, Charlotte Hug, Butch Morris, Roger Turner, Okkyung Lee, Peter Evans, Carlos Zingaro, Gunter Müller, Jaap Blonk, Barry Guy, Lucas Niggli, Sylvie Courvoisier, Han Bennink, Rhodri Davies, Paul Lovens, Dorothea Schürch, Phil Minton, Elliott Sharp, ... Jacques Demierre received the Music Prize of the City of Geneva in 2007. His scores are available on SME/EMS. His work is documented on Tzadik, Héroslimite, Psi, Victo, Jazzwerkstatt, Leo, Plainisphare, Creative Sources, INSUB., Intakt, Bocian Records, Bardem, Unit Record, ASM-STV.

Bryce Dessner

BRYCE DESSNER is a composer, guitarist and curator based in New York City, best known as the guitarist for the acclaimed rock band The National. Their last two releases both reached number three on the US Billboard Chart and their most recent record, *Trouble Will Find Me* (2013) was nominated for a Grammy for Best Alternative Album. Dessner has also received widespread acclaim as a composer and guitarist, performing and recording with some of the world's most creative musicians including songwriter Sufjan Stevens, composers Steve Reich, Philip Glass and David Lang, and the contemporary ensembles Kronos Quartet and eighth blackbird. Dessner has also collaborated extensively with visual artist Matthew Ritchie. Dessner's recent commissions include *Murder Ballades* for eighth blackbird, *Music for Wood and Strings*, a 40-minute for So Percussion commissioned by Carnegie Hall in November 2013, and *Black Mountain Songs*, a collaboration with Brooklyn Youth Chorus celebrating the artistic endeavors of the Black Mountain College. In November 2013, Anti- released *Aheym*, an album featuring recordings of Dessner's compositions for the Kronos Quartet. In March 2014 Deutsche Grammaphon released *St. Carolyn by the Sea*, a collection of his orchestral works recorded by the Copenhagen Philharmonic with Andre de Ridder. Other noteworthy works include a collaborative song cycle with Sufjan Stevens and Nico Muhly called *Planetarium*, a string orchestra composition for the Amsterdam Sinfonietta entitled *Lachrimae*, and *The Long Count*, an origins story told in music and video commissioned by BAM. In May 2015 Dessner will premiere a new orchestral work with the Los Angeles Philharmonic. Dessner is the founder and Artistic Director of the acclaimed MusicNow Festival in Cincinnati, Ohio, which will present its ninth season in 2014. In addition, Bryce and his brother Aaron produced the Red Hot Organization's extensive AIDS charity compilation, *Dark was the Night*, which has raised over 2 million dollars for AIDS charities as of January 2012. Dessner is Composer-in-Residence at Muziekgebouw Eindhoven.

DU YUN, born and raised in Shanghai, China, currently based in New York, is a composer, performer and performance artist, who practices her works at an artistic crossroads of orchestral, chamber music, opera, theatre, cabaret, storytelling, pop music, dance, visual arts and noise. Selected commissions and venues: Seattle Symphony, Detroit Symphony, Mann Center for the Performing Arts (Philadelphia), Whitney Museum, Berkeley Symphony, Festivals für Neue Musik & aktuelle Kultur (Switzerland), Fromm Foundation, Chamber Music America, Festival d'Avignon, Ultima Norway, Salle Playel Paris, Darmstadt, Musica Nova Helsinki, Carnegie Hall, Lincoln Center, RedCat, Kimmel Center, International Contemporary Ensemble, Trinity Wall Street, Shanghai Symphony, Shanghai Opera Orchestra, Muziekgebouw aan 't IJ, Philharmonie Luxembourg, Salzburg Aspekte Festival, BAM NextWave. Off-Broadway: *Kung Fu* (Signature Theatre). In art: Guangzhou Art Triennial, Sharjah Biennial (UAE), Auckland Triennial (New Zealand), Istanbul Biennial, Ullens Art Center (Beijing).

Clarinetist and composer BEN GOLDBERG grew up in Denver, Colorado. He received his undergraduate music degree from the University of California, Santa Cruz and a Master of Arts in Composition from Mills College. He was a pupil of the eminent clarinetist Rosario Mazzeo and studied with Steve Lacy and Joe Lovano. From 1992, when his group New Klezmer Trio released *Masks and Faces* to 2013's simultaneous release of *Subatomic Particle Homesick Blues* and *Unfold Ordinary Mind* Ben Goldberg has shaped a career through the relentless pursuit of musical truth across many genres and styles. In 2012 Ben premiered *Orphic Machine*, a ten movement song-cycle based on the poetical writings of Allen Grossman. Commissioned by Chamber Music America's New Jazz Works and performed by an all-star 9-piece band with Carla Kihlstedt on vocals, *Orphic Machine* was recorded for a 2014 release with the help of a grant from the Shifting Foundation. Ben currently leads the following groups: Orphic Machine; Unfold Ordinary Mind featuring Nels Cline and Ellery Eskelin; DIALOGUE, a duo with pianist/composer Myra Melford; Go Home featuring Charlie Hunter, Ron Miles, and Scott Amendola; the Ben Goldberg Trio with Greg Cohen and Kenny Wollesen; Ben Goldberg School; and Ben Goldberg's Brainchild, an 11-piece ensemble performing Ben's on-the-spot compositions. He also runs BAG Production Records.

Du Yun

Ben Goldberg

James Ilgenfritz

Bassist and composer JAMES ILGENFRITZ has worked in New York's experimental music community for 10 years, interacting with visual artists, improvisers, composers, and literary figures. As an improviser James has performed with Anthony Braxton, John Zorn, Elliott Sharp, Anthony Coleman, Jin Hi Kim, Jon Rose, Nate Wooley, Jeremiah Cymerman, Brian Chase, and Steve Swell. As an interpreter of notated music, he has also worked with composers Lukas Ligeti, JG Thirlwell, Annie Gosfield, Pauline Oliveros, Ted Hearne, David T. Little, Karin Rehnqvist, Duane Pitre, Kevin Norton, Brian Griffeath-Loeb, Jeffrey Treviño, and Gordon Beeferman. He recently completed a tour of the Midwest and northeast with his jazz quartet MiND GAMeS (with Denman Maroney, Andrew Drury, Angelika Niescier). His debut solo recording *Compositions (Braxton) 2011*, features his distinctive solo bass interpretations of the music of Anthony Braxton. Current projects include the avant-jazz quartet Colonic Youth (with Dan Blake, Philip White, and Kevin Shea), Hypercolor (with Lukas Ligeti and Eyal Maoz), Red Triangle (with Chuck Bettis and Nonoko Yoshida), The Curators (with Joe Hertenstein and Mikko Innanen) and Kid Typo (with Jason Ponce). In 2011 James was Artist-in-Residence at Issue Project Room, where he premiered his opera *The Ticket That Exploded* (based on the 1962 William S. Burroughs novel of the same name). A recording of *The Ticket That Exploded* is due in 2014. James Ilgenfritz holds degrees from University of Michigan and University of California San Diego, and is on faculty at Brooklyn College Preparatory Center and Brooklyn Conservatory.

Travis Just

Travis Just (b. 1976) comes from a background in improvised music and experimental composition. His work often uses texts, gesture and unconventional technologies in addition to instruments and electronics. His music has been presented around the world at numerous festivals, theaters and galleries. Travis is also active as an improviser, performing regularly with musicians in New York and internationally. Travis studied music and composition with Andrew Cyrille, James Tenney, Wadada Leo Smith, Michael Pisaro and Johannes Fritsch at Mannes College of Music/New School University, California Institute of the Arts and Hochschule für Musik, Köln. He has worked for composer La Monte Young and from 2008–2010 he designed and engineered sound for theater director Richard Foreman. In addition to his compositional work, Travis is Co-Director (with writer/director Kara Feely) of the New York-based performance group Object Collection. Founded in 2004, Object Collection presents original hybrid theater-music performances, which take the shape of large-scale projects, smaller mobile performances and installations. For Object Collection, he has composed three operas, *Problem Radical(s)* (2009), *Innova* (2011) and *No Hotel* (2013) and is working on a fourth entitled *cheap&easy October*. He adapted Robert Ashley's studio composition *Automatic Writing* for a live, staged version (2011) and was Music Director for Jennifer Walshe's opera *The Geometry* (2010). He has composed music for additional Object Collection pieces including: *New York Girls* (2012), their live-film piece *Actua 1* (2013), *Gun Sale* (2009), *Famous Actors* (2007), *Evoke Memories of a Golden Age* (2006). Object Collection's work has been produced throughout New York and has toured internationally. For more information, please see www.objectcollection.us

Tim Keiper is a drummer, percussionist, composer and astrologer based in Brooklyn, NY. He grew up in Red Bank, NJ, and studied under Anthony Braxton and Pheeroan akLaff at Wesleyan University and Joey Baron in New York City. In 1999, he met mentor and bandleader Cyro Baptista who taught him infinitely about music, percussion and building instruments. Baptista introduced Keiper to anthropophagy—the concept of cultural cannibalism first put forth by Brazilian poet Oswald de Andrade in his *Manifesto Antropófago* (*Cannibal Manifesto*), which became the impetus behind the formation of Banquet of the Spirits. Keiper spent formative years on the road as the only Westerner in the band of Malian guitarist Vieux Farka Touré. Experiencing a reality much different from his own, he was introduced to West African animism and syncretism, learning about the mysteries of the Niger River and the spirits that live beneath it. Travels in Mali presented Keiper with the opportunity to study the donso ngoni, and he has immersed himself in the instrument ever since. Keiper also leads his own band, Eclipticalia, influenced by the sounds of New York City, Timbuktu and outer space.

Only a select few artists have the ability to convey their message to the back row, to galvanize an audience with a visceral power that connects on a universal level. David Krakauer is such an artist. Widely considered one of the greatest clarinetists on the planet, he has been praised internationally as a key innovator in modern klezmer as well as a major voice in classical music. Known simply as "Krakauer" to his fervent following, he is nothing less than an American original who has embarked on a tremendous journey transforming the music of his Eastern European Jewish heritage into something uniquely contemporary. That journey has led Krakauer to an astounding diversity of projects and collaborations ranging from solo appearances with orchestras to major festival concerts with his own improvisation based bands. He has shared the stage with a wide array of artist s such as the Klezmatics, Fred Wesley, Itzhak Perlman, Socalled, Eiko and Koma, Leonard Slatkin and Iva Bitova while being sought after by such composers as Danny Elfman, Osvaldo Golijov, David Dell Tredici, John Zorn, George Tsontakis, Mohammed Fairouz and Wlad Marhulets to interpret their works. In addition, he has performed with renowned string quartets including the Kronos, Tokyo and the Emerson and as soloist with orchestras such as the Orchestre de Lyon, the Orquestra Sinfonica de Madrid, the Phoenix Symphony, the Brooklyn Philharmonic, the Dresdener Philharmonie and the Detroit Symphony, among many others.

Tim Keiper

David Krakauer

Jon Madof

Jon Madof is a guitarist and composer based in New York. He leads the 13-piece band Zion80 and the trio Rashanim, both on Tzadik Records. Performances include the Jewish Culture Festival (Krakow, Poland), Saalfelden Jazzfestival (Austria), Tzadik Festival (Poznan, Poland), Off New York Festival (Germany), Leipzig Jazz Festival, Glatt Und Verkehrt Festival (Austria), Washington, D.C. Jewish Music Festival, Brooklyn Academy of Music and elsewhere in the US and Europe. For more information, please see www.Zion80.com

Billy Martin was born 1963 in New York City to a Radio City Rockette and concert violinist. He is a percussionist, visual artist, composer, producer, teacher and carpenter. His endeavors with groundbreaking bands like Medeski Martin & Wood and The John Lurie National Orchestra have propelled him from the Downtown venues in New York City outward continually defying category along the way. Recent endeavors include producing *The Road to Jajouka* (Howe) a benefit recording for the Master Musicians of Jajouka, an exhibit of his original art and music for the Cartegena De Indias Bienal in Columbia and an original score for the feature film *Mirage* directed by Szabolcs Hajdu.

Composer, producer, filmmaker and trans-media storyteller Raz Mesinai (aka Badawi, Sub Dub, The Heretic of Ether) has been a cult figure in underground New York City music scene for over 20 years, utilizing aspects of Dub music production, sound design, contemporary composition, improvisation, sound system theory, science fiction and trans-media storytelling to create, what Mesinai refers to as "Dub Fiction." Mesinai's work has caught the attention of a wide range of artists, from filmmakers Ridley Scott (*Black Hawk Down*), Darren Aronofsky (*The Wrestler*, *The Fountain*), Yaron Zilberman (*A Late Quartet*) and Jonathan Demme (*The Truth About Charlie*), to such diverse musicians and producers as John Zorn, Meat Beat Manifesto, The Kronos Quartet and Kode9 among many others. Raz Mesinai's longtime interest in graphic novels, which spurred him to penn a short story that was published by Marvel Comics back in 1993, has re-emerged as an integral part of his current artistic practice. For more information, please see www.dubfiction.com.

Pat Metheny is a musician from Missouri who lives in New York.

James Moore is a versatile guitarist and multi-instrumentalist. A native of the San Francisco Bay Area, he has been active in New York since 2006. He is a founding member of the electric guitar quartet Dither, and performs internationally as a soloist and ensemble player. James has worked with John Zorn to perform and record *The Book of Heads* for solo guitar, and several of his game pieces. Other notable projects include playwright Richard Maxwell's *Neutral Hero*, for which James is an onstage musician and actor, and *PLAY/PAUSE*, a collaborative piece with composer David Lang and choreographer Susan Marshall. James performs with groups of all types including two new projects Forever House and The Hands Free.

Billy Martin

Raz Mesinai

Pat Metheny

James Moore

Thurston Moore

Thurston Moore moved to NYC at 18 in 1976 to play punk. He started Sonic Youth in 1980. He edited the music and literary fanzines *KILLER*, *Sonic Death*, and *Ecstatic Peace Poetry Journal* and started the Ecstatic Peace records + tapes label. He is senior editor of Ecstatic Peace Library, the poetry imprint Flowers & Cream and has edited books at Rizzoli and Abrams. He has been on faculty at the Naropa University summer writing program since 2011. His own writings have been published through various imprints. He has worked collaboratively with Yoko Ono, Merce

Cunningham, Cecil Taylor, Rhys Chatham, Lydia Lunch, John Zorn, Takehisa Kosugi and Glenn Branca. He has composed music for films by Olivier Assayas, Gus Van Sant, and Allison Anders. He presently records and tours both solo, with various ensembles and with his own band. His most recent recording is to be released by Matador Records September 2014. Thurston currently resides in London.

JOE MORRIS is originally from New Haven, Connecticut. He began playing guitar in 1969 and double bass in 2000. He lived and worked in Boston on and off from 1975 to 2001, where he co-founded Boston Improvisers Group (BIG) in 1981; he started Riti Records and released his first recording *Wraparound* in 1983. Morris cites Cecil Taylor, Eric Dolphy, Leroy Jenkins, Thelonious Monk, Jimi Hendrix, Anthony Braxton, Jimmy Lyons, Ornette Coleman and traditional West African string music as major influences. He has performed and/or recorded with Anthony Braxton, Matthew Shipp, William Parker, David S. Ware, Joe Maneri, Marshall Allen, Ken Vandermark, Barre Phillips, Sunny Murray, Leroy Jenkins, Rob Brown, John Butcher, Eugene Chadbourne, Mats Gustafson, Dewey Redman, Lawrence "Butch" Morris, Malcolm Goldstein, Andrew Cyrille, Lowell Davidson, Mat Maneri, Nate Wooley, Barry Guy, Agusti Fernandez and many others. Morris has performed extensively throughout North America and Europe. He currently leads various groups and performs in collective ensembles, as well as performing solo, and as a freelance guitarist and double bassist. He is featured as leader, co-leader, and sideman on more than 100 recordings to date. In addition to his own Riti Records, he has recorded for the labels SoulNote, AUM Fidelity, Thirsty Ear, Ayler, Knitting Factory, Okka Disc, OmniTone, Avant, Incus, HatHut, ECM, Leo, Homestead, About Time, Clean Feed, Skycap, No Business, ESPdisk, NotTwo, Relative Pitch, Broken Research, Porter and Rogue Art. Morris is on the faculty in the Jazz and Contemporary Improvisation departments at New England Conservatory, and in the Modern American Music department at Longy School of Music of Bard College. He has also taught improvisation and/or guitar at Tufts University Experimental College, Southern Connecticut State University and New School University.

MICHAEL NICOLAS is a cellist in New York City. He has performed all over the world at the most prestigious music festivals and venues and is recognized as a brilliant soloist, chamber musician, recording artist and teacher. He has worked with many distinguished composers—Milton Babbitt, Elliott Carter, Mario Davidovsky, Steve Reich, Kaija Saariaho, Charles Wuorinen, John Zorn—as well as countless others of his own generation. He is a member of the International Contemporary Ensemble (ICE) and Ensemble Ditto. His debut solo record will come out in 2015.

Joe Morris

Michael Nicolas

Aya Nishina

Drawing inspirations from diverse forms of visual art and her experiences in the natural world, NYC and Sendai based artist AYA NISHINA composes concert music and soundscapes for moving image, site-specific installation and performance art. She has collaborated with her mentors including John Zorn, Ryuichi Sakamoto and with organizations such as Canadian Opera Company, UNICEF, California Academy of Sciences, Electronic Music Foundation, among many others. Her works have received awards from: Alto Riot *Best of 2013: Choral Recording of the Year*, Taukai Edizioni Musicali *Contemporanea Japan 2011*, The International Alliance Women in Music *Patsy Lu Prize 2010*, Essentially Choral 2007 (VocalEssence—American Composers Forum), Interlochen Center for the Arts *Artist Award 2001*, *Neil Rabaut Memorial Composition Award 2000* and have been featured in some of the leading international festivals. She has studied music composition with Akira Nishimura, Julia Wolfe, Giampaolo Bracali, Nils Vigeland, John Boyle, Elaine Broad, Shu Yashima, and electronic music with Joel Cadabe. A registered composer at ASCAP, her recorded works are published by Tzadik. For more information please see www.ayanishina.org

Aaron Novik is a composer/clarinetist who lives in the Bay Area.

Chris Otto is a violinist and composer from Champaign, IL, now living in Montclair, NJ. As a violinist, he is a founding member of the JACK Quartet, with whom he has performed contemporary music throughout the world and worked closely with composers such as Helmut Lachenmann, John Zorn, Matthias Pintscher, Georg Friedrich Haas, Steve Mackey and Derek Bermel. JACK's recordings include the complete quartets of Iannis Xenakis and albums of the music of Alex Mincek and Ken Thomson, and upcoming releases include the music of Helmut Lachenmann, Lewis Nielson, Miguel Frasconi, Jason Eckardt, Matthew Barnson and Ha-Yang Kim. He also performs with ensembles such as Signal, Ne(x)tworks, the Knights, Talea and the Cellar and Point. He has premiered and recorded several chamber works by John Zorn, and performed as a soloist in Zorn's violin concerto *Contes de Fées*. He has also performed the violin solo in Ferneyhough's *Terrain* with Ensemble Signal. His violin teachers include Cyrus Forough and Timothy Ying. He is a founder, with his wife Emily DuFour, of Hutchins East, an ensemble performing on a set of eight proportionally-sized string instruments made by Carleen Hutchins, and has written and arranged several works for the ensemble. He studied composition at the Eastman School of Music with Robert Morris, David Liptak, Martin Bresnick and James Willey. He has written works for string quartet, violin duo, violin octet and violin with electronics. His violin duo was recorded by Erik Carlson, and is available on soundcloud along with his violin octet. He can be reached at christopherotto@gmail.com.

Aaron Novik

Chris Otto

Hilda Paredes

Hilda Paredes firmly established as one of the leading Mexican composers of her generation, made her home in London since 1979 and her music is now performed widely around the world. As an active participant in master classes at Dartington Summer School, studied with Peter Maxwell Davies and Richard Rodney Bennett as well as attending Franco Donatoni's classes at the Accademia Chigiana in Siena. After graduating at the Guildhall School of Music, she obtained her Master of Arts at City University in London and completed her PhD at Manchester University. She continues to be involved in the musical life of her native country, teaching at the University in Mexico City and several other music institutions and was also a radio producer of new music in the early '90s. She has been recipient of important awards, such as the Arts Council of Great Britain fellowship for composers, the J.S. Guggenheim Fellowship in the USA and the Sistema Nacional de Creadores, (FONCA) in Mexico. Hilda now lives in London as a freelance composer and has taught composition and lectured at several Universities and was appointed the Darius Milhuad Visiting Professor at Mills College in the US, at Centre Acanthes in France, at the Escola Superior de Música de Catalunya in Barcelona, amongst others. Recently completed works include *La tierra de la miel*, a collaborative opera project commissioned by Susan Narucki and premiered in May at UCSD. She is currently working on her third quartet for the Ardittis fortieth anniversary in 2014. Her works are published by University of York Music Press: www.uymp.co.uk Hilda Paredes has been commissioned by soloists, ensembles and orchestras around the world. Her music has been performed by internationally renowned ensembles has been widely performed at important international festivals around the world.

JOSHUA RUBIN is a founding clarinetist and the Program Director of the International Contemporary Ensemble (ICE), where he oversees the creative direction of more than sixty concerts per season in the United States and abroad. Joshua has worked closely with many of the prominent composers of our time, including George Crumb, David Lang, John Adams, George Lewis, Philippe Hurel, Kaija Saariaho, John Zorn, Magnus Lindberg, Steve Lehman, Nathan Davis, Tyshawn Sorey, and Mario Davidovsky. His interest in electronic music throughout his career has led him work on making these technologies easier to use for both composers and performers. Joshua can be heard on recordings from the Nonesuch, Kairos, New Focus, Mode, Cedille, Naxos, Bridge, New Amsterdam, and Tzadik labels. His album *There Never is No Light*, available on ICE's Tundra label, highlights music that uses technology to capture the human engagement of the performer and the listener. In the past season he has been featured as a soloist with the Seattle Symphony and at the Mostly Mozart Festival at Lincoln Center, in engagements with the Nagoya Philharmonic Orchestra and the Saint Paul Chamber Orchestra, and has given solo performances of new music in New York, Chicago, Los Angeles, São Paulo, Rome and Berlin. He holds degrees in biology and music from Oberlin College and Conservatory, and from the Mannes College of Music. For more information, please see thisroom.org

Joshua Rubin

Dave Scanlon

DAVE SCANLON is a composer and guitarist. He is a member of the experimental rock band killer BOB and the avant-garde group Pet Bottle Ningen. He frequently performs and collaborates with the dance-pop band Leverage Models. He often performs and records under the moniker Girls and God. Girls and God is a combination of stark songs, solo guitar pieces and chamber works. Dave Scanlon has performed throughout the United States, Japan and Canada; including performances at The Stone (New York), Roulette (New York), Jazz Art Sengawa (Tokyo), Shinjuku Pit Inn (Tokyo) and Casa Del

Popolo (Montreal).

Born in San Diego, CA and raised in Sacramento, CHES SMITH came up in a scene of punks and metal musicians who were into jazz and free improvisation. He studied philosophy at the University of Oregon before relocating to the San Francisco Bay area in 1995. After a few years of playing with obscure bands and intensive study with polyrhythm guru Peter Magadini, he enrolled in the graduate program at Mills College in Oakland at the suggestion of percussionist William Winant. There he studied percussion, improvisation and composition with Winant, Fred Frith, Pauline Oliveros and Alvin Curran. One of Winant's first "assignments" for Ches was to sub in his touring gig, Mr. Bungle (here he met bassist/composer Trevor Dunn who would later hire him for his Trio-Convulsant and Trey Spruance who would do the same for his Secret Chiefs 3). During his time at Mills, Ches co-founded two bands: Theory of Ruin (with Fudgetunnel/Nailbomb frontman Alex Newport) and Good for Cows (with bassist Devin Hoff). He currently performs and records with Ceramic Dog, Mary Halvorson, Xiu Xiu, Tim Berne's Snakeoil, Secret Chiefs 3, the Darius Jones Quartet and La Troupe Makandal. He leads a quintet called These Arches (with Tim Berne, Mary Halvorson, Tony Malaby and Andrea Parkins), a solo percussion project called Congs for Brums and a trio with Mat Maneri and Craig Taborn. He lives in Brooklyn, NY.

Ches Smith

Matt Shipp

MATT SHIPP (b. December 7, 1960) is an American pianist, composer and bandleader. Shipp was raised in Wilmington, Delaware and began playing piano at 6 years old. His mother was a friend of trumpeter Clifford Brown. He was strongly attracted to jazz, but also played in rock groups while in high school. Shipp attended the University of Delaware for 1 year, then the New England Conservatory of Music, where he studied with saxophonist/composer Joe Maneri. He has cited private lessons with Dennis Sandole (who also taught saxophonist John Coltrane) as being crucial to his development. Shipp has been very active since the early 1990s, appearing on dozens of albums as a leader, sideman or producer. He was initially most active in free jazz, but has since branched out, notably exploring music that touches on contemporary classical, hip hop and electronica. At the beginning of his career Shipp was stylistically compared to some of his predecessors in the jazz piano pantheon but has since been recognized as a complete stylistic innovator on the piano. Shipp was a long-time member of saxophonist David S. Ware's quartet. He has recorded or performed with many musicians, including William Parker, DJ Spooky, Joe Morris, Daniel Carter, Roscoe Mitchell, Mat Maneri, High Priest and Beans of Antipop Consortium and El-P. In February 2011, Shipp released a double-disc album entitled *Art of the Improviser*. Shipp has been continuously improving his repertoire from touring the world, writing new compositions and, since 2011, has been collaborating with Barbara Januszkiewicz. Together they are exploring new territory through an avant-garde film called *The Composer* with Matthew Shipp/Barb Januszkiewicz. On September 24, 2013 Thirsty Ear Records released a solo piano CD by Shipp called *Piano Sutras*.

GEORGE STEEL is musician living in New York City. He has worked in New York and around the world as a conductor, composer, singer, pianist, teacher, musicologist, and impresario. He is founder and conductor of two groups, the Vox Vocal Ensemble (1990) and the Gotham City Orchestra (1998). Some of his notable concerts include Stravinsky's orchestral music at the Park Avenue Armory, Bach's *B-Minor Mass* in New York and at Caramoor, Feldman's Rothko Chapel in a live radio broadcast, *Treasures of the Sarum Rite* with the Trinity Church choir, and an all-John Zorn program in Helsinki with the Avanti! Orchestra. For 4 years as General Manager and Artistic Director, he led the fight to save New York City Opera. During those troubled final years of the Company, he produced some of its most vital work. For 11 years, he ran the Miller Theater at Columbia University, where he produced dance, opera, theater, music, and intellectual programs. While there, he created the Composer Portraits series, which is credited with changing the musical landscape of New York City. As an advocate for new music he has commissioned dozens of works from composers. Steel was a founding member of FACE, the French-American Cultural Exchange, a member of the Young Leaders Forum of the National Committee on US-China Relations, and the chair the Music Panel of the New York State Council on the Arts. He has lectured widely, including invitations to the Aspen Music Festival, the Eastman School of Music, the Operahögskolans in Stockholm, Yale College, and classes at Columbia University as adjunct professor of music. For his work, Steel has twice received the Chamber Music America Award for Adventurous Programming, as well as the inaugural Trailblazer Award from the American Music Center and the ASCAP Concert Music Award.

George Steel

Kent Tritle

KENT TRITLE is one of America's leading choral conductors. He is Director of Cathedral Music and Organist at the Cathedral of St. John the Divine in New York City; Music Director of the Oratorio Society of New York, the acclaimed 200-voice volunteer chorus; and Music Director of Musica Sacra, the longest continuously performing professional chorus in New York City. In addition, Kent is Director of Choral Activities at the Manhattan School of Music and is a member of the graduate faculty of The Juilliard School. He is the host of the weekly radio show *The Choral Mix with Kent Tritle*, a weekly hour-long radio program on New York's Classical 105.9 WQXR and www.wqxr.org. An acclaimed organ virtuoso, he is also the organist of the New York Philharmonic. Kent is co-chair of the New York Choral Consortium, an advocacy organization for the choral arts composed of more than fifty New York City-based groups. Kent Tritle has made more than a dozen recordings on the Telarc, AMDG, Epiphany, Gothic, VAI and MSR Classics labels. His recent CDs with the Choir of St. Ignatius Loyola, *Cool of the Day*, an a cappella program of music ranging from Gregorian chant, Palestrina, and spirituals to Strauss's *Deutsche Motette*, and Ginastera's *The Lamentations of Jeremiah* and Schnittke's *Concerto for Choir*, have been praised by Gramophone, the American Record Guide, and *The Choral Journal*; his most recent disc is *Messages to Myself*, a recording with Musica Sacra of five new works. Kent Tritle founded the *Sacred Music in a Sacred*

Space concert series at New York's Church of St. Ignatius Loyola, and led it to great acclaim from 1989 to 2011. From 1996 to 2004, Mr. Tritle was Music Director of the Emmy-nominated Dessoff Choirs, winners of the ASCAP/Chorus America award for adventurous programming of contemporary music.

KENNY WERNER is a world-class pianist and composer. Born in Brooklyn, NY on November 19, 1951, Kenny began playing and performing at a young age. He is currently an Artist-in-Residence at New York University and was the Artistic Director for the Banff Center Jazz Program for 1999–2002. Kenny Werner's influence is unsurpassed, impacting generations of musicians and artists. Despite his creative output, Kenny is still focused on the music. "I am still more and more aware of the true purpose of the music and the people who play it: to heal and unite the planet." In 1996 he published *Effortless Mastery—Liberating the Master Musician Within*. Using his life experiences as a microscope into the artist's mind, *Effortless Mastery* is a guide to distill the emotional, spiritual and psychological aspects of an artist's life. The book has since been translated into several languages and is regarded as an essential read for artists of any kind. He has performed or recorded with: Toots Thielemans, Michel Legrand, Gunther Schuller, Marian McPartland, Dizzy Gillespie, Stan Getz, Elvin Jones John Scofield, Bill Frisell Nigel Kennedy, Lee Konitz, Pat Metheny, Michael Brecker, Randy Brecker, Joe Henderson, Archie Shepp, Sonny Fortune, Dave Liebman, Bob Brookmeyer, Tom Harrell, Kenny Wheeler, Eddie Henderson, Dave Douglas, Chris Potter, David Sanchez Tim Hagans, Mark Feldman, Bobby Hutcherson, Ron Carter, Eddie Gomez, Dave Holland, Charlie Haden, Marc Johnson, Ray Drummond, Rufus Reid, Mel Lewis, Jack DeJohnette, Billy Hart, Ed Blackwell, Paul Motian, Peter Erskine, Steve Gadd, Joey Baron, Idris Mohamad, John Abercrombie, Joe Williams, Bobby McFerrin, Lou Rawls, Joe Lovano, Betty Buckley. Published Works: *Effortless*, *Free Play*, *Channeling Music*, *Playing for the Right Reasons*, *Hostile Triads*. DVDs: *Effortless Mastery: The 4 Steps*, *Effortless Mastery: Melody and Harmony and Rhythm*.

Kenny Werner

Theresa Wong

THERESA WONG is a composer, cellist and vocalist actively exploring the intersection where music meets with the creative spirit of experimentation, improvisation and the synergy of multiple disciplines. Her works include *The Unlearning* (Tzadik), 21 songs inspired by Francisco Goya's *Disasters of War* etchings which premiered with visual projections by filmmakers Daria Martin and Mao Mollona at Roulette in December 2013, *O Sleep*, an improvised opera exploring the conundrum of sleep and dream life and *Meet Me At The Future Garden*, a piece for 2 voices and 8 Italian Futurist Intonarumori. Raised in upstate New York and the San Francisco Bay Area, Wong studied classical piano and cello from an early age but took a hiatus to pursue design, leading her to Stanford University's product design program, the University of Applied Arts in Vienna and finally to a fellowship at Fabrica, a creative laboratory in northern Italy. While living in Venice Italy, Wong realized her vision to unite music with the inquisitive process of design, in search for the transformative potential of performance. Venice as a city was a mirror to conjure the impossible, absurd and ephemeral in art and to recognize its vital importance to daily life. Upon returning to the US, Wong completed an MFA at Mills College where she studied with Fred Frith, Joan Jeanrenaud and Joëlle Léandre. She collaborates with many singular artists, including Ellen Fullman, Luciano Chessa, Søren Kjærgaard, Carla Kihlstedt, conceptual artist Jonathon Keats and dance pioneer Anna Halprin. She has presented her work internationally at venues including The Unlimited 21 Festival in Wels, Austria, Cafe Oto in London, Area Sismica in Forlì, Italy and The Stone in New York City. She is currently based in Berkeley, California. For more information, please see www.theresawong.org

JEFFREY ZEIGLER was the cellist of the internationally renowned Kronos Quartet for eight seasons. One of the most celebrated ensembles of our time, Zeigler has performed over a thousand concerts worldwide, has premiered over 200 works and has collaborated with many of the world's most innovative composers and performers. Zeigler has been the recipient of the Avery Fischer Prize, the Polar Music Prize, the President's Merit Award from the National Academy of Recorded Arts and the Chamber Music America Richard J. Bogomolny National Service Award among others. Notable premiers include pieces by John Adams, John Corigliano, Henryk Gorecki, Steve Reich, Terry Riley and John Zorn. Notable collaborations include Laurie Anderson, Noam Chomsky, the Merce Cunningham Dance Company, Philip Glass, Hauschka, Glenn Kotche (of Wilco) and Tom Waits. Mr. Zeigler has appeared as a soloist with the Los Angeles Philharmonic, the Toronto Symphony, the Royal Danish Radio Symphony and the Hard Rubber Orchestra and has performed under the batons of Seiji Ozawa, Christoph Eschenbach, Michael Tilson Thomas, Leonard Slatkin, Sir Roger Norrington, Mstislav Rostropovich, Peter Oundjian and Dennis Russell Davies. Mr. Zeigler has released over a dozen recordings for Nonesuch Records, Deutsche Grammophon and Smithsonian Folkways and has appeared with Norah Jones on her album *Not Too Late* on Blue Note Records. Jeffrey Zeigler holds a Bachelor of Music degree from the Eastman School of Music where he was a student of Stephen Doane, and a Master of Music degree from Rice University where he served as the Teaching Assistant for Paul Katz. He then continued his studies at Indiana University under Janos Starker. Zeigler is currently a member of Cello Faculty at Mannes College The New School For Music.

Jeffrey Zeigler

John Zorn

Drawing on his experience in a variety of genres, including jazz, rock, hardcore punk, classical, klezmer, film, cartoon, popular, and improvised music, JOHN ZORN has created an influential body of work that defies academic categories. A native of New York City, he has been a central figure in the Downtown scene since 1975, incorporating a wide range of musicians in various compositional formats. He learned alchemical synthesis from Harry Smith, structural ontology with Richard Foreman, how to make art out of garbage with Jack Smith, cathartic expression at Sluggs, and hermetic intuition from Joseph Cornell. Early inspirations include American innovators Ives, Varèse, Cage, Carter, and Partch, the European tradition of Berg, Stravinsky, Ligeti, and Kagel, soundtrack composers Herrmann, Morricone, and Stalling, as well as avant-garde theater, film, art and literature.

RECOMMENDED LISTENING

Irvine Arditti
Berio Complete Quartets Montaigne
Birtwistle Complete Quartets Aeon
Cage Complete Quartets Mode
Carter Complete Quartets Et Cetera
Ferneyhough Complete Quartets Aeon
Harvey Complete Quartets Aeon
Complete Lachenmann Quartets Kairos
Ligeti Quartets Sony
Stockhausen Helicopter Quartet Stockhausen-Verlag
Violin Concertos Berio, Mira, Xenakis Bis

Chuck Bettis
Early Ambient Slowdime
ESP Organism Tzadik
Sublingual Glossectum Rock is Hell
Urgency Renewal Don't Trust The Ruin
Community of Commotion North East Indie
Sonic Sigils Scarcelight
Chatter Blip Acheulian Handaxe
Cold Planet Living Myth
Meta-matics: Complete Discography Troubleman
Fantasy Horizon Don't Trust The Ruin

Shanir Ezra Blumenkranz
Psychomagia Tzadik
A Playlist Without Borders Sony Masterworks
Abraxas Tzadik
Mount Analogue Tzadik
Caym Tzadik
Kef Tzadik
Blasphemy and Other Serious Crimes Tzadik
Hope and Destruction Tzadik
The Gathering Tzadik
Banquet of the Spirits Tzadik

Rob Burger
Lost Photograph Tzadik
City of Strangers Tzadik
Memory is an Elephant Angel
Helium Angel
The Rodeo is Eroded Ropeadope
Book of Silk Ropeadope

Jay Campbell
On the Torment of Saints, the Casting of Spells and the Evocation of Spirits Tzadik
The Alchemist Tzadik
Invisible Lilacs Tzadik
Beethoven/Debussy/Stravinsky/Matthias Pintscher CAG Records
Enter Houses Of Tzadik

Eugene Chadbourne
Volume Two Solo Acoustic Guitar

House of Chadula
Great Duo Live with John Zorn House of Chadula
The English Channel (Orchestra) House of Chadula
There'll be No Tears Tonight House of Chadula
He is Insane! House of Chadula
Corpses of Foreign War House of Chadula
Vermin of the Blues House of Chadula
We are Together Again with Jimmy Carl Black House of Chadula
Insect and Western Box House of Chadula
Horror Part III: X the Man with the X-Ray Eyes House of Chadula

Gloria Coates

At Midnight Tzadik
Indian Sounds (Symphony No.8) New World Records
Symphony No. 2 CPO
Symphony No. 15 Naxos
Symphonies Nos. 1, 7, and 14 Naxos
Symphonies 1, 4, and 7 CPO
String Quartet No. 9 Naxos
String Quartets Nos. 1, 5 and 6 Naxos
String Quartets No. 2, 3, 4, 7 and 8 Naxos
Gloria Coates Complete Quartets Naxos

Jacques Demierre

Breaking Stone Tzadik
Almost Even Further Leo
Öcca Bocian
Pièces sur Textes Héros-limite
One is Land Creative Sources
Avenues Unit
LDP—Cologne Psi
Gad Gad Vazo Gadati Héros-limite
Deux Pianos Intakt
Avec Plainisphare

Bryce Dessner

St. Carolyn by the Sea Copenhagen Philharmonic dir. Andre de Ridder Deutsche Grammaphon
Aheym Anti-
Trouble Will Find Me 4ad
High Violet 4ad
Boxer 4ad
Alligator Neuma 4ad
Sad Songs for Dirty Lovers Brassland
The National Brassland
The Creatures in the Garden of Lady Walton Brassland

Du Yun

Shark in You New Focus
Abandoned Time New Focus
In 27 Pieces: the Hilary Hahn Encores Deutsche Grammophon
Aliento New Focus
Figment Oxingale
Forum 2004 ATMA Classique
100 Names New Focus

Ben Goldberg

Unfold Ordinary Mind BAG Production
Subatomic Particle Homesick Blues BAG Production
Baal Tzadik
Go Home BAG Production
Speech Communication Tzadik
The Door, The Hat, The Chair, The Fact Cryptogramophone
Short for Something Tzadik
What Comes Before Tzadik
Melt Zonk Rewire Tzadik
Masks and Faces Tzadik

James Ilgenfritz
Compositions (Braxton) 2011 Infrequent Seams
The Ticket That Exploded—An Ongoing Opera Infrequent Seams
MiND GAMeS OutNow
Urbana: Awayland Infrequent Seams
Thank You Engine Studios
Introspective Athletics Engine Studios
Anagram Ensemble Earthtones

Travis Just
No Song Khalija Records
Eight Miles High (for Guido Henneböhl on Karl-Marx-Allee Object Collection
Famous Actors Object Collection
Eickhoff, Just, Vortisch Object Collection
National Reform Object Collection
Rooms and No Titles Object Collection

Tim Keiper
Gravity is the Enemy Arctic Rodeo
Mount Analogue Tzadik
The Secret 6 Degrees
Caym Tzadik
Ali and Toumani Nonesuch
Fondo 6 Degrees
Banquet of the Spirits Tzadik
Vieux Farka Touré World Village
New Attitude Marriage Records
Beat the Donkey Tzadik

David Krakauer
The Big Picture Table Pounding Records
Checkpoint Label Bleu
Pruflas Tzadik
Tweet Tweet Table Pounding Records/Label Bleu
Klezmer, NY Tzadik
A New Hot One Label Bleu
The Twelve Tribes Label Bleu
Krakauer Live in Krakow Label Bleu
Bubbemeises: Lies My Grandma Told Me Label Bleu
The Dreams and Prayers of Isaac the Blind Nonesuch

Jon Madof
Rashanim Tzadik
Masada Rock Tzadik
Shalosh Tzadik
The Gathering Tzadik
Zion80 Tzadik

Billy Martin
Percussion Duets Amulet
Black Elk Speaks Amulet
Drop the Needle Amulet
Shackman Gramavision
Combustication Blue Note
The Dropper Blue Note
Starlings Tzadik
Zaebos Tzadik
Life on Drums Vongole
The Road to Jajouka Howe

Raz Mesinai
Dancehall Malfunction Asphodel
Original Masters '92–'97 The Agriculture
Sub Dub Instinct
Bedouin Sound Clash ROIR
Soldier of Midian ROIR
Clones And False Prophets ROIR
Unit of Resistance ROIR
Before the Law Tzadik
Resurrections for Goatskin Tzadik
Cyborg Acoustics Tzadik

Pat Metheny
Bright Size Life ECM
80/81 ECM

Travels ECM
The Road to You ECM
Song X (with Ornette Coleman) Nonesuch
Question and Answer Nonesuch
Beyond the Missouri Sky (with Charlie Haden) Verve
The Orchestrion Project Nonesuch
Unity Band Nonesuch
Tap Tzadik/Nonesuch

James Moore
Dither Henceforth Records
Touch Five Touch Music
The Book of Heads Tzadik
Game Pieces Tzadik

Thurston Moore
Confusion is Sex Neutral Records
Barefoot in the Head Forced Exposure
Psychic Hearts
Piece for Jetsun Dolma Les Disques Victo
Trees Outside the Academy Ecstatic Peace
Demolished Thoughts Matador
Comes Through the Call Hold Fast Speaking Music/Ecstatic Peace
Yokokimthurston Chimera Music
Last Notes Open Mouth
"@" Tzadik

Joe Morris
Wraparound Riti
No Vertigo Leo
Singularity Aum Fidelity
Age of Everything Riti
Sensor No Business
High Definition Hat Hut
Colorfield ESPdisk
Camera ESPdisk
Mess Hall Hat Hut

Michael Nicolas
Music and Its Double Tzadik
What Thou Wilt Tzadik
Verklaerte Nacht Naxos
Ditto Hits Universal Korea

Aya Nishina
Flora Tzadik

Aaron Novik
Secrets of Secrets Tzadik
Floating World Vol. 1 Porto Franco
Our Band Could be as Serious as Your Life
The Samuel Suite/Dancing Into One Evander

Chris Otto
Complete Quartets of Iannis Xenakis Mode
Complete Quartets of Helmut Lachenmann Mode
Ken Thomson: Thaw Canteloupe
Alex Mincek: Lift-Tilt-Filter-Split Carrier
Lemma Tzadik
On the Torment of Saints, the Casting of Spells and the Evocation of Spirits Tzadik
Fragmentations, Prayers and Interjections Tzadik

Hilda Paredes
The Seventh Seed Mode Records New York
Tañendo Recio Quindicim
Canciones de Luna Vol. 1 Euram Records
Aí Tencargo Luna Negra
México Contemporáneo: Música Para Voz y Piano Ediciones Pentagrama
Salsa Nueva Somm Recordings

Listen How They Talk Mode Records New York
Agueda González: XX–XXI Música Mexicana Para Clavecín Quindicim
No Time At All CD Baby
The School of Natural Philosophy Move Records

Joshua Rubin
There Never is No Light Tundra
ice Kairos
Ensemble Works 3 Mode
On the Torment of Saints, the Casting of Spells and the Evocation of Spirits Tzadik
The Bright and Hollow Sky New Focus Recordings
Enter Houses Of Tzadik
Undersong Mode
Abandoned Time New Focus Recordings

Dave Scanlon
Girls and God Of Plants
(o)N(o) repeat self-released
Non-Recyclable Tzadik
Fear May Be A Builder Primary Records
Pet Bottle Ningen Tzadik

Matt Shipp
Symbol Systems No More
Before the World FMP
Songs Splasc(h)
One Thirsty Ear
Un Piano RogueArt
4D Thirsty Ear
Creation Out Of Nothing (Live in Moscow) SoLyd
Piano Sutras Thirsty Ear

Ches Smith
Hammered Clean Feed
Finally Out of my Hands Skirl
International Hoohah Fortune
Psycho Predictions 88
Noise to Men
Audumla Web of Mimicry
Bebop Fantasy Asian Man
Nina Graveface
Your Turn Northern Spy

Kent Tritle
Messages to Myself MSR Classics
Hans Werner Henze's Symphony No. 9
Cool of the Day MSR Classics
Wondrous Love MSR Classics
Alberto Ginastera's Lamentations of Jeremiah/Alfred Schnittke's Concerto for Choir MSR Classics
Sergei Rachmaninov's Vespers AMDG Recordings
Maurice Durufle's Requiem & Suite for Organ MSR Classics
Kent Tritle at the Old Dutch Church of Sleepy Hollow: Organ Works by Buxtehude, Bach, Walther, Sweelinck www.rctodc.org
The Romantic Organ Epiphany Recordings
Kent Tritle at St. Ignatius Loyola Gothic

Kenny Werner
Me, Myself and I Justin Time Records
No Beginning, No End Half Note Records
Listening Lawn Chair Society Blue Note Records
Peace, Live at the Blue Note Half Note Records
Beauty Secrets BMG
Paintings Pioneer LDC

Uncovered Heart Sunnyside Records
Introducing the Trio Sunnyside Records
Ken Werner Plays the Music of Bix Beiderbecke, Duke Ellington, James P. Johnson and George Gershwin Finnadar Records

Theresa Wong

The Unlearning Tzadik
Venice Is A Fish Sensitive Skin Music

Jeffrey Zeigler

Kronos Plays the Music of Bryce Dessner Anti
WTC 9/11 Nonesuch
Floodplain Nonesuch
Cusp of Magic Nonesuch
Body Maps Tzadik
Not Too Late Blue Note
String Quartet No.3 Nonesuch
Oceana Deutsche Grammophon
Y34RZ3R0R3M1X3D Interscope Records
Music by Clint Mansell Nonesuch

John Zorn

The Testament of Solomon Tzadik
Psychomagia Tzadik
The Alchemist Tzadik
Myth and Mythopoeia Tzadik
The Holy Visions Tzadik
On Leaves of Grass Tzadik
In the Hall of Mirrors Tzadik
Fragmentations, Prayers and Interjections Tzadik
The Last Judgment Tzadik
The Hermetic Organ vol. 2 Tzadik